CHRISTOPHE
King of Haiti

Also by Hubert Cole

JOSÉPHINE
FIRST GENTLEMAN OF THE BEDCHAMBER

CHRISTOPHE
King of Haiti

Hubert Cole

New York / The Viking Press

to
Susan and David

Contents

Illustrations

Acknowledgements and thanks are due to the following for permission to reproduce photographs:
BIBLIOTHÈQUE NATIONALE, PARIS: PLATE II; HAITI NATIONAL TOURIST OFFICE: PLATES VII, VIII; NATIONAL PORTRAIT GALLERY: PLATES VIa, VIb; RADIO TIMES HULTON PICTURE LIBRARY: PLATES I, III.

CHRISTOPHE
King of Haiti

I

October 1820

Behind the palace the mountain lifted steeply to the sky, topped by
the twin-peaked Bishop's Mitre on which ships' captains, coming
in from the long Atlantic voyage, took bearings for the harbour
entrance at Le Cap. Beside the Bonnet-à-l'Evêque, amazingly
perched on the Pic de la Ferrière, the Citadel thrust its massive
stone prow through the clouds, the tropical sun etching its case-
ment embrasures in black intaglio and striking menacing glints
from the brassy lips of the scores of cannon that squatted four-
tiered within the walls.

Below the great fortress, plunging more than two thousand
feet to the foothills on which the palace stood, the sharp facets of
the precipices and gullies that scored the mountain's sides were
hidden beneath liana-tangled trees. Over and down them, through
bushes and creepers and moss, streams trickled and tumbled to the
lower slopes, where a system of pipes marshalled the ice-cold
waters into the ornamental conduits that ran through the queen's
pleasure gardens and then plunged out of sight again, dispersed
beneath the palace floors, carrying the freshness of the mountain
with them so that even now, in the dry end-days of summer, it
was cool and wonderful to walk barefooted across the strips of
polished mahogany amid the magnificence of crystal and marble
and gilt, the sumptuousness of tapestries and curtains, paintings
and fine furniture, with which Christophe had embellished his
favourite residence. The water reappeared once more, gushing out
from under the great arch that supported the building on the
forward slope, streaming down a blue-tiled chute between the
double flights of steps and forking into two blood-red culverts
before continuing its twelve-mile course across the plain to the
Rivière du Haut-du-Cap and the sea.

This was Sans-Souci, the finest of the many palaces of Henry

Christophe, King of Haiti. Before he came it had been called Millot, a place that was scarcely a village, merely a huddle of huts beside an isolated plantation. Even today the village itself, down the slope beyond the forecourt of the palace, was no more than seven or eight score houses, often of lath and plaster though with splendidly appointed interiors, lodgings for the nobility when the king was in residence. Barely a hundred yards away the dense vegetation began again.

Seen from the village, the palace lacked dignity. From the fretted iron gates, ill-placed in the north-east corner of the outer courtyard just beyond the bishop's palace and the old round church, the carriageway ran beside the long, low building that served as the royal council chamber and swung right-handed to the broad, central flight of steps. At the top of the first flight, where the cooling stream splashed out over its bright blue tiles, the stairs branched right and left, mounting upward and outward and then turning inward again to converge on the terrace before the main entrance under the long white portico. Except for the central arch through which the stream flowed and which was surmounted by a great gilded sun with the legend *Je vois tout et tout voit par moi dans l'univers* (I see all, and all in the universe see by me), there was nothing but the stone sentry boxes and the filigree railings of the double flight of steps to break the bleak background of stone wall and buttresses.

From the terrace itself the building took on a more imposing aspect. The six tall french windows under the portico were flanked on either side by nine similar windows giving on to the salons and banqueting rooms. Above them was the long balcony of the audience chamber, with the apartments of the queen and the two princesses on one side, those of the king on the other.

The king's suite, his library, study and bedroom, ended in a small balcony leading off his bathroom, and it was Christophe's habit to stroll here in the morning, looking out from the palace that he had created in the hills, over the wide, fertile plain that he had made once more the richest in the whole West Indies, to the capital city that he was still rebuilding after it had twice been almost totally destroyed by fire. But for seven weeks now – ever since he had been struck down during the celebrations of the queen's patronal festival – he had been unable to get out on to the balcony unaided and would not let himself be helped.

Tended by the queen and his two daughters, and by the Scotsman, Duncan Stewart, Professor of Anatomy at the Royal College and *maréchal de camp* commanding the Royal Haitian Medical Corps, he continued to rule the kingdom with his old severity. To suggestions that he should set up a council of regency with the Prince Royal at its head he responded with such a blaze of fury that nobody dared raise the subject again. Since he could not make his own way down the long flights of steps to the council chamber, and would not be carried, his ministers brought documents to his bedside for approval and signature. On formal occasions or for matters of great moment he would drag himself on the arm of an equerry to his study or the library, where he was painstakingly and painfully enthroned in the great chair of state, embellished with the royal arms and surmounted by a massive gilded crown.

It was here that he received a messenger from Romain, governor of the Artibonite District, on Wednesday, October 4. The man, breathless with running up the long flights of steps and with the terrifying knowledge that he carried unwelcome tidings, brought word that the 8th Regiment of Foot had mutinied at Saint-Marc and had murdered the garrison commander. The news enraged but did not at first alarm Christophe. As he sat propped awkwardly upright in the tall chair, a pair of pistols by his left hand, there was nobody at the council table who had courage enough to comment or even to meet his eyes. Some, for certain, were involved in the plot against him; others must have been aware of it but remained silent, from fear or because their loyalty had worn thin.

They lowered their eyelids, stared at the table and waited for the royal commands. When they came, the king's impeded vocal chords gave a harsh inflection to the words. He expelled them slowly, distorted and metallic. Guerrier was to march to Romain's aid with six thousand men; the mutiny was to be stamped out and as many men as necessary punished on the spot; the ringleaders would be brought to Le Cap to answer to a military court.

He turned to other affairs, apparently unconcerned, but during the afternoon he cancelled an audience that he had promised to Sanders for the following day. The significance of this was not lost on those around him, for the subject was close to his heart: Sanders had been making the final arrangements for bringing in the first batch of Negro emigrants from the northern states of the USA, where they had found freedom but no happiness – and Sanders's departure for Philadelphia, already once postponed, was set for Friday evening.

The messengers who galloped over the rough mountain road from Saint-Marc during Thursday brought dark tidings. Romain reported that he had been warned of unrest and had ridden over from La Petite-Rivière to harangue the troops – but the mutiny had exploded in his face. He narrowly escaped with his own life after the garrison commander had been shot down in the street, and he was now besieged in a perimeter fortress with the two hundred cavalrymen of his escort. This was no longer a mutiny against regimental officers, ignited by some obscure domestic grievance; it was a revolt against the governor, perhaps against the government itself.

Confirmation came during the night: the mutineers were believed to have sent representatives south across the border asking the Republicans for help. Now Guerrier must reach Saint-Marc and crush the revolt before the Southerners, hacking their way through the twenty-mile no-man's-land of jungle, caught him between two fires. On Friday, Christophe ordered Richard, governor of the North Province, to muster all his available troops and send them to reinforce Guerrier.

But for the paralysis that crippled the whole of his right side, he would by now have been spending hours in the saddle, harrying his generals and ministers, perhaps leading troops in person to Saint-Marc, at least hustling about Le Cap, doling out thwacks from his silver-knobbed cane and threats of forced labour in the Citadel, intimidating everybody into wonders of enthusiasm. Instead, dragged painfully from bedroom to study on a servant's arm, he was forced to let others carry out his commands, snarling and ranting at them in the hope that a little of his rage would be communicated to those who had to take action.

The mutiny of Saint-Marc was grave – but of insignificant importance compared with the trouble that now broke out close at hand. At first light on Saturday morning, the orderly officer rode down to Le Cap with the daily instructions from the king – and at the gates of the capital found himself halted at bayonet point by the sentinels. He shouted to them that he was on the king's business and was answered with yells of, "There is no king! Tyranny is ended! Haiti is free!"

A crowd had collected for this great moment: soldiers, students, shopkeepers, clerks and workmen who had been kept awake by the night's commotions, and their wives, sisters and mothers in their big madras headscarves. "No king!" they chanted. "No king!" The generals had deposed the king, they roared – ended the monarchy. Richard had taken over command, with Prophète and Gros-Morne as his aides.

The mob was singing and screaming itself into a mood of truculence; the jeers turned to threats of rough handling and the orderly officer swung his horse round and galloped back to the palace. When he arrived there he was too frightened to deliver his news. He dismounted and stood in the courtyard trembling. He told the duty officers, who ran up the long flights of steps to the palace, but eventually he was forced to enter the king's presence himself, crouching in terror, to tell him all that he had heard.

Christophe refused to believe him. Of Richard, with whom he had clashed and whom he had punished severely on at least one recent occasion, he was willing to believe that he was capable of treason and might even dare it; but he flatly denied the possibility that Prophète, commander of the Royal Light Horse, his companion in the long, bloody fight for freedom, would ever turn against him.

He was wrong; and as the day wore on and more reports came in, he was forced to admit it to himself. The treasury at Le Cap had been plundered, his châteaux had been looted, they had set fire to his plantations – looking out from Sans-Souci he could see the smoke and flames billowing and spurting up from the burning sugar canes, as they had in the early, dreadful days of the revolution, and again when he had defied Bonaparte's brother-in-law and the veteran soldiers of France. He exploded with rage, cursing his servants and the wrecked body that would not obey his will.

He ordered rum to be brought from the royal distillery down the hill and to be heated, gallons of it in iron pots with oil of pimento added. He had himself assisted to a room on the ground floor and lay for an hour in a bath of this fiery concoction while servants rubbed him with flannel, scouring the dead nerves and muscles back into life with the heat and smart of the liquid, the stimulation and insistence of the friction and towelling. He called for his full-dress uniform as colonel-in-chief of the Haitian Guard: the long red coat with black revers, collars and cuffs, white lining and braid, red epaulets, white knee breeches, white stockings, the shako trimmed with red silk lace, red braid and red pompom, and a gold badge bearing the royal arms – a crown with two lions rampant guardant and the motto 'God, my Cause and my Sword'.

They pulled on his half-boots and laced them. As they drew back and pretended not to watch, he placed his left hand on a servant's shoulder and dragged himself to his feet.

He stood stock still for a moment, the muscles of his jaw rigid with the effort of holding his balance. Then, his face gleaming with sweat that sprang from exertion and the realisation of triumph, he took a step forward, and did not fall.

He shouted for his horse to be brought to the terrace, for the companies of the guard to be paraded at once. He was himself again; he could ride at the head of his soldiers once more. His face was transfigured with joy.

The palace filled with noise: clamour for the king's horse, for the king's guard, whispers that grew to murmurs and then rose to more shouting as the news flew round of the king's miraculous recovery. This was the true, the invincible Christophe; the old Christophe who scattered trinkets in the streets to catch thieves and had now perhaps been shamming paralysis for seven weeks to catch traitors. Heads sprouted round doorways, eyes squinted through the filigree of bannisters and balustrades, all trying to catch a glimpse of this wonder of wonders. In the midst of this commotion the king walked uncertainly but upright towards the great french windows that opened on to the terrace.

Facing the doors a groom stood with the richly-caparisoned charger, its saddle-cloth decorated with the royal device of a crowned phoenix and the motto "I rise again from my ashes". Behind him was ranged the first demi-brigade of the Gardes Haitiennes, the grenadier companies of the Royal Guard. They stood motionless, their eyes wide with the rumour they had heard but not believed, great startled circles of white in blank black faces – and in their minds a new fear of the unknown powers that this broken man could summon up. Here was real vaudou, the magic that could surpass all physical bounds.

Christophe paused in the great doorway, slowly surveying his soldiers, his gaze raking their faces, straining to bore into their thoughts, peer into their hearts, distinguish the faithful from the faithless, friend from foe. The hubbub behind him had dwindled; the terrace was so still that the sharp ear caught the sigh of intaken breath as he emerged from the doorway and strode towards his horse. Not a single pair of eyes was directly upon him; all stared straight to the front at their own height. Yet for each of them somewhere in their field of vision was the blurred figure of this man moving, the crippled man who had now proved himself so incontestably superhuman, and their king.

As he moved, as his misty outline approached the horse, the image crumpled. There was the metallic clatter of scabbard tip and sword hilt striking the stones. At once each pair of eyes swivelled towards him, to where he lay face downward on the ground. A second sighing gust of caught breath swept across the terrace, the first rush of autumn wind before the gale that snaps off dead branches and uproots old trees.

The officers of the household ran forward to pick up their master, jerking and shouting on the ground. The commander of the grenadiers swung round and screamed orders. The men marched off the terrace into the Cour d'Honneur and swung leftwards to their barracks. Their eyes were still wide and unwinking, the image of the collapsing man etched upon them.

His valets undressed him and put him to bed. Duncan Stewart came to make a pretence of ministering to him, though all that he could offer were a few gruff words of comfort. For a moment Christophe was stunned by his failure, as broken in spirit as in body. But then the old temper and determination revived; he sent for Prince Joachim, *grand maréchal du palais*, and spoke to him with authority, his voice harsh and brusque, though with pleading in his eyes.

Tomorrow, he said, he would confront the troops again, address them and remind them of their duty; and then Joachim would lead them against the mutineers at Le Cap. Joachim would carry with him a letter from the king, summoning them to submit, to throw themselves on the royal mercy. In the face of this firm action it was likely that the rank and file would return to their allegiance. If not, Joachim was to destroy them.

Throughout the night Christophe lay restless, reliving the dreadful moments on the terrace, knowing that even in the palace there were now many who were ready to turn against him, wondering how long fear would hold them back.

Soon after daybreak the Haitian Guard paraded on the terrace once more, the startled expression gone from their eyes, heavy lids hiding all emotion. Riché, their commander, brought them to attention and accompanied Joachim on his round of inspection before a stir beneath the balcony announced the arrival of the king. At his right side an equerry supported the crippled body and urged forward the paralysed leg; in his left hand he carried a pistol.

He moved slowly, his right boot slurring and grating across the stones. His face was set, not the slightest twitch of a muscle betraying the intense pain of this rough handling of withered sinews and locked bones. As he passed along the front rank he halted before each man, glaring into his eyes. The wiry hair stood out from under the sides of his shako, like white wool framing his dark chestnut-coloured face; his right eyebrow, rising in a steep curve from the bridge of his broad nose, slanted suddenly and asymmetrically downward, as did the right corner of his thick-lipped mouth.

There were twelve hundred men on parade. After he had inspected the front rank of the first company, he shuffled back to the great door of the palace, turned, and began to speak. Beyond them, beyond the village, away to left and right in a vast semi-circle wherever his glance rested, huge billows of smoke rose from the plantations, black clouds tinselled with the glowing filaments of burning cane, bending and twisting under the morning off-sea breeze.

He wanted to tell them of the things that he had still to do for Haiti, the first nation of the Blacks, the kingdom that he had built with his own will and with the courage of their fathers. These were young soldiers. Scarcely one of them had fought in the great rebellion against the whites and, if any of them had been born in slavery, there were few who had any memories of it. They had grown up in the simple acceptance of the astounding fact that their fathers had thrown off for ever the chains with which their white masters had bound them. There was no surprise, no shock, in the thought that they were the first black slaves to succeed in the struggle for freedom – perhaps, indeed, the first slaves of any colour, in all the history of the world, to triumph in such a cause. It was difficult for him to explain, to find his way to them across this barrier of the generations; and hard, too, to find words, for they were illiterate and Creole a limited language.

Besides the thought and the words there was the manner – he could no longer simply command but must woo, cajole, persuade. And beyond this there was the fear that his mouth, his tongue and teeth and palate, might no longer obey him, that though he willed himself to speak, opened and closed his lips and flexed his vocal chords, nothing would come but a meaningless chatter and mumble. He concentrated desperately, trying to distinguish the words that came out of his mouth from those that he formed in his mind, as if it were another man's throat within the black satin collar of his uniform jacket, somebody else's voice that began to echo back from the terrace balustrade.

A voice . . . sounds . . . and sounds that were distinguishable as words, though the tone was discordant and the consonants blunted. It had the nasal quality that had marked Toussaint's voice, and he remembered how Toussaint had once said that a vaudou priest had put a curse on his nose. There were many in the silent ranks in front of him who believed in vaudou, practised it in the secret conventions that were held in the hills and in the forests, shaking and chanting themselves into sexual ecstasy and stupor, worshipping the serpent and the dark mysticism of the *papaloi* and *mamaloi*. They would practise it openly if this rebellion succeeded, reverting to the superstitions of their ancestral Africa, for their new leaders would tolerate all manner of abuses if that were the only way to hold fast to power and the riches that came with it.

Power and riches – he was familiar with both. There was a great fortune hidden at Sans-Souci, and an even vaster one up in the Citadel on its cloud-shrouded mountain peak. He had used power to accumulate his riches, but he had used those riches for the good of his people. He had used them to bring out teachers from England and to set up schools; to rebuild the burned and shattered cities; to reclaim the devastated plantations that had three-quarters reverted to jungle; to enforce law and morality and the code of civilised nations.

He had seen the wonder and admiration in the visiting foreigners' eyes, to find all this done by Blacks, by men who had been born not even men but slaves. It was for this that he had driven the field hands so relentlessly and had kept half the nation under arms. So that they, who hated the name of Negro but exulted in the title of Black, might hold up their heads among the whites who were once their masters. It was for this that his subjects had been flogged and imprisoned and sometimes shot – not for his personal glory but for the honour of them all.

He could have lived as well, swaggered with the same pomp, reigned with great popularity and only half the effort, if he had given way, agreed that they had won the battle and could now lounge the sunny days away in idleness. That was what this rebellion was about. The rebels promised them more leisure and less discipline. He could offer them only more toil, more effort – and the admiration of the world. Was he to descend to being the headman of a pack of lazy field hands – he who was King of the Blacks?

There had been two battles. There was the battle that Toussaint had begun and Dessalines continued, the battle for liberty and then for independence, the battle that had been fought with matchets and barrel-hoops sharpened into swords, with muskets and cannon, with burning and torture, with hangings and dogs trained to tear men to pieces – and in all this he had played his part. But then there had remained the second battle, the battle whose command had fallen to him, after Toussaint had been murdered in the twilight of his icy French fortress-prison and Dessalines hacked to pieces in the bright hot sunlight beside the Pont-Rouge.

It was this second battle that he was still fighting: the battle for recognition; the battle of pamphlets and propaganda; the battle of letters to England, to Clarkson and Wilberforce, to the pale, powerful Tsar of all the Russias; the battle to establish schools and universities; the battle to substitute the plough for the mattock and pointed stick. The battle to show the world that a nation could be black and yet be as good as the white. That a king of the Blacks could be black himself, and still be the equal of other kings.

This is our triumph, that we who are black can do all these things. Although we are black. Because we are black. *Noir . . . Noir . . . Noir. . . .*

As he spoke he forgot his impediment and overcame it. His thoughts became words and the words rattled louder and louder across the parade ground. The harshness and the distortion were still there, but the message was clear and the tone compelling. When he had done, Riché saluted and turned to call upon the soldiers for a cheer for the king. They responded with a crashing *Vive le roi!*

He listened closely, seeking a note of insincerity, but could find none. Then he gestured to orderlies in the palace behind him and they brought out boxes of coins, running with them to the company commanders, who distributed them to their men: four *gourdes* each, more than most of them had ever received at one time before. They settled their tunics and again removed their shakos to cry *Vive le roi!* Riché gave the order for them to march and company by company they turned and wheeled away down the double staircase to the courtyard, across the courtyard to the village, and through the village northward towards the city, their scouts running before them to spy out ambushes in the plantations on either side.

As each company marched out of the courtyard it broke into the song of the grenadiers:

> *Grenadiers, à l'assaut!*
> *Ça qui mouri zaffaire à yo,*
> *Qu'y a point papa,*
> *Qu'y a point maman!*
> *Grenadiers, à l'assaut!*
> *Ça qui mouri zaffaire à yo!* *

The strong young voices rose in the sunshine of the early Sunday morning. The dust stirred and curled into clouds under their feet. He watched until they were out of sight.

---

* *Grenadiers, to the attack!*
Those who die, that's their affair,
They have no father,
They have no mother!
Grenadiers, to the attack! (etc.)

II

The Beginning

1

The colony of Saint-Domingue was Bourbon France's fairest and richest overseas possession. Shaped like a scorpion's claw, the upper prong pointing at Cuba and the lower at Jamaica, it covered the western coastal plains and mountains of the great crumpled island between the Atlantic and the Caribbean that Columbus discovered in 1492 and named Española. One hundred and twenty-five miles from north to south, with an area of 10,000 square miles – a little less than Belgium, a little more than the state of Vermont or the counties of Yorkshire, Lancashire, Westmorland and Durham combined – the colony was divided into three provinces. The south, with its capital at Les Cayes, was almost entirely confined to the rocky, 100-mile-long lower peninsula. The north occupied the upper peninsula and possessed the island's richest land – the six hundred square miles of the immensely fertile Plaine du Nord – as well as its biggest port, Cap-François, more commonly called Le Cap. The west bordered the Bight of Léogane, the vast bay contained between the two peninsulas, with the rich Plaine du Cul-de-Sac stretching back from its capital, Port-au-Prince.

Around this long coastline lay a dozen ports, busy with the traffic that used the sea in preference to the rough and inadequate roads. Inland, across the plains and up into the valleys and foothills, the plantations marched neatly, rank upon rank and acre upon acre, sugar, coffee, cotton, indigo, each great house flanked by mill and storage sheds and kitchen garden, and backed by the lines of huts, thatched with cane haulms, in which the workers lived. Deep verandahs threw a cool barrier of shade against the torrid sunlight; and from the garden, bright with the quavering wings of multi-coloured butterflies, came the scent of jasmine and orange blossom. *Rich as a Créole*, they said in Paris; and this was to all appearances a colony to be proud of and a way of life that most Europeans would envy.

Le Cap, the oldest of the island's settlements, facing the Atlantic and sheltered by steep hills to north and west, owed its prosperity to its convenience for the French trade and the magnificent harbour in which as many as five hundred ships had been known to ride at anchor. Along the half-mile of harbour-front, its quays and jetties and battery-positions built up on the marshes with stone brought down from the mountains, the government offices and white-washed warehouses rippled with the faint blue reflections of the sea. Behind them the straight streets criss-crossed at right angles, with six feet of pavement on either side of the middle kennel, then gravel and a brick or pebble sidewalk in front of the houses that were set four to a block.

The greater part of the houses were constructed of stone, often French stone, brought by vessels that came out in ballast from Nantes, and roofed with tiles from Anjou and Normandy. The symmetry of streets and roof-tops was broken by the tree-lined public squares, the arsenal, the former palace of the governor, the great church of Notre Dame (the colony, still regarded as a mission field, had no bishop but an apostolic prefect from Rome). To the north of the church opened the place d'Armes, one hundred yards square and shaded with alleys of pear trees. Eastward, in the main shopping streets of the rue de Penthièvre and the rue du Vieux Gouvernement, the latest novelties from Paris could be bought with only the delay of six or seven weeks necessary to bring them across the Atlantic. Westward, up the rue Notre Dame, past the printing works and newspaper office, lay the place Montarcher, with the theatre in its north-west corner, where the twelve actors and eight actresses of the permanent company played on Sundays, Tuesdays and Thursdays, with occasional benefits for themselves on Satur-days. Westward again, beyond the place Montarcher and the town's longest and widest road, the rue Espagnole, lay the govern-ment buildings, taken over from the Jesuits after their expulsion in 1763. Here most of the civil departments of the colony had their offices and even the governor and intendant spent the greater part of the year in preference to Port-au-Prince, the official capital, still recovering from the earthquake of 1770.

Beyond the Gouvernement, the barracks faced the Champs de Mars and the men's section of La Providence, the public hospital. Eastward along the ravine that separated the town from the Morne

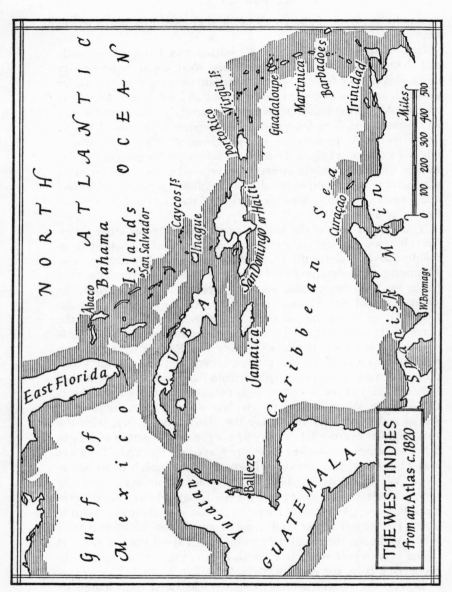

1. The West Indies

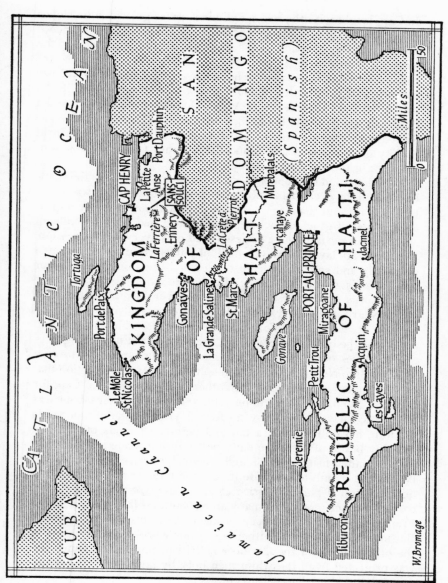

2. The Kingdom of Haiti and the Republic of Haiti

du Cap, bright with the green of Guinea grass grown on its slopes for fodder, the prison intruded between the chapel of La Providence and the women's section of the hospital. On the other side of the place du Gouvernement the nuns of the Congregation of Notre Dame had established their school for young ladies. For further encouragement of healthy minds (the body was catered for in the public baths in the rue de la Vieille Joaillerie and the place La Luzerne) there were bookshops in the rue Dauphine, the rue Saint-Domingue and the place d'Armes, while both the Royal Society of Arts and Sciences and the Literary Circle were accommodated in the rue de Vaudreuil.

Whether amid the sophisticated urbanities of Le Cap or the rustic luxuries of the great plantation mansions, the *colon* had it within his power to live out the elegant, kindly days without worry or regret: an epitome of gracious living, an existence that only the affluent and dominant can find in a society based on slavery and repression. Yet over all lay the sweet smell of putrefaction that emanated physically and spiritually from the lesser beings on whose labour the colony's wealth depended. In this decaying paradise whose dawn chorus was the crack of the slave-driver's whip and the howl of the Negro, the misery of the slave was often matched by the discontent of his master. For one, life was miserable, brutish and short; for the other it was vicious, brutish and not much longer.

The slaves outnumbered the masters by almost twelve to one: half a million Negroes to less than 40,000 whites, a proportion that was far higher on the plantations than in the towns (Le Cap, for instance, had 8,000 whites to only 12,000 slaves). Their labour was not particularly cheap. Allowing for the yearly issue of four yards of cloth, a woollen shirt, a hat and eighteen pounds of salt, the monthly bottle of *tafia*, the daily bottle of lemonade and ounce of meat or salted fish, a plot of land on which to raise vegetables and two days a month to cultivate it, and the interest and depreciation on the original purchase price of 2,000 livres, the average slave cost his master more than many an agricultural labourer earned in France. He was also, in theory, protected by Louis XIV's *Code Noir*. But in practice he fared neither better nor worse than the slaves in the other islands of the Caribbean, British, Spanish or Dutch: he was protected from the white men only by laws which the white men were seldom disposed to enforce.

Thus a master would with impunity shoot one of his slaves to demonstrate the accuracy of a pistol newly arrived from Europe, or bury another up to his neck and use his head as the jack in a game of bowls. And then, as a natural precaution against reprisals from these creatures who nursed and attended him throughout his life, prepared all his food and ministered to all his needs, he would increase the severity of his punishments, piling horror upon horror with a disgusting ingenuity that often forbids description.

On the Gallifet plantation the manager poured brine and pepper into the open wounds of slaves who had been flogged; a planter at La Grande-Rivière nailed a refractory Negro to the wall by his ears, then sliced them off with a razor, had them grilled and forced the man to eat them; another, in the Plaine des Gonaïves, was nicknamed Master Wooden Leg because, when he recaptured a runaway slave, he would order one leg to be cut off and – if the man survived – replaced by a wooden one.

The simplest and most common instrument of torture was the whip: the long bullockhide cart whip of which it was said that, while the British cat o'nine tails would take the skin off a man's back, this would take the flesh off his bones. The slave, stripped naked and forced face downward on the ground, was tied by wrists and ankles to four posts set in a rectangle; the slave-driver, under the threat of a beating himself if he laid on too lightly, administered the number of lashes with which the master or steward or overseer had ordained that the unfortunate creature should be *taillé* – the grim word that haunted the history of the island and meant "to cut or hew or whittle" a man until he was a bloody mess. White women were as free in allotting the punishment of the whip as the men, one of them taking pleasure in dripping molten sealing wax into the slave's wounds. And black women were whipped as readily as black men, though on some plantations a pregnant Negress received special consideration: a hole was scraped out of the ground to accommodate her distended belly before she was stripped and flogged.

Between the Negro slaves and the white masters lay the free Negroes and the *petits blancs*, the white artisans and shopkeepers, sailors, good-for-nothings and small farmers with less than twenty slaves. And beyond these there were the many layers of black and brown and yellow and pink, ranged from *Nègre* to *sacatra* to *griffe* to *marabou* to *mulâtre* to *quarteron* to *métis* to *mamelouc* to *quarteronné* to the almost white *sang-mêlé*, distinctions based on a scale of 128 gradations in the blood and pitifully perpetuated as much by the coloured as the white. *Mulâtre* was used as a general term for all the last six subdivisions, and mulattos made up the bulk of the colony's total of 27,000 *gens de couleur libre*,* often loosely referred to as *sang-mêlés*† or *affranchis*,‡ which was more properly the term for a free Negro.

These people, free but not white, were often well-to-do. The men were merchants, craftsmen, small planters; the women traditionally became the mistresses of white men. (It was a commonly held belief, warmly propounded by the planters themselves, that a white man must have a Black or coloured mistress so that she could inform him of the plots that his slaves were hatching against him.) But their legal freedom was little more than an exemption from slavery; no white man would accept them socially or politically as equals.

It was a land of discontent: slaves longing for the simplest human rights; mulattos craving equality; *petits blancs* resenting the dominance of the *grands colons*; the *grands colons* themselves casting envious glances northwards to the United States and dreaming of a day when they too might be able to snap the shackles in which their mother-country held them – for the law restricted all trading to France and, rich though the profits were, the cream was skimmed off them by the fat merchants of Nantes and La Rochelle and Bordeaux.

There were many masters who treated their slaves well, according them at least as much consideration as they would to a pet animal; and they were almost certainly in the majority, although in a society where atrocious inhumanities were permitted and practised, it was the evil men who were remembered rather than the good. Except on those plantations where the owner was vicious by nature, the most coveted posts were those of the house-servants, exposed to gusts of temper but relieved of the brutal labour of the fields. Better still was employment in the towns, where even the largest houses had few slaves and a Negro who worked as a personal servant might preserve a sense of individuality. It was thus that Henry Christophe was employed at Le Cap in the days when the great revolution in France hurled Saint-Domingue into a decade of unimaginable horror.

He was a robust young man in his early twenties, broad-shouldered, a little above middling height, with a frank open face, a sharp, aggressive eye, and a spirit that had never been broken. He was born on October 6, 1767, on the island of Grenada, formerly

* Free coloured people.   † People of mixed blood.   ‡ Freed slaves.

French but ceded to Britain by the Treaty of Paris four years before. For political reasons he was always imprecise about his family background, but it seems probable that one of his parents was not of pure Negro blood (his own complexion was not black but a deep red-brown) and that he was born free. Even as a child he was flinty, argumentative, unbiddable. Before he was ten years old his father sent him to sea as cabin boy to the French skipper of a coasting vessel, who in turn found him too much of a handful and got rid of him to a Saint-Dominican sugar planter named Badêche who farmed at Portelance in the district of La Petite-Anse, from whose port a long chain of reefs stretched northward and westward to protect the harbour of Le Cap.

Badêche set the small boy to work as a scullion in his own kitchen and, soon getting reports of his neatness and energy, decided to train him as a cook. Young Christophe's eagerness and manifest suitability for a job which demands much devotion and exactitude and thrives on irascibility suggested to Badêche that he might be well employed at the 'Couronne', an hostelry at Le Cap that he owned in partnership with a Mademoiselle Mongeon. The hotel was popular and well-sited, on the right-hand side of the long broad rue Espagnole that continued the main road from Port-au-Prince up to the place du Gouvernement and the place Montarcher. To the west of the rue Espagnole the land was still being developed and there were no buildings of great consequence – with the exception of the Amitié lodge built by the Freemasons – between the girls' school and the cemetery of La Fossette just inside the town gates. Eastwards, however, between the hotel and the quays, lay the rue de Saint-Louis, rue Royale and rue de Vaudreuil and the busy place Clugny, bordered with fig trees under which on Sundays as many as 15,000 slaves from the plantations on the plain would squat to barter the produce from their kitchen gardens. The Couronne was new and bustled with the town's prosperity, but here again Christophe's initial stay was short, for he went off at the age of eleven in a regiment of light infantry that the Comte d'Estaing raised from mulattos and free Negroes to aid the insurgent American colonists. He was slightly wounded at the siege of Savannah – as a free-born infantryman or, according to other accounts, as a slave-orderly to a French officer. Yet another story says that it was his service at Savannah that won him his freedom. It is indeed likely that, whether born free or not, so young a child would have had difficulty in retaining or proving his freedom. On the other hand, within ten years of his return to the Couronne at the end of the campaign he was in effect managing the hotel – improbably swift progress for a slave.

When the hard-pressed Louis XVI decided to summon the States-General in 1788, the white inhabitants of Saint-Domingue insisted on sending delegates to set forth their grievances. The existing government was identified for them with restrictions on trade and unfair profits for France; and the arrival in the following year of news that the Bastille had fallen was greeted with a blossoming of tricolour cockades and such boisterous enthusiasm that one eccentric who sported the royal favour had his head cut off and carried round the streets on a pike. Yet most of the political aims of the Revolution were meaningless in Saint-Domingue – the intolerable privileges of the nobility and church did not exist there. It was economic emancipation that the colonists wanted and they soon found that liberal policies cut both ways.

The National Assembly decreed universal franchise for all tax-payers over the age of twenty-five – and the mulattos promptly demanded votes and seats in the provincial assembly of Saint-Domingue. They were met with a scornful refusal. But the new revolutionary spirit was as intoxicating to coloured heads as to white. From Paris a young mulatto firebrand named Vincent Ogé crossed to England in 1790, tried in vain to meet the cautious Wilberforce, and managed instead to borrow money from Thomas Clarkson, the originator of the campaign to abolish the slave trade. With this Ogé sailed to the United States, bought weapons in Charleston, and continued to Le Cap. He landed without being recognised, continued on to his home at Le Dondon, in the North Province close to the Spanish border, and from there a few days later turned back towards Le Cap with three or four hundred armed mulattos, sending word in advance that he was coming to demand for the *gens de couleur* the political rights that had been granted them by the National Assembly in Paris.

Five hundred soldiers from the garrison struggled uncon-cernedly out to disperse this rabble – and were themselves put to rout. It had been unthinkable that the mulattos should demand their rights. It was incredible that they could fight for them. In an atmosphere approaching panic in the town, volunteers were called for. Christophe, who is known to have served about this period as an artilleryman and as a dragoon, was probably a member of the force of 1,500 which this time successfully smashed the rebels.

Ogé, with his lieutenant, Chavannes, and many of their supporters, escaped across the Spanish border, but the Spaniards handed them back to the provincial assembly of Le Cap, which put them on trial. Thirteen were sent to the galleys, twenty-two to the gallows. For Ogé and Chavannes a special punishment was decreed: "They are to be taken to the place d'Armes, and to the opposite side to that appointed for the execution of white criminals, and have their arms, legs and ribs broken, while alive, upon a scaffold erected for that purpose, and placed by the executioner upon wheels, with their faces turned towards heaven, there to remain as long as it shall please God to preserve life; after this, their heads to be severed from their bodies and exposed upon stakes."

Even in this excruciating death they were not to be granted equality with the whites. It was a declaration of war. But for the moment the mulattos of the North Province were intimidated by the ferocity of the sentences. Small risings in the West and South Provinces collapsed. The attitude of whites to coloureds became more harsh, more contemptuous.

In Paris, news of the horrible vengeance so moved the National Assembly that it passed a new edict in May 1791 specifically decreeing that all *sangs-mêlés*, born of a free father and a free mother, were to be admitted to the parochial and colonial assemblies. The white colonists of Saint-Domingue replied by electing their own all-white Colonial Assembly and, after convening at the South Province capital of Léogane, agreed to hold their first full session at Le Cap on August 25, 1791.

The mulattos of the West Province conspired in secret, collected arms, and decided on August 26 as the day when they would strike again.

2

Two days before the white colonists met at Le Cap to hurl defiance at the government in France, three days before the mulattos embarked on their rebellion in the West, the whole of the Northern Province went up in flames. While their masters, white and brown, plotted against each other, the disregarded nine-tenths of the population – the Black slaves – broke into bloody and terrifying revolt.

They came from many different parts of Africa. The harsh conditions of slave life, the aborting effects of venereal disease, the natural check which inhibits animals from breeding in captivity – these factors kept the birth-rate below that of mortality. There was, too, a compassionate unwillingness to inflict such a life on a child, which led to so many procured miscarriages, abortions and smotherings of new-born babies that, on some plantations, if any pregnancy did not bear lasting fruit the midwife and the mother were both flogged and the mother was put into an iron collar until she was pregnant again. During the past century a million Negroes had been brought across the ocean and sold in the markets of Saint-Domingue, yet the slave population remained at less than half that figure, the island-born Créole slaves far outnumbered by those born in Africa and shipped over from the great slave factories that dotted the coast from Senegal to Mozambique.

Just as the white planters despised the merchants, and the merchants the *petits blancs*; just as the mulattos were the most meticulous in preserving the distinctions between the mixtures of black and white blood; so among these poor kennelled creatures a sense of class and origin stayed strong. The Créole slaves held themselves superior to the African-born 'Congos', and these in turn claimed precedence according to their tribes. The Senegalese, intelligent, clean, thin-lipped and highly prized house-servants, looked down their straight noses upon the backward tribes who filed their teeth and were said to eat human flesh. The sturdy, deep-chested warriors of the Gold Coast despised the lanky, indolent Quiambas and the happy, yellow-eyed real Congos, whose frenzied dancing of the noisy, lascivious *chica* contrasted so strangely with their normal marked preference for idleness. The Nagos, their cheeks incised with tribal markings, were notorious thieves, but even they were higher in the social scale than the melancholy Ibos, whom slavery made so sad that they would sometimes hang themselves in batches, believing that in death they would return to the African homes where they were born. The only way in which a wise master could prevent this wholesale suicide was to cut off the nose or ears of the first one who killed himself, and threaten the others that they too would begin life again in the same mutilated state. *

Most of them came as savages. With them they brought old, dark superstitions that in their new land were commingled in the rites of vaudou, a magic woven around the worship of many spirits,

* The description of the various tribes comes from a contemporary account, Métral, *Histoire de l' Insurrection* . . . (1818).

and in particular Damballah, the sacred serpent served by priest-kings and priestess-queens, the *papaloi* and *mamaloi*, who had the power of bringing the dead to life in the form of *zombies*. The lesser gods were multitudinous and when the drums beat and the congregation began to dance, the *crise de loa* would seize many of them. Shaking, shivering, drenched in sweat, they contorted themselves to strange rhythms and the gods spoke, snarled, snapped and sang with their voices. The possessed passed on their sacred frenzy to those not yet inspired, rubbing them with their heads, spitting into their faces or grasping their hands. The hysterical *mamaloi* spoke oracles, made promises, uttered threats. They scattered rum and flour on the ground as food for the serpent god. They worshipped him in small, obscene idols made of wood or stone. They sacrificed chickens and young goats to him and drank the blood.

It was a mystery that they were forbidden to reveal. Rapidly it became the heart of a secret society that linked all slaves on all plantations. The *papaloi* and their lesser priests, the *hougans*, were natural leaders recruited from among the superior house-slaves or the *commandeurs*, the drivers who whipped the others to work in the fields. It was one of these *commandeurs*, a British-born slave named Buckman, who led the first uprising in the great Plaine du Nord.

Buckman's plan to use the vaudou network to synchronise risings throughout the colony was imperilled by the eagerness of his followers. During June and July there were outbreaks of disobedience and illegal gatherings in the West Province. Retired plantation stewards had to be called in to man the gallows and supervise the whipping grounds before these disturbances were put down. The planters did not regard these as portents of serious trouble, but Buckman summoned an assembly of conspirators from each of the North plantations at the end of July to impress on them the need for unity and unison.

They met in the Cayman wood – appropriate for its sacramentally reptilian name as well as for its inaccessibility – not far from the Gallifet plantation on the outskirts of La Grande-Rivière. There, to the rolling thunderclaps of a fortuitous storm, Buckman performed the vaudou rites and, in rocking ecstacy, screamed that the time was drawing nigh for the destruction of their white masters. His *mamaloi* slit the throat of a black boar. Their faces gleaming in the lightning flashes, their lips sticky with the blood of the pig, the conspirators swore an oath of obedience to Buckman and his three lieutenants: Jean-François, Biassou and Jeannot.

Once more over-eagerness led to premature risings. Early in August the Chabaud plantation was set on fire and the steward at Lagossette was murdered. Buckman, fearful lest the whites should take punitive measures which would crush the revolt before it began, summoned another meeting on August 14 at the Lenormand plantation near Morne Rouge, only five miles from Le Cap. He harangued the two hundred representatives from all over the Plaine du Nord, celebrated with them the sacred paroxysms, and once more received their oaths of obedience. But this time he set a date for the rising: August 22.

On that night Buckman the slave-driver summoned his fellow slaves on the Turpin plantation – not with a whip but with a torch; not to work in the fields but to murder and destroy. Across the whole of the northern plain the slaves ran from their barrack huts to burn, kill and rape. By the glow of the flames from cabins and mansions and the crackling sparks of the sugar canes, they hunted their ferocious masters and repaid them with a ferocity that was as wild and evil.

On some plantations the slaves remembered past kindnesses and smuggled their masters to safety. On others no whites escaped at all. Elsewhere they had sufficient warning to flee to some better fortified plantation and fight off the attacks. Almost all of those who made for Le Cap were cut down and so little information reached the provincial capital that for some hours the inhabitants believed that only a small and isolated mutiny had occurred.

Odeluc, the manager of the Gallifet plantations who had won notoriety with his trick of sprinkling pepper and brine into the wounds of his flogged slaves, had spent the evening at Le Cap and on hearing the news he at once collected a few of the town guard and set off for his plantation. Convinced that his own slaves were too cowed ever to risk his anger, he intended to use them to stamp out the disturbance. When he arrived at the plantation he found that they were among the leaders of the uprising, and that they carried as their banner the naked body of a white child impaled on a stake. He was captured and killed, with most of his companions, though one or two escaped to carry the horrible news back to the city.

It was by now unnecessary to sound a general alarm, for the exulting bands of slaves, intoxicated with murder and devastation, had spread like molten fire across the plain; the night sky was bright with the holocaust of a score of plantations; new flames burst upward every minute, climbing the slopes of the surrounding mountains and creeping closer and closer to the encircled city. Sailors were brought off the ships in the harbour to reinforce the garrison troops. The white women and children were sent aboard the vessels for safety, after having run panic-stricken about the streets.

The number and fury of the slaves were so great that it was clear that even the superior fire-power and discipline of the garrison might not prevent them from reaching the city and setting it ablaze. While detachments of artillery were sent out along the approach roads, the ferry boat at the south-east corner of the town, linking it to the Petite-Anse road across the Haut-du-Cap river, was brought over to the west bank and put under guard, and all the remaining townsmen were called out to set up palisades and *chevaux de frise*. As they worked through the night, word came in that in some parishes the mulattos had joined forces with the Negroes – whereupon the whites turned against the mulattos and a new massacre began inside the town.

There were details, too, of the horrible vengeance that the slaves were exacting. An officer of the *maréchaussée* had been nailed alive to a plantation gate and his limbs chopped off with an axe; a carpenter had been bound between two boards and sawn in half; over and over again there came reports of men being pinioned and forced to watch the violation of their wives and daughters before the whole family was slashed to pieces with cane knives, stolen cutlasses or sharpened lengths of rusty iron barrel-hoop.

Dawn came up black and cheerless for Le Cap. The flames that lit the night sky gave way to great rolling clouds of smoke, enveloping the landscape in a sombre shroud while gusts of blazing cane-straw, like a burning snow-storm, threatened to set fire to the houses in the town and the ships in the harbour. For three weeks this alternation of flames and smoke continued to illumine and overcast the sky; and six weeks later the ashes of the burnt plantations were still glowing.

The slaves captured some of the coastal defence guns and dragged them into position on the approach roads to Le Cap. Their knowledge of their new weapons was so primitive that at first they put the powder in front of the cannon balls; but they fought with a frenzy that came partly from faith in the protection from bullets conferred by the incantations of their *hougans* and partly from realisation of the fate that awaited them if they were taken prisoner. For Le Cap was a city given over to death and retribution. In the place Clugny alone five gallows had been erected for the hanging of captured rebels and two scaffolds where they were broken on the wheel, the white onlookers refusing the executioner permission to give the *coup-de-grâce* after he had placed the victim, with folded, broken limbs, on the upturned wheel to die under the scorching sun. On the periphery of the North Province, the planters were fighting back. The whites had made a short-lived truce with the mulattos in the West and South, and many who had fled across the frontier to the eastern two-thirds of the island, which was a Spanish colony, had returned with reinforcements. Captured slaves were tied to ladders and shot and the roads were hedged with severed black heads. Those who surrendered voluntarily were branded on the cheek with the letter R.

The colonists blamed the liberal policies of the National Assembly in Paris for their troubles. Many who called themselves republicans before were royalist now; more still were reluctant to continue their allegiance to either party. Scorning to turn to France for help, the Colonial Assembly at Le Cap raised three new regiments of its own, equipped them with the round English hat and gave them a black cockade instead of either the revolutionary tricolour or the royalist white. A mission sailed to Jamaica to ask the governor, Lord Effingham, to take the colony under his protection – a request as flattering as it was unwelcome, for Lord Effingham, while by no means wishing the revolted slaves to gain control, was equally averse to assuming the temporary custody of a desirable possession which, with continuing troubles both in the colony and in France, might well eventually fall into his government's hands as a permanent acquisition. He increased the naval patrol along the western shores – as a precaution against the infection spreading to Jamaica – and sent a derisory gift of 500 muskets and 150 pounds of bullets.

This niggardly response served to moderate what would otherwise have been a rough reception for the commissioners from the National Assembly who arrived at the end of November 1791. The three men, Mirbeck, Roume and Saint-Leger, had originally been appointed to enforce the decree of May, granting free mulattos full rights, but news of the bitter fighting between whites and coloured had prompted the nervous Assembly to change its mind and, in September, to ordain that such questions should be left to the

Colonial Assembly. This about-turn delighted the *colons* – but their mood changed again when they learned that the commissioners had decided to open negotiations with the rebellious slaves.

The contending parties were bewilderingly split into factions. Circumstances differed in each province and each parish, but in general the mulattos had sided with the slaves in the North and with the whites in the West; while in the South the whites had armed their own Negro slaves to attack the mulattos. So perplexing had loyalties and labels become that the rebel slaves now called themselves *les gens du roi* and fought under the white royalist banner, and their leaders, Jean-François and Biassou, styled themselves Grand-Admiral of France and Viceroy of Occupied Territories respectively. Buckman was captured early in the uprising, his body burned in the sight of his followers and his head displayed as a trophy, stuck on the end of a pike in the place d'Armes at Le Cap, the eyes still open in death, staring with unquenched malevolence at the passers-by. Jeannot, like Biassou a vaudou adept, grew more and more insane, conducting nightly orgies at his camp-fire, surrounded by twirling witches, cats, snakes and human bones. At last his ferocity against friend and foe alike became so unbridled that his followers put him to death.

A late arrival was now rising to prominence in the leadership, a wizened little postillion named Toussaint Bréda. He could read and write a little and had doctored the horses on the Bréda plantation where he had been born into slavery. On the strength of this he allotted to himself the title of *médecin des armées du roi*. He was a member of the deputation of slaves which met the commissioners during the closing days of 1791 and offered to bring the rebels back to obedience in return for pardons for all and the grant of liberty to the leaders. But the white colonists forbade the commissioners to treat on these terms and the slaves resumed their fight, striking from their camps in the mountains through the defensive cordon that the whites had set up to protect the plains, often threatening Le Cap and Port-au-Prince but never quite daring to make a full-scale attack.

So the guerilla war continued into the spring, summer and autumn of 1792, the white colonists failing to quell the rebellion and dissipating their energies in quarrels with the mulattos and the commissioners. In September three new commissioners arrived from France, Sonthonax, Polverel and Ailhaud, tougher men with instructions to enforce a tougher policy, for in April 1792 the

National Assembly had gyrated once more and had again decreed equal rights for freemen of all colours.

The mulattos were at once the allies of the new commissioners and their eager instruments in smelling out 'royalist plots' among the disgruntled whites. With the 6,000 fresh troops that they brought with them, the commissioners drove back the rebel slaves and pushed the defensive cordon higher up into the mountains, completely freeing the Plaine du Nord. They restored the authority of the republic at Port-au-Prince and in the spring of 1793 they moved on to the pacification of the South Province, where the struggle between whites and mulattos had reached such extremes of savagery that the whites paraded a captured mulatto leader through the streets in a cart with his feet nailed to the floorboards before breaking him on the wheel and burning his broken body alive, while mulattos ripped open a pregnant white woman and threw her unborn child to the hogs, and then decapitated her husband and sewed up his severed head in her womb.

Already the brutish horrors inflicted by each colour upon the others exceeded the most bloody and perverted inventions of Elizabethan melodrama, yet the sickening story was still only beginning. Its next chapter opened with the arrival at Le Cap in May 1793 of a new governor-general, Galbaud, married to a Créole from Saint-Domingue and determined to oppose equality for the *gens de couleur*. The commissioners ordered him to return to France. In reply he called out the white National Guard. With them and the sailors from the ships in port, he took over control of the city. The commissioners, helpless because most of their forces were committed in the West and South, resorted to the desperate and appalling expedient of calling on the rebel slaves for help.

The proposal was so wild and improbable that Jean-François and Biassou rejected it, suspecting a trap. But two of the lesser chieftains brought their followers into the city and, as three thousand slaves ran through the streets with flame and sword, the dreadful, familiar scenes of murder and rape were repeated. This time it was from the mountains, in the cordon posts that still held back the bulk of the rebels, that white onlookers saw great billows of smoke and towers of flame; and this time they rose not from the plain but from the city itself. Le Cap burned for four days. At the end of that time more than half its buildings were destroyed and almost all the white inhabitants, including Galbaud, had fled to America.

The commissioners were the undisputed masters of the smouldering city; but their troubles were far from ended. In February 1793 France had declared war on Britain and Britain had shortly afterwards been joined by Spain. The colony was now open to attack across the sea from Jamaica and, much more immediately, across the eastern frontier from the Spanish part of the island. Once more Sonthonax, the dominant figure among the three commissioners, called on the slaves for help – and this time he did not offer them liberty as a future reward but granted it to them as an immediate right. Henceforward all slaves were free!

The response was disappointing. Jean-François and Biassou already had more freedom than they had once dreamed of, and they calculated that the rewards would be greater and more certain if they took their followers over to the Spanish invaders' side. This they did, declaring that they owed allegiance to three kings: the king of France, their lord (though he was in fact already dead); the king of Spain, their employer; and the king of the Congo, in whose lands they had been born. With them went the wizened little ex-postillion, who had now changed his name to Toussaint Louverture. On the same day that Sonthonax decreed the emancipation of the slaves, Toussaint issued his first recorded proclamation, calling on his fellow Negroes to join him against their liberator:

Turel Camp, August 29, 1793

Brothers and Friends,

I am Toussaint Louverture. My name has perhaps become known to you. I am bent on vengeance. I desire the establishment of liberty and equality in Saint-Domingue. I strive to bring them into being. Unite with us, brothers, and fight with us in the common cause.

Your most obedient and humble servant,

Toussaint Louverture,

General of the King's armies, for the public weal.

In the South Province the white colonists renewed their approaches to the government of Jamaica. On September 3, 1793, General Sir Adam Williamson signed a convention with the leading planters, taking the province under the protection of King George III for the duration of the war. On September 20 a squadron of the Royal Navy under Commodore Ford landed a detachment of the

13th Regiment of Foot at the port of Jérémie where, as Ford reported to the Admiralty, "they were received by the inhabitants with every demonstration of joy and fidelity . . . and the British colour hoisted under a royal salute."

It was agreed between Britain and Spain that Britain should take the South Province and the whole of the western bay as far as the great fortified naval base of Môle Saint-Nicolas at the tip of the northern peninsula while Spain invaded the remainder of the North Province and the hinterland of the West. Môle Saint-Nicolas surrendered two days after Jérémie; by December, the British and their French *colon* supporters had captured almost the whole of the West Province except its capital, Port-au-Prince, and the Spaniards had taken all of the North with the exception of Le Cap and three lesser ports.

In June 1794 Port-au-Prince fell and the three French commissioners left in a ship that had been sent to take them home for impeachment. In the South a mulatto, André Rigaud, continued to fight on for the republic, though his lack of weapons restricted him to guerilla raids. In the North another mulatto, Commandant Villatte, held out at Le Cap, defying the attacks of the Spaniards but also refusing to acknowledge the authority of the acting governor-general, Laveaux, a man of revolutionary principles who had arrived with Sonthonax as commander of the Orléans Dragoons and was now cooped up at Port-de-Paix, west of Le Cap, so short of supplies that his soldiers received only six ounces of bread a day and paraded in bare feet.

The whole colony was virtually lost to France.

3

At this moment the little Negro, Toussaint Louverture, made the astonishing decision to desert the Spaniards and join the French. He had risen in the Spanish service to the rank of colonel, commanding a regiment of four thousand men who were outstanding for their efficiency and discipline; with these he garrisoned La Marmelade, a small town in the mountains between Le Cap and Les Gonaïves. On June 25, 1794, after a secret exchange of letters with General Laveaux, Toussaint declared his support of the French, massacred those troops in his vicinity who refused to join him and, with the leaders of the other neighbouring regiments, delivered to Laveaux a great swathe of territory that included the towns and parishes of Plaisance, Le Gros-Morne, L'Ennery, Le Dondon, L'Acul and Le Limbé.

Toussaint's motives for this defection will probably never be known. His detractors have said that they were envy and ambition: envy of his superior, Jean-François, whom the Spaniards had appointed general; ambition to be a general himself – a rank that Laveaux had promised him. His admirers have claimed that it was because his employers the Spaniards, like their allies the British, were committed to the maintenance of slavery. But he had not up to this point shown any more interest in universal emancipation than had the other Negro commanders.

During the negotiations of 1791 he had claimed freedom for himself, as one of the leaders, but not for his followers. His superior officer, Jean-François, had been in the habit of selling captured Negroes into slavery with the Spaniards and Toussaint had raised no protest. It is unlikely that so shrewd a man would have taken Sonthonax's declaration of emancipation as more than a desperate gamble for support, though it is true that news of the National Convention's abolition of slavery on February 4, 1794, would have reached Saint-Domingue by this time. But even this was of doubtful value: the National Convention, the National Assembly, the Legislative Assembly had each passed such conflicting and contradictory laws that none was to be relied upon. Whatever Toussaint's motives, and they almost certainly included some element of idealism as well as ambition, there is no doubt that the decision demanded a great deal of confidence and courage.

Leaving a rear guard at La Marmelade, Toussaint made a swoop across the mountains and established his headquarters on the west coast at the Descahaux plantation near Les Gonaïves. From here he drove the Spanish forces out of the Artibonite valley and back over their frontier, and began to push the British towards the sea. On the north coast, Laveaux and Villatte linked their two commands by capturing Le Borgne and Port-Margot. The French, instead of being penned into a few coastal towns, were now masters of a broad corridor whose strongpoints were firmly based on the mountain ranges; the Spaniards were on the defensive and the British-held peninsula of Môle Saint-Nicolas had been converted into an island. Toussaint had well merited his reward of being appointed *général de brigade* in the French army. But he needed more men if he was to continue his triumphant career and, with Laveaux's approval, he raised and trained four new regiments; a task in which he was aided by another stern disciplinarian, Captain Henry Christophe, seconded to him from the garrison of Le Cap.

Christophe never served with the rebel bands or in the Spanish army – another indication that he was a free Negro and not a slave. He remained at Le Cap and, after the fire of 1793 – which destroyed the Auberge de la Couronne – and the departure of most of the white population, he was appointed a captain of infantry. In the same year he married the daughter of the proprietor of a local dram shop, Marie-Louise Coidavid, a jolly, plump, fifteen-year-old girl with a very black face and classically Negroid features: thick lips, wiry black hair and splayed nostrils. She, too, was the off-spring of Negroes who had been free for many years. Their first son, François-Ferdinand, was born in 1794, when Christophe, irked by being cooped up with little food and less fighting, had gone to sea as the commander of a corsair.

Christophe's military gifts soon made an impression on Tous-saint. His days as a head-waiter had made him a stickler for punctuality and precision, while his natural aggressiveness provided him with dash and ferocity on the battlefield. In November 1794 he was promoted major, in a batch of appointments with which Toussaint honoured several of his subordinates who were later to become famous: Dessalines, Clervaux, Maurepas and Toussaint's nephew, Moyse; and on January 25, 1795, Toussaint wrote to Laveaux from Les Gonaïves praising Christophe for an ambush that he had carried out on British troops four or five days earlier in the Artibonite.

The campaign that opened so briskly in June 1794 flagged in 1795. Toussaint was short not only of men but also of ammunition. Although some was smuggled to him through the British blockade – he reported to Laveaux in July that he had bought 8,000 pounds of powder from the skipper of an American vessel, Captain Watt – it was not enough for more than defensive actions and a few guerilla raids. He was distracted, too, by Villatte's attempts to lay claim to some of his territory. Although he had little of the average Negro's dislike and distrust of mulattos, he intended that nobody should rival him or whittle away the smallest part of his power. In June 1795 he protested to Laveaux that one of Villatte's officers, Flaville, was trying to take command of the troops at La Marmelade and bring them under the control of Le Cap, where the mulattos were becoming daily more powerful. But it was of little use to complain to Laveaux, who seemed incapable of disciplining his subordinate and meekly accepted the most insolent letters from Villatte without rebuke.

Fortunately for Toussaint, the Spanish and British were unable to take advantage of this dissension. Spain had come to terms with France and, by the Treaty of Bâle in July, surrendered its part of the island. The news did not arrive until October 4, 1795, but the Spanish troops were already almost as short of supplies as were the French and had no inclination to launch a new offensive. The British, who had landed at Jérémie two years before to such encouraging acclamation from the white population, were now at loggerheads with their planter allies.

The planters were dissatisfied at not being reinstated more rapidly on their former plantations and indignant at not being allotted a share of the booty when Port-au-Prince surrendered (the value of the vessels and cargo in the port were assessed at anything between £40,000 and £500,000 and the British naval and military commanders were locked in conflict over the prize money). The British, on the other hand, had discovered that the planters' assurances – that their slaves, whom they depicted as unhappy and insecure without the guidance of the drivers and their bullockhide whips, would come flocking back to the plantations and that the revenue from taxes on the produce would cover the expenses of the British forces – were more notable for Gallic enthusiasm than for accuracy. The drain on the exchequer was great; and even greater was the drain on the man-power, not from battle casualties but from the fever which raged during the summer months and against which the European troops had no immunisation.

It was becoming clear that the campaign had been ill-advised and ill-considered. At its beginning Major-General Williamson was full of optimism. "You see what we have done and are still doing, with literally a handful of men," he wrote to the War Office in February 1794. "They are choice lads, that's true, and five thousand such, I think, would beat all the *sans culottes* – the damned brigands [the rebellious slaves] and white scoundrels do not like the brightness of our bayonets." But by the time that Spain surrendered he was having to report that "at Saint-Marc they cannot mount a sergeant's guard of British, from the great sickness and mortality."

Williamson's solution to the problem was the compulsory recruitment of slaves, in those parts of the South and West where they had remained on the plantations, buying them from the planters at two thousand livres (about £83) a head in the ratio of one slave for every fifteen on the plantation, irrespective of sex. This proposal to arm slaves produced consternation among the planters of Jamaica. Their alarm turned to indignation when they learned that the slaves were promised liberty at the end of their five-year engagement. But Williamson, who had been appointed governor of the British-occupied parts of Saint-Domingue in October 1794 and had gone there to take command in person in April 1795, stuck to his guns. "At the expiration of that period," he wrote to Henry Dundas, the Secretary of State for War, "probably very few of these individuals will be alive to partake of the terms now offered to them. The French having proclaimed a general liberty to them all, it has been judged prudent to hold out something like it to those who take up arms in defence of their masters' property."

Since the truly prudent general must take into account the possibility that he may not lose all his men, he pointed out to Dundas that it was likely that "after the term of five years is expired and [the Negro] is supposed to be entitled to his freedom, he will ever after prefer a military life as the most agreeable and least to do." On economic grounds Williamson was convinced of the soundness of his plan: "a soldier costs as much before he arrives here as the purchase of the Negro, and most probably in less than six months he is unfit for service from sickness. The Negro, except from the casualties in the field, is seldom sick. . . ."

There was a flaw in Williamson's argument, though he was not yet aware of it. The French colons who were obligingly raising these Black regiments (derisively nicknamed the royal goudrons) and giving their friends commissions in them, were also enlisting great numbers of their own and their friends' slaves, putting them on the pay roll and then sending them home to continue work on the plantations. However, Williamson was right when he continued: "The whites never can follow the brigands into the mountains, they are only fit to guard the towns and support the government."

At Port-au-Prince alone, forty officers and more than six hundred other ranks died of the fever within two months. But in August 1795 Sir Adam believed that he had lighted on a cure. "The 82nd Regiment which landed yesterday are perfectly healthy," he wrote, "notwithstanding they were some months at Gibraltar. It is evidently owing to their drinking wine and not spirits. I understand the wine costs about five pounds a cask. I do not know the price of wines in general . . . but some very good Teneriffe wines might be contracted for at a very reasonable rate – the loss of hundreds, nay thousands, of valuable men might be saved."

He did not get approval from Dundas for his admirable project. The Secretary of State for War was coming under increasing fire for his support of the Saint-Dominican adventure, although the criticism was not entirely fair. Throughout the century, Britain had been the only European country to make substantial gains from war – and had done this by seizing her enemy's colonies. India, Canada and a rich assortment of islands in the Indian and Atlantic oceans were already harvested. Cape Colony joined them in 1795 and the Royal Navy was keeping a watchful eye on South America. That Dundas should try to add the immensely valuable Saint-Domingue to the collection was understandable and laudible. But Parliament was alarmed at the costliness of the operation in money even more than in men. It was gushing out in pay, in provisions, in the purchase of Negroes, in bribes paid to unspecified 'brigand chiefs' but more often sticking to the fingers of the *colon* go-betweens and in any case producing no visible results. Reinforcements were being retained in Jamaica by Williamson's successor, Lord Balcarres, to deal with a rebellion by the Maroons, the former Spanish slaves who lived in the hills. The fresh troops who reached Saint Domingue at the end of the year failed to dislodge Rigaud from the port of Léogane in the south. It was plain that General Williamson had failed. He was appointed a Knight Commander of the Bath and the Army List was consulted for a successor.

Fortunately the situation was not acutely grave, for the French commanders were quarrelling among themselves. Laveaux, much to Villatte's resentment, had returned from Port-de-Paix to the mulatto-dominated city of Le Cap to exercise his offices of governor and commander-in-chief. Villatte, refusing to relinquish control of the city, increased his whispering campaign against Laveaux. On March 20, 1796, the mulattos struck.

Laveaux later sent Toussaint a description of what happened when

at ten o'clock that morning I was in my bedroom seated at a table, talking with the chief engineer. Some seven or eight persons entered through the door of the study on the left, and about a hundred through the salon, *all coloured men, not a single Black, not a single white!* I supposed it was a quarrel that they had brought for my judgement.

I got up calmly. They formed a circle round me. I asked them, what do you want, citizens? Immediately the ringleader aimed a punch at my head. I dodged it, jumped on him and brought him to the ground. I said to the others: Assassins, I have no weapons! At the same time a dozen jumped on me saying, In the name of the people, we will drag him to the cells. I asked them: Where is the municipal council?

You've no need of it – move, rascal, they answered. No, I said, you are not the people. There are neither Black citizens nor white citizens here, you are assassins.

At this, they rained blows on me. I fought back furiously and for an instant threw them off. I called for my *aide-de-camp*, who came running. They struck him with sticks and he could not reach me. I then seized one of them and threw him down. He was armed with pistols and daggers.

They overwhelmed me with truncheon-blows on the arms, they dragged me by the hair, they hammered their fists on my chest and grabbed me by the skin of my belly. I was in my slippers. I lost them in the struggle and hoped for help but none came, for all the entrances to Government House were guarded. Finally, barefooted and bareheaded, I was dragged out by my hair and my arms and taken to the town prison.

He was thrown into a cell and kept there incommunicado until half-past eight the following evening, when the town council came to see him. The councillors, however, were either too frightened or too much in the pockets of the mulattos to do more than offer their condolences and promise that they would look into the matter. Since they proposed to consult all the other town councils in the colony, Laveaux seemed likely to remain long enough in prison for Villatte to establish his hold not only over Le Cap but also throughout the North Province.

The mulatto *coup* was effected so successfully and secretly that it was almost three days before Pageot, the white French general commanding the North Province, heard of the governor's arrest and sent a messenger at once to Toussaint at Les Gonaïves. The warning was unnecessary. The Black colonels and generals stationed in the region of Le Cap were all among Toussaint's devoted followers, and on hearing of the arrest of the governor-general (whom Toussaint, they knew, was in the habit of addressing as 'my father') they took action without waiting for further orders.

All refused to accept Villatte's authority; Colonel Léveillé rode through the streets of Le Cap, calling on the Negroes to come to the aid of their protector, while Colonel Pierre Michel, commanding the garrison at Le Haut-du-Cap, sent word that unless Laveaux was released he would march in at the head of his troops and 'destroy everything alive'. The bearer of this ferocious message was Major Henry Christophe. He delivered it with such emphasis that at nine o'clock on March 22 the municipal council marched in procession to the city jail, released Laveaux and conducted him back to the town hall where he received the plaudits of the citizens.

Though Toussaint had not stirred from Les Gonaïves, nobody – least of all the governor-general himself – had any doubt of whose hand had foiled the *coup*. A few days later Toussaint made a triumphant entry into Le Cap at the head of two battalions of infantry and 800 horsemen and on April 1, at a great parade in the place d'Armes, Laveaux proclaimed his gratitude to Toussaint, "the saviour of established authority, the Black Spartacus, the Negro predicted by Raynal as the avenger of the injuries suffered by his race", and appointed him lieutenant-governor. Toussaint replied with a cry of "After God, Laveaux!" and his army thundered their appreciation. He rode off with Laveaux's permission to form three new regiments of infantry, two of cavalry, and a personal bodyguard. He was the most powerful man in the island. His faithful subordinates received promotion: Léveillé and Michel to the rank of *général de brigade*, Christophe to a colonelcy, with command of the district of La Petite-Anse, where he had once worked as a scullion in Monsieur Badêche's kitchen at Portelance.

From France, where the flames of the revolution had dwindled to the sooty corruption of the Directory, a new set of commissioners arrived on May 12, 1796, including Sonthonax, the Paris lawyer who had been tried and exonerated for his part in the colony's troubles of three years before. With them came three thousand fresh troops and two generals, to whose authority Toussaint was no more prepared to submit than he had been to mulatto domination. He quarrelled with one of them, Rochambeau, whom Sonthonax sent home to France. The other, Desfourneaux, was dispatched to the South Province to cooperate with Rigaud; but Rigaud, furious at the honours heaped on Toussaint by Laveaux, refused to have anything to do with him and Desfourneaux returned to be employed in the North Province, discreetly out of Toussaint's way.

Three months after the commissioners' arrival, elections were held to nominate representatives to the Corps Legislatif in Paris. Toussaint was accused at the time by representatives of the South Province of rigging the voting in favour of Sonthonax and Laveaux because they were his friends, and has since been accused of having done it in order to get rid of them because they were his rivals. It seems probable that he brought pressure to bear on the electors in his own district around Les Gonaïves and in the North Province where Colonel Christophe and General Michel were very active on his behalf. (It is again indicative of Christophe's status that the pamphlets denouncing Toussaint's manoeuvres refer to 'le Noir' Christophe and 'le Nègre' Michel – the nouns specifically used for freeman and slave respectively.) But neither Sonthonax nor Laveaux showed any reluctance to accept nomination, both wrote letters of thanks after their election, and Sonthonax would have accompanied Laveaux and the others to France had not his fellow commissioners begged him to remain "to save the colony and rescue the remaining Europeans from a general massacre". It is clear that Toussaint's ambitions were limited at this time. In July he sent his son and stepson to be educated in France, and he was scarcely cold-hearted and calculating enough to offer them unnecessarily as hostages in this way; and the French authorities still had faith in him, for in December he was promoted to *général de division* and in January 1797 publicly presented with a sabre and a pair of pistols made at the national arsenal at Versailles.

The crisis which prompted the other commissioners to beg Sonthonax to remain in the colony was an outbreak of guerilla warfare in the district of La Vallière and La Grande-Rivière, led by some of Jean-François's former followers. Furnished with money and munitions by the British, the dissident Negroes threatened both the neighbouring Fort-Liberté and, via Les Perches and Le Trou, Le Cap itself. The situation was sufficiently menacing for Toussaint to leave his headquarters at Les Gonaïves, facing the regular British forces, and return to Fort-Liberté to deal with the threat, while Desfourneaux, back from his unsuccessful mission to Rigaud, was given charge of three columns which marched up into the mountains, commanded by Colonels Christophe, Moyse and Grandet. The campaign, which was successful in quelling the revolt, resulted in the three colonels being cited by Carnot in a report to the *Conseil des Anciens* – the first and last occasion on which Christophe was ever to be officially commended by a member of the French government.

To Christophe himself the occasion was more memorable because it brought him into closer cooperation with Colonel Vincent, the French engineer officer responsible for the colony's fortifications and the man who had drawn up the plan of attack for Desfourneaux. Christophe never regarded warfare as an end or a pleasure in itself as did many of the Negroes who had risen to high rank in the army. He understood and shared Toussaint's determination to rebuild the island's economy and to lead it back to peace and prosperity. In Vincent he found a collaborator and fellow-enthusiast and when Christophe returned to his command at La Petite-Anse the two men threw themselves into a project for the regeneration of the colony's agriculture after six years of rebellion and war.

The system of *fermage* which they instituted was destined to save the economic life of the colony and to form the basis of the many *codes rurales* which succeeded it. The abandoned plantations were taken over by the government and let out to rent, usually to senior army officers and public officials. The tenant was required to distribute one quarter of his gross revenue among the workers on the plantation and to provide lodgings and nursing services. The government undertook to enforce a code of work under which the field hands were required to labour for a set number of hours each week and were not allowed to quit their employment without permission. Idle workers were punished and inefficient tenants were deprived of their plantations. Christophe, always enthusiastic for tidiness and industry, was soon establishing, overlooking and enforcing the new projects throughout the district under his control; and within eighteen months the sugar produced on one plantation had increased almost tenfold.

With the crushing of the British-inspired revolt, the North Province was at peace. In the South, during the early part of 1796, the British tried to bribe Rigaud into handing over the capital, Les Cayes; but, though he was willing to surrender the town, and with it the province, his terms were too high. In the West, Toussaint returned to the attack during March and recaptured the Mirebalais district, for which Sonthonax rewarded him with the title of *général-en-chef des armées de Saint-Domingue,* a post that had been vacant since Laveaux's departure. But in May his advance was held up by Major-General Simcoe, who had replaced General William-son as commander-in-chief in December. Toussaint returned to the defensive and, leaving the approaching fever season to hold the British at bay, turned his attention to Le Cap.

Here Sonthonax was still in the saddle, despite his assurance to his fellow deputies that he would be joining them in Paris in the spring. Once again it is difficult to distinguish truth from slander and to decide what influence Toussaint had on Sonthonax's even-tual departure, but it is clear that, while Sonthonax was becoming more inclined to remain on the island, Toussaint had less reason to desire his presence. He accused Sonthonax of interfering in military affairs and undermining his authority. Sonthonax, although agree-ing to promote Toussaint's nephew, Moyse, to the rank of general, refused to grant several other of Toussaint's requests. Sonthonax also ordered the arrest as an *emigré* of seventy-year-old Bayon de Libertat, the former steward on the Bréda plantation, who had returned to the island from the USA at Toussaint's invitation. Bayon had been one of Toussaint's greatest benefactors during his slave days, providing him with the opportunity to pick up the rudiments of reading and writing and giving him a sheltered job as a postillion; in gratitude, Toussaint had organised the Bréda slaves in opposition to the rebels in 1791 and had held them off for a month until he could get Madame Bayon in safety to Le Cap.

Whether as a result of these incidents or not, rumours began to circulate, first in the army and then among the civil population, that Commissioner Sonthonax was an enemy of the Negroes and intended to deprive them of their liberty. In August Toussaint marched towards Le Cap at the head of a large force of men – much larger than any military requirements would indicate. Son-thonax took the hint, if hint it was, and went aboard one of the ships in the harbour, en route for France and the seat on the *Conseil des Anciens* that had awaited him for almost a year.

Toussaint was the undisputed master of the North and West Provinces. Only one rival remained: Rigaud in the South. But before he settled accounts with him Toussaint must deal with the British. They were still apparently firmly implanted at strategic points right down the curve of the great western bay from Môle Saint-Nicolas through Saint-Marc and Port-au-Prince to Jérémie at the tip of the southern peninsula. But Whitehall was in fact only too eager now to rid itself of the burden of this ill-judged expedition. The government was short of men to resist Bonaparte in Europe, and had already lost 10,000 soldiers and 5,000 sailors in Saint-Domingue. It was short of money and had been forced to suspend payment in gold by the Bank of England in February, 1797. This campaign alone had cost five million pounds and was continuing at the rate of three-quarters of a million a year. On May 18, 1797, the Commons debated, and somewhat reluctantly rejected, a motion to abandon the campaign at once.

To the long list of commanders and acting commanders, most of whom had lost their reputations on the island, were now added two more names: those of General Nesbitt and his remarkable second-in-command: 'King Tom' Maitland.

4

Brigadier-General the Honourable Thomas Maitland, brother of Lord Lauderdale, was thirty-eight years old, strong-willed, irascible, courageous and supremely contemptuous of all mankind. His fellow-Scotsman, Dundas, found his outspokenness refreshing in contrast to the mealy-mouthed servility that he received at the War Office from most senior officers. He had also been impressed by the alacrity with which Maitland had resigned his seat as Member of Parliament for the Haddington Burghs in favour of one of Dundas's nominees. He knew that Maitland was acquainted with Saint-Domingue, where he had served as lieutenant-colonel commanding the 62nd Foot in 1794, and in 1797 he sent him back there as aide to General Simcoe with orders to submit confidential reports. Maitland's trenchant comments on the mismanagement and corruption that he claimed to have observed prompted Dundas to send him out again in 1798 with Nesbitt. He was allowed to see Nesbitt's secret instructions, which were to reduce expenditure to a maximum of £25,000 a month, even if this meant evacuating any or all of the positions at present held – with the exception of the valuable naval base at Môle Saint-Nicolas.

Maitland arrived alone – Nesbitt having had to be put ashore seriously ill at Madeira, where he later died – and at once began to deluge Dundas with a stream of confidential letters in which he lambasted everybody – his French allies, whom he accused of theft and extortion; his fellow generals: "I shall not enter into details, because it would only lead to unpleasant explanations, but generally

I am forced to say that Churchill's conduct, to make the best of it, has been childish to a degree"; his enemies: "every attempt the Brigands have yet made clearly proves how unfitted they are for any regular attack on any place decently fortified, for tho' there are instances of their coming on with bravery when intoxicated with liquor, yet they are totally unfit to undertake the labour and fatigue of a general siege"; even casual acquaintances of superior rank: "I do myself the honour to acquaint you that on my passage to this place I touched at Barbadoes and Martinique, where, from every information I received, it would seem that His Majesty's Service would not essentially suffer if ill-health or any other circumstance should render it necessary for Lieutenant-General Cuyler to return to England."

'This place' was Môle Saint-Nicolas, where 'King Tom' arrived on March 11, 1798, and whence he at once reported to Dundas that "our situation is worse than even I, who was never sanguine respecting it, could have possibly imagined". He criticised the existing commander-in-chief, General Whyte, for his "superciliousness of manner and hauteur of demeanour, at all times unpleasant, but which must be peculiarly abhorrent to the [French colonists] in their situation." Since he was equally rude to Whyte himself and flatly refused to let him know the contents of Nesbitt's secret instructions, Whyte shortly sent him down to Port-au-Prince, which was now threatened by a two-pronged drive led by Colonels Christophe and Dessalines under Toussaint's direction.

On April 4 Maitland sent Whyte a report of the successes his troops had gained against the 'brigands' at L'Arcahaye which was as misleading as it was boastful, for in less than three weeks he was writing to Toussaint offering to surrender Port-au-Prince with all its defensive and public works undamaged if Toussaint would undertake not to interfere with the evacuation by sea of the British forces and any inhabitants who wished to accompany them, and would further guarantee the lives and properties of any who wished to stay behind. To Whyte, Maitland had his chief-of-staff write an impertinent note informing him of what had been done and adding, "if you think proper to interfere and counteract any of his [Maitland's] measures, he will no longer become responsible for the consequences or even the life of any individual in this place".

In Port-au-Prince he declared martial law, "to save legal expenses," as he explained to Dundas, and lost no time in impressing the inhabitants with his determination to be obeyed. A proclamation from King's House on April 26 announced that a local citizen had been found guilty of seditious conduct and that the Honourable Brigadier-General Maitland "hereby directs the said Sieur Peyrade to be executed this evening at five o'clock, and that the severity of the example may deter others from involving themselves in a similar situation, the mode of execution will be by blowing him from the mouth of a cannon on the heights of St Robin" – a refinement of local government that 'King Tom' had picked up during earlier service in India.

Toussaint, who hurried from Grand-Bois to his headquarters at Les Gonaïves as soon as he heard of the arrival of the *parlementaire* whom Maitland had sent on April 23, was very ready to give his word to safeguard the whites who wished either to stay or leave. He was no revolutionary; the laws against *emigrés* meant nothing to him and he had already quarrelled with Sonthonax when he tried to enforce them. Indeed, Toussaint recognised that the colony's economy would benefit from the experience of the ex-planters and it was his policy to encourage them to return. So long as they did not obstruct his ambition, all men to him were equal and acceptable, black, brown or white. He agreed to Maitland's proposals and on May 6, 7 and 9 the British evacuated Saint-Marc, L'Arcahaye and Port-au-Prince.

Nesbitt's instructions were to hold on to the naval base at Môle Saint-Nicolas because it dominated the westward passage from the Atlantic to the Caribbean and was impregnable from the sea. It was, however, difficult to defend on the landward side because of the hills that encircled it. Maitland decided that Jamaica could be as well protected by the capture of Tiburon in the south as by the retention of Môle Saint-Nicolas in the north, and accordingly again tried to buy Rigaud's cooperation.

He was encouraged to believe that his offer would be accepted because he had recently paid Toussaint's adjutant-general, Idlinger, one thousand pounds for a complete muster-roll of Toussaint's forces (and never discovered that, after consultation with Toussaint, Idlinger had fooled him by grossly exaggerating their number). Rigaud, however, was determined to hold on and prove to the Directory that he was a better man than Toussaint. He refused. Maitland launched an attack on Tiburon in June. It was a failure; the troops that succeeded in getting ashore met with fierce resistance and the naval vessels that were to have bombarded the forts were dispersed by a storm.

Despite vigorous protests from Admiral Hyde Parker, com-manding the Jamaica station, Maitland decided to evacuate the whole island. By handing over Port-au-Prince to Toussaint instead of to Rigaud, Maitland had not only ensured that Rigaud was too weak to attack Jamaica but had also provided him with an additional grievance against Toussaint. For the same reason – to split the contending leaders in the island – he surrendered Môle Saint-Nicolas to Toussaint instead of to the new commissioner whom the Directory had sent out to replace Sonthonax: General Hédouville.

Hédouville, who was then enjoying a great reputation as the man who had brought peace to the Vendée, very soon appreciated that Toussaint was not prepared to accept a master in the island. Like Maitland, he counted on weakening Toussaint by fanning the flames of his rivalry with Rigaud and invited both men to confer with him at Le Cap. Toussaint, shrewdly suspecting what Hédou-ville was at, journeyed to Le Cap in Rigaud's carriage and proposed to him that they should concert their efforts against the white man. But Rigaud was too suspicious, too deeply and emotionally com-mitted to his fight against the Blacks. On arrival at Le Cap he was tricked by Hédouville into denouncing Toussaint, whom Hédou-ville had left within earshot. The struggle between the mulatto and the Black was now intensified and could only end in the total defeat of one of them.

On October 3, 1798, the last of the British troops withdrew from Môle Saint-Nicolas and Toussaint had his hands free to deal with Hédouville. The strange whispers that had plagued Sonthonax's later days in the colony were now repeated about the new com-missioner. The general was an enemy of the Blacks. . . . He planned to re-introduce slavery. . . . As before, the whispers spread from the army to the civilians. On October 20 bands of Negroes began to march on Le Cap. On October 23 Hédouville prudently embarked for France, after a stay of just six months.

Maitland's return to England was accompanied by rumours that he had entered into a secret commitment under which Britain recognised Toussaint as the ruler of an independent Saint-Dom-ingue in return for a monopoly of the ex-colony's trade – a threat to United States interests which brought anxious inquiries from Rufus King, the American Ambassador in London. Dundas assured King that he had been misinformed: the secret clause was only a mutual pact of non-interference in each other's affairs and a promise that the British blockade would be slackened to allow provisions and produce to pass in and out of Saint-Dominican ports. But this, from King's point of view, was almost equally unacceptable, since the French corsairs who used the Saint-Dominican ports would now be better supplied for their attacks on American shipping. He asked for an additional paragraph banning privateers from ports under Toussaint's control.

Toussaint had already written to President Adams in November, suggesting a resumption of the trade that had been suspended because of America's difficulties with France, and in December he sent his treasurer, Joseph Bunel, to Philadelphia for extended talks. He realised that both the British and the American governments were under pressure – from their West Indian colonists and Southern planters respectively – to discourage and quarantine the 'republic of Blacks' that seemed to be emerging in Saint-Domingue; but he knew, too, that there was just as strong a pressure from the merchants of both countries to get their hands on the valuable Saint-Dominican trade. By playing one against the other he intended to strengthen his own position and his country's economy.

Maitland, who had persuaded King as well as Dundas that he was an expert on Saint-Domingue and Toussaint, was sent to Philadelphia to put to Timothy Pickering, the American Secretary of State, the British proposal of setting up a joint Anglo-American company to monopolise the trade with Saint-Domingue and to restrict this trade to a single port – thus simplifying the task of the Royal Navy in maintaining a cordon round the island. But he soon found that a government-controlled company was unacceptable to the free-enterprise merchants of the northern states. "Our policy is to protect, theirs to destroy, the present colonial system," he wrote despondently to Dundas. "With such fundamental differences existing, it is not very likely they will enter cordially into our views; but as it fortunately happens they cannot carry their own views into effect without our assistance, that is without our taking off the naval blackade of Saint Domingo, they will, I fancy, be induced to give a reluctant consent to a restricted intercourse, but never to a closed company."

As for America as a whole, his views were as forthright as ever. "To me it appears to be in a deplorable state of national debility. The executive government without energy, the people without the smallest feeling of national honour, all occupied in accumulating money, and he not only the best but the ablest man who gets the

most, tho' possibly in the unfairest manner. From such a government and such a people, we can expect nothing either vigorous or
beyond the narrow limits of their paltry views of their immediate
interests. War they will never declare, and insult they will ever
submit to."

In the end, it was agreed that Britain should drop the demand for
trade to be confined to a single company, but that it should be
restricted to two ports – Le Cap and Port-au-Prince – except for
vessels specially licensed by local British or American agents.
Maitland sailed from Philadelphia to Le Cap and then – because
Roume, the only survivor of the many agents that France had sent
to Saint-Domingue, had now returned there from the Spanish part
of the island and Toussaint was unwilling to conduct negotiations
with an enemy under his nose – he continued on to Les Gonaïves
where the new terms were accepted by Toussaint.

"If I have not succeeded as far as I could have wished," Maitland
wrote to Dundas on the eve of his return to England on June 25,
1799, "I think I may venture to say I have done as much as could
be effected, and should no other good arise out of it, it has had at
least this effect, to have set the chiefs in the island fairly by the
ears, and to have turned the attention of Rigaud from Jamaica to
this island." And thus to a typical Maitland conclusion: "With
regard to the island of Jamaica I fairly confess to you I was not a
little astonished at the state in which I found it, and have no hesitation in saying that whether it be considered with a view to its
defence against attack, or with a view to its internal government,
it requires the immediate and vigorous interposing hand of His
Majesty's Government to save it from ruin."

Maitland's self-congratulation on having "turned the attention
of Rigaud from Jamaica" was based on a report he had received
from Edward Stevens, the American consul-general at Le Cap,
that Rigaud, still hoping to gain favour with the Directory, was
planning to invade the British colony. Since Stevens received his
information from Toussaint, there is every reason to doubt its
truth. Toussaint was well aware that the basic purpose of British
policy was to protect Jamaica and he seldom missed an opportunity
of rasping the colonists' fears; he was also aware that it was highly
unlikely that Rigaud would embark on any foreign adventure.
Toussaint had denounced him as a traitor in April and in June
Rigaud replied by assuming the title of Governor of the South
Province and setting his troops on the move against the northern

forces. The long-expected war between the Negroes and the mulattos had begun.

5

Toussaint's troops were far different now from the ill-armed, disorganised, untrained bands of field hands who had risen to fight against their masters in the early days, trusting to vaudou charms to bear down a volley of grapeshot or to change it to water, plunging their arms into the mouths of guns to hold back the cannon-balls. The less likely soldiers had been released to work on the reviving plantations; the remainder had been brought to a pitch of training that quite amazed one British officer who, posing as an American, went ashore at Le Cap during the spring of 1799.

"At a whistle, a whole brigade ran three or four hundred yards," he wrote, "and then, separating, threw themselves flat on the ground, changing to their backs and sides, and all the time keeping up a strong fire until recalled. . . . This movement is executed with such facility and precision as totally to prevent cavalry from charging them in bushy and hilly countries." The training was organised and stringently supervised by Henry Christophe, now commanding the city of Le Cap and already creating such a reputation for his men that they were usually referred to not under their designations as demi-brigades but as 'Colonel Christophe's army'. Captain Marcus Rainsford, the British officer who was so impressed by their field training, shortly afterwards became more closely acquainted with Christophe, for he was denounced as an Englishman, charged with spying, and condemned to death by a court-martial over which Christophe presided with gravity and consideration. It was only after much pleading that Rainsford's American friends secured his release and he was expelled from the country.

Rigaud synchronised with his advance in the South a number of mulatto risings in other parts of the colony and Toussaint no sooner moved from his headquarters at Les Gonaïves to join Dessalines at Port-au-Prince than he learned that Rigaud's sympathisers had taken over Môle Saint-Nicolas. He turned northwards again to deal with this, and in July wrote to Christophe warning him that he had secret information of a similar *coup* planned at Le Cap, where there were still many mulattos among the population.

"I rely more than ever on your unwavering severity," he wrote.

"Let nothing escape your vigilance." Christophe's court-martial sat continuously throughout August. At night squads of his soldiers marched through the streets, arresting suspects and taking them to the *savane de la Fossette*, a piece of waste ground just outside the town, where they were shot without trial and tumbled into waiting graves. By September 3, Toussaint had crushed all resistance at the Môle and was able to order Christophe to take the bulk of his troops to Jacmel, where he was to reinforce Dessalines.

At Port-au-Prince, on his way south, Christophe met the British vice-agent, Hugh Cathcart, who was as impressed as Rainsford had been by the quality and appearance of his soldiers: "By far the best dressed and armed of Toussaint's troops." Of Christophe's personal bodyguard of one hundred and fifty cavalrymen, fifty were dressed as hussars. The two demi-brigades of infantry, some 3,000 men, included a battalion of white troops, all that were left of the thousands that had been sent to the colony during the past decade. At his own expense, from the profits of the plantations that he farmed, Christophe brought with him enough pay, provisions and ammunition for three months: 1,800 gold doubloons, 500 barrels of flour and 100 barrels of pork, clothing, 400 cannon balls for a brass 12-pounder and a brass 16-pounder; and ball and powder for pistols and muskets – shipped round the coast in the brig *Rebecca*, which he had chartered from Dr Stevens at Le Cap.

Cathcart found that Christophe, neat, compact, businesslike, presented a sharp contrast to Toussaint, whose skinny form was almost ludicrously clad in "a kind of blue spencer, with a large red cape falling over his shoulders, and red cuffs, with eight rows of lace on his arms, and a pair of large gold epaulets thrown back from his shoulders, a scarlet waistcoat, pantaloons and half-boots; a round hat with a red feather and national cockade; and an extremely large sword suspended at his side." There was an air of authority about Christophe that impressed Cathcart. "He appears to possess fully as much influence and power as Dessalines or Moyse (although he ranks only as a *chef de brigade*), he is equally as ambitious and far superior to either of them in abilities, knowledge of the world (if I may be allowed to use the expression) and his own resources."

Cathcart had a bone to pick with Christophe. Three British vessels, carrying cargoes from Port-au-Prince, had been requisitioned on arrival at Les Gonaïves and sent north to Le Cap. There they were used to transport some of Christophe's infantrymen down to Port-au-Prince. When the captain of one of the vessels protested, he was beaten by Christophe's soldiers. Cathcart made a strong protest to Toussaint who promised that, if the facts were true, Christophe would apologise.

This Christophe did, very civilly, and added composedly: "But you know, Mr Cathcart, if the master of that ship had been a Frenchman and had conducted himself in that manner, I should have shot him out of hand." It was clear that he was very surprised that Cathcart should have taken the matter so seriously.

Toussaint told Cathcart that he was determined not to receive any more commissioners from France and that he had a vessel waiting at Le Cap to send Roume back there "and that he would have done it long before this time, was he not afraid that he might find his way to Rigaud and turn the tables upon him". Toussaint was appealing to Lord Balcarres, governor of Jamaica, for large quantities of arms and ammunition – among them 6,000 muskets and bayonets, 100,000 pounds of gunpowder – but Cathcart thought him in no urgent need of them. He reported, however, that Toussaint had left off disposing of mulattos by blowing them from cannon and had recently had six hundred taken out to sea in lighters, tied back-to-back, bayonetted and then thrown overboard with weights attached to their feet.

Cathcart, a colonial, had an inbred distrust of Toussaint and was for ever dreaming of the day when the British government would be able to end its association with him. His superior, John Wigglesworth, the principal agent, had come out from Britain as an army contractor and held a much higher opinion of the general, particularly since he had recently shown his good faith by denouncing to the Jamaican government two French spies who had been sent over by Roume. Toussaint had supplied not only their names but also such accurate descriptions of their appearance that they were captured and condemned to death just before Christmas 1799. Nevertheless, Wigglesworth was very worried at this time by a report that Roume was attempting to bring about a reconciliation between Toussaint and Rigaud. It would be necessary, Wigglesworth suggested, to send arms to Rigaud at once if the war were to be kept going.

"To feed the enmity of the contending chiefs but not to suffer either the one or the other to gain entire military ascendancy" was, as he well knew, the principal aim of British policy. On the other hand, he advised doing everything possible to retain the friendship of Toussaint, who had lately been grievously offended by the Royal

Navy's action in capturing and putting up for sale as prizes several vessels which he had furnished with papers declaring that they were being used solely for the transport of troops and munitions in his campaign against Rigaud. The navy was perfectly within its rights in seizing ships sailing under the French flag but Wigglesworth suggested that to placate Toussaint the government should buy in the ships and return them to him. This Admiral Hyde Parker dismissed as "totally inadmissible", adding that he had no faith in Toussaint's word. Wigglesworth, already sick with yellow fever, was in no condition to press his argument and a few days later he died.

Cathcart had forecast at the end of November that the task of defeating Rigaud would take Toussaint longer than he expected, and as the months dragged by and the mutual slaughter of Negro and mulatto continued, it became clear that he was right. The southward drive was held up by the determined resistance of Pétion, a mulatto officer who had recently deserted from Toussaint's forces, in the fortified town of Jacmel which guarded the entrance to the south peninsula. Toussaint had more artillery brought from the north, and personally supervised the arduous, dangerous work of dragging it over the mountains, often leaping from his horse to put his shoulder to a wheel or strain on a rope as the guns were manoeuvred along the precipitous and ill-made roads. He returned to Port-au-Prince and implored Cathcart and Ritchie, the American agent, to ask their governments to sell him a frigate so that he might bombard Jacmel from the sea. But neither the British nor the American government intended to be so foolish as to trust this Black man with a ship of war.

The besiegers built redoubts along the shore from which their coastal batteries prevented the provisioning of Jacmel from the sea. Pétion and his army of 3,000 men, though short of rations, still had enough ammunition to repulse every attack launched against them – several led by Colonel Christophe in person at the head of the 2nd demi-brigade. Toussaint finally managed to charter armed American merchant ships and these he sent down to blockade and shell the town. Dessalines ordered Christophe to attack again, but again the defenders threw him back.

By March 1800, however, it was apparent to Pétion that his situation was hopeless. Rigaud had been unable to send him help either by land or by sea. The garrison was reduced by two-thirds; food was so short that a slice of horse or dog or cat, garnished with stewed grass, had become a luxury. The hatred between Negro and mulatto was now so bitter that surrender was out of the question and Pétion ordered a general break-out to be attempted during the night of March 12, to be covered by a feint demonstration from one redoubt manned by a rear guard. Since he was well aware that spies were passing between the lines, he let the information leak out that the escape route would be along the Baynet road, and was gratified to learn shortly afterwards that Dessalines had begun moving troops in that direction.

At nightfall on March 12 Pétion revealed to his junior commanders that they were to escape not along the Baynet road but on a path that skirted the last redoubt. At eight o'clock the force of nearly one thousand soldiers, followed by four hundred women and children, began to move stealthily through the outer ring of shattered houses and along the muddy road. Suddenly they were met with a blast of fire from Christophe's 2nd demi-brigade: Pétion's plan had been revealed to Dessalines by a white doctor who had slipped through the lines and the escape route was blocked.

From the last-manned redoubt the rear guard opened covering fire that was soon beaten down by the weight of musketry opposed to it. In the blackness the flash of discharging muskets was accompanied by the rattle of steel and the screams of hand-to-hand fighting. Christophe sent an assault party to capture the redoubt and brought up two 18-pounders with which he volleyed grapeshot into the column of escapers. Caught on one side by fire from the captured redoubt, they found themselves attacked with bayonet charges on the other. Soon the stream of refugees was cut in two. Pétion and four hundred grenadiers managed to fight their way across a river and into the safety of wooded country. The remainder, including many women and children, were shot or cut down.

The road to the South Province lay open. But as Toussaint's troops began to pour along it Rigaud gave orders for a 'desert of fire' to be created between the two armies. The land itself was burned, tortured, destroyed, as its inhabitants had been before it.

Rigaud had no strong defensive positions left and his forces were far outnumbered by Toussaint's. Toussaint, moreover, proclaimed that "like the father of the prodigal son" he would receive all repentant mulattos with joy. Although Rigaud appealed for more men to come forward "to continue the struggle against the butcher, the devastator of Saint-Domingue and slave of the English", resistance was on the point of collapse when, in June

1800, Toussaint received fresh support from an unexpected quarter – Napoléon Bonaparte who, seven months before, had overthrown the Directory and appointed himself First Consul. Not yet ready to take strong measures against Toussaint, Bonaparte sent out a commission to report on the state of the island and to confirm him in his title of commander-in-chief.

Among the members of the commission were Christophe's former associate, Colonel Vincent, whom Roume had sent back with reports some time before, and Raymond, a mulatto economist who had been a member of Sonthonax's second triumvirate. Toussaint, suspicious of their intentions and instructions, had them arrested 'by mistake' soon after they landed and used this opportunity to go through their papers. Finding nothing incriminating, he greeted them warmly and ordered Colonel Vincent to proceed to Les Cayes and summon Rigaud to surrender.

It was a perilous errand, undertaken in a small boat with a safe conduct on the doubtful authority of Roume, who was now undisguisedly Toussaint's prisoner at Le Cap. When Vincent arrived and explained his mission, and added that Bonaparte had confirmed Toussaint's appointment as commander-in-chief, Rigaud flew into such a fit of fury that his staff officers thought that he would kill Vincent. Refusing to continue in the island with a Negro as his superior, he left on July 28, 1800, in a ship for Saint-Thomas and thence to France. On August 1 Toussaint made a ceremonial entry into Les Cayes and, after hearing a *Te Deum* in the cathedral, went into the pulpit and spoke to the congregation on the forgiveness of sins. On August 5 he declared a general amnesty.

The sufferings of the unfortunate mulattos were far from over. Dessalines was appointed governor of the South Province – an action that casts doubts on Toussaint's good faith, for he was fully aware of Dessalines's violent and bloodthirsty character – and those mulattos who were not shot or impaled on bayonets were flogged into cringing submission. Toussaint, turning northward, halted at Léogane to order the execution of 300 prisoners. Desperate revolts flared up in the Artibonite, the Cul-de-Sac and the mountains of the south, but they were put down by Dessalines with such cruelty that soon all opposition flickered out. In October the heavens opened and the rain deluged unceasingly down, swelling the rivers, choking the irrigation ditches, bursting through dams and levées, washing away plantations on the hillsides and drowning men and animals in the plains.

At Port-au-Prince Toussaint reorganised his general staff, many of whom were white officers, and formed a personal guard of two thousand men, their officers drawn from men of all colours, the infantry commanded by a Negro and the cavalry by a mulatto. Escorted by this guard of honour and preceded by trumpeters in silver helmets with scarlet plumes, he made his entry into Le Cap on November 22, passing beneath a specially erected *arc de triomphe* to be welcomed by a beautiful white woman, a member of one of the colony's oldest families, who recited a congratulatory verse and embraced the small, ugly, elderly ex-slave. The crowd, white, brown and black, roared its approval and struck up the 'Marseillaise', to which new verses had been written in the commander-in-chief's honour, including one that celebrated his triumph over the British:

> Les Anglais, ces foudres de guerre,
> Ont éprouvé nos bataillons;
> Leur sang a rougi la poussière,
> Leurs corps ont comblé nos sillons.
> Armé d'un courage intrépide,
> Toussaint partout guidait nos pas,
> Et dans l'action de nos combats,
> Son panache était notre guide.
> Terrible aux ennemis,
> Humain pour ses amis,
> Toussaint, Toussaint, reçois nos voeux,
> Par toi, tout est heureux.*

Three days later he accused Roume of encouraging dissension and disturbing the tranquillity of the colony. He had him arrested and sent to France. There was now no doubt who ruled in Saint-Domingue. Two months later Toussaint trebled the size of his domain by a lightning invasion of the Spanish part of the island.

* *The English, those thunderbolts of war,*
Have suffered the weight of our battalions;
Their blood has reddened the dust,
Their bodies have covered our fields.
Armed with intrepid courage,
Toussaint guided our steps everywhere,
And in the heat of our battles,
His helmet was our guide.
Terrible towards his enemies,
Humane towards his friends,
Toussaint, Toussaint, accept our troth,
Through your efforts, all is well.

Moyse led the major body of troops along the northern coast while Toussaint struck across the Mirebalais. Resistance was feeble and on January 27 Toussaint made yet another triumphant entry – this time into Santo-Domingo, the former Spanish capital, to the joyful clamour of cathedral bells.

The clergy had reason for their rejoicings, for Toussaint showed a marked devotion to the Catholic faith. Regular in church attendance himself, he demanded that his senior officers should go to communion at least once every week as well as holding church parades for their troops. Among the parish priests of pre-revolutionary days, there were several who had remained with the slaves and, even in the bloodiest days of the revolt, continued their ministrations, often acting as spokesmen and secretaries for the illiterate leaders of the rebel bands. These Toussaint favoured, although the church was still legally proscribed, and he shortly reintroduced the Gregorian calendar, though this too was illegal in France. Although he had many mistresses of all colours, he was a stickler for the outward observance of marriage vows and threatened with cashiering any officer who openly formed an adulterous association or continued in an irregular union. Vaudou he constantly tried to stamp out, sending soldiers to break up the secret ceremonies and beat or even kill the celebrants – but whether this was because of devotion to the Christian faith, or because he despised the cult as reminiscent of the old slave days, or because he feared it as a secret society, nobody ever discovered.

It was Toussaint's great strength that he was always ready to offer forgiveness – at least temporarily – to his enemies, and to treat them handsomely so long as they were of use to him. Just as he brought back the white planters to restore the agricultural prosperity of the country, and installed others as administrators in his secretariat and in government offices, so he now made his peace with the mulattos. On May 28, 1801, he assembled in the church at Le Cap all those who had been put in prison or conscripted into the army (where they had been treated with extreme brutality by their Negro commanders and comrades) and harangued them from the pulpit.

"Partisanship has led you into error; I speak to you as a father; I grieve for the ills that you have suffered and I offer you a generous pardon. . . . Take heart, return to the bosom of your families."

He had always preached tolerance to his fellow Negroes. More than five years before, when the mulattos were trying to gain control of the North Province as well as the South, he had written to a Negro officer, Pierre Dieudonné, urging him to "forget all personal animosity, reconcile yourself with our brothers Rigaud and Beauvais, they are brave defenders of our common liberty". It was a mulatto general, Clervaux, whom he appointed as Commander of the Army of the East – the former Spanish colony – with a white man, Pageot, and his brother Paul Toussaint, as brigadiers; in the North, Christophe, now promoted to brigadier, served with Maurepas, another former free Negro, under Toussaint's nephew, Moyse; while in the West and South Dessalines, with an army of 11,000, twice as large as either of the others, exercised his terrifying rule with Belair and Laplume as his brigadiers.

With all opposition crushed, the army's principal task was to enforce the agricultural laws, ensuring that all field hands returned to their former plantations and that they were joined by any others who had no trades. Discipline was as severe for the *cultivateurs* as for the soldiers. Officers inspecting plantations would order idlers to be stripped and to run the gauntlet between files of soldiers. Incompetent overseers were liable to receive the same treatment. Persistent offenders were hanged. Dessalines, in whose province agriculture improved with great rapidity, sometimes varied the punishment by burying the offenders alive; and where he was dissatisfied but could find no specific complaint or offender, he had the victims chosen by lot.

The system of *fermage* which Christophe and Vincent had introduced in the North Province had proved to be immensely successful – both for the colony and for the plantation tenants, who were making great fortunes. In November 1799 Cathcart reported that Christophe himself was believed to be worth nearly two hundred and fifty thousand dollars. The national economy was advancing by leaps and bounds. Toussaint, guiding and inspiring this recovery, worked twenty hours a day, rode a hundred miles from dawn to dusk, his saddle padded with feather cushions, his underlings never secure from an unexpected pouncing visit, in the cause of his own ambition and his country's prosperity.

He delighted to receive white guests at the *petits cercles* over which he presided in the evenings, dressed in the traditional planters' uniform of white jacket and breeches, and with a madras scarf wrapped around his head. His Negro guests he impressed with a gallimaufry of Latin phrases recalled parrot-fashion from the psalms. At the full-dress receptions that he held from time to time he wore his general's uniform and the whole company, male and female, was obliged to rise when he entered the room. He had now gone a long way towards throwing off all control from France. The conquest of the Spanish part had been carried out in flat defiance of instructions that it was not yet to be brought under French rule. His institution of compulsory church parades was contrary to the spirit of the revolution, and so was the favourable treatment that he gave to the non-juror priests. Finally he ordered a new issue of coins which, though still carrying the inscription 'République Française', also bore a replica of his own head.

For some he had already gone too far; for others not far enough. His principal lieutenants, Moyse and Dessalines, were both extremists; they urged him to declare the whole island independent, to throw off the shackles not only of the French but of all white men and to create a wholly Negro state. Christophe and Vincent, on the other hand, totally opposed this project, seeing in it no advantage to the country and fearing reprisals which might deprive the Negroes of everything they had so far gained.

They watched with alarm as Toussaint appointed an Assemblée Centrale of ten men to examine the colony's problems. They reluctantly admired the artistry by which he entirely excluded Negroes from the assembly and instead chose seven whites and three mulattos who had all been zealous advocates of independence at the time of the revolution. On May 9, 1801, they learned with the deepest foreboding that the Assembly had agreed upon a new constitution for Saint-Domingue. The island was recognised to be a French colony; but Toussaint was appointed governor-general for life, with the right to nominate his successor. The Assembly was empowered to accept or reject laws set before it by the governor, but not to initiate legislation. Finally, "in view of the urgent need to emerge from our perilous state and to reestablish agriculture, the governor-general is authorised and requested to put the constitution into effect".

Vincent was at Les Gonaïves when he heard the news. He boldly warned Toussaint that Bonaparte – whom he had met during his last journey to France – was too vain a man to accept this affront, and that the injury was aggravated by the fact that the constitution had been published without even the pretence of being submitted to the consulate for approval.

"If there is anything they do not approve, they will send commissioners to discuss it with me," Toussaint replied.

"You mean," said Vincent, "that you want them to send you *chargés d'affaires* and ambassadors, which is what the Americans, Spaniards and even the English will certainly do."

"You shall take the constitution to France yourself," Toussaint answered curtly, "and explain it."

He whisked out of the room, leaped on his horse and was away on one of his urgent mysterious errands. Vincent was left in no doubt that he was in disgrace. Toussaint refused to see him again before his ship sailed from Le Cap, sending word to him to collect from the President of the Assembly a sealed envelope which Vincent rightly assumed contained the draft of the constitution. In reply, Vincent asked Christophe to send on to Toussaint a letter in which he urged him to beware of the men who were pressing him to take over supreme power. Vincent left the letter unsealed, so that Christophe might read it. When he had done so, he looked up and said, with unusual emotion: "You are the only white man who really loves the Saint-Dominicans. You have always spoken the truth to us. This constitution has been drawn up by our most dangerous enemies."

Toussaint was not to be swayed by argument. On July 8 the new constitution was publicly proclaimed on the place d'Armes at Le Cap by Borgella, the white President of the Assembly, Toussaint giving his approval and crying, "*Vivent à jamais la République Française et la Constitution Coloniale!*"* As the magistrates and public officials advanced to embrace him the guns on the place d'Armes boomed out the signal for the forts and ships in the harbour to offer their salutes. Observant onlookers noted that, although the official salute to the republic was twenty-two guns, today there were twenty-three: Saint-Domingue was to be in no way inferior to France. The chief magistrate, also a white man, addressed Toussaint as "the saviour and restorer of the colony". Toussaint led the way to church and, after mass, to the military commander's house, where Christophe, scarcely able to conceal his disquiet, entertained them to a banquet.

In the four weeks that followed the proclamation of the new constitution, Toussaint put forward – and the Assembly accepted without discussion – a series of laws on the reorganisation of the departments throughout the island, municipal government, the judicial, financial and ecclesiastical administration. The sweep and perspicacity of Toussaint's work is astonishing. He had received no

* "*Long live the French Republic and the Colonial Constitution!*"

education beyond a smattering of reading and writing picked up in the slave-barracks when he was a child. Until the age of nearly fifty he had remained a slave. His appearance was unprepossessing: short, thin, protuberant-jawed, a scarf wrapped round his head ("that maggot in a rag", Hédouville's officers called him) and his small hat overhung with too many black and white plumes; his coat too lavishly decorated with gold braid, his gold epaulets too heavy for his narrow shoulders.

He would have been a figure of fun – except for the swiftly-darting eye, the inexhaustible energy, the confidence and ruthlessness with which he enforced his commands. The ability to make do with only two hours' sleep a day, a brilliant brain, and a flair for secrecy and deception – with these he had restored equilibrium and peace to the island. He had divided the offices of influence between the contending castes – whites in the administration, Negroes in the army, a few mulattos in both – and had retained supreme power for himself. After a decade of uninterrupted agony, the island seemed set upon the path of recovery.

6

Toussaint's new constitution had worried Christophe by its rashness and its unnecessary flouting of the authority of France; Dessalines and Moyse, on the other hand, were disappointed by its moderation. Both were men of violence. Dessalines, who bore the indelible weals of many vicious floggings on his back, had been the lowest and most despised of all creatures – the slave, not of a white man, nor even of a mulatto, but of a free Black. He was born on the Cormiers plantation in the district of La Grande-Rivière and at first named Duclos, after the owner. His parents either died or were sold to another plantation (though it was illegal under the *Code Noir* to separate a family) and he was brought up by his aunt, until she was sold and taken to the West Province. At the age of thirty-three he was himself put up for sale, and bought by a Black *affranchi* who had formerly worked for a Frenchman named Des Salines. His new owner, who seems to have been a jack-of-all-trades, working at various times as a carpenter, a tiler and a potter, described his slave assistant as *"bon ouvrier, mais mauvais chien."* *

With a fierce hatred of all authority, of all whites, of all mulattos, Dessalines was happiest when humiliating them, torturing them,

* *"Good worker, bad character."*

or, with his coat off and his sleeves rolled above his elbows, slashing at them with a sabre in the forefront of his men.

Moyse, whose original name was Gilles-Bréda, was one-eyed, impetuous, with the same qualities of savagery and courage as Dessalines. He had known Toussaint from childhood, had been pampered by him and had always addressed him as 'uncle'; for this reason he was universally referred to as Toussaint's nephew although there was in fact no blood relationship between them. His position as heir-apparent to Toussaint had been secure until a year or two before, but the rising star of Christophe threatened to dim his own and this served to increase the bitterness with which he denounced the policy which he claimed Toussaint was pursuing and which he knew Christophe favoured. "He is always talking about the interests of the mother-country – but these are the interests of the whites, and I shall never love the whites until they give me back the eye that they made me lose during the fighting."

The rift between them was being continually widened by Toussaint's scoldings over the decline in output from the plantations of the North Province where Moyse was in command; for here the former field hands, having fought harder for their independence than those of the West and South, were all the more determined to enjoy it. In a climate where sufficient food to satisfy a man would grow almost without attention, they saw no reason why they should labour unwillingly in the fields all day instead of sleeping the sunny hours away, storing up their strength for nights of dancing. Since Sonthonax's declaration of liberty, the ex-slave who was summoned to work was likely to reply, "*Moé pas esclave, moé pas travayé. Li Noir pas besoin, li mangé patate, li mangé banane; blanc mangé pain, li travayé.*" "I'm not a slave, I don't want to work. The Black doesn't need to, he eats sweet potatoes and bananas; but the white man eats bread, he has to work. . . ." When Toussaint complained, Moyse remarked: "Whatever my old uncle may do, I am not prepared to persecute my own colour." This and many similar retorts soon circulated among the dissatisfied labourers. Then, following a familiar and ominous pattern, the whisper began to run that Christophe had plans to reintroduce slavery, and that Toussaint was of the same mind. Moyse had decided to strike.

During the afternoon of October 29, 1801, a white warrant-officer of the National Guard called at Christophe's headquarters at Le Cap and asked to see the general. When he was taken in to Christophe's orderly room he reported that he had just made a tour of some of the guard posts and had found them manned by Negroes whom he had never seen before in his life. The story seemed odd and Christophe at first suspected that the heat had affected the man's brain. However, he sent a messenger to the town major, another white man, named Barada, and asked him to make inquiries. At nightfall, Barada reported that he could find nothing wrong but that there was an air of disquiet in the streets and he feared that some secret affair was brewing.

Christophe, accompanied by one or two gendarmes and some men from his personal corps of guides, set out in the darkness to inspect the town. As the party of horsemen clattered round the corner of the rue du Conseil at the northern end of the city, there was a flash farther down the street and the sharp crack of a musket shot. The ball whistled past Christophe's head. He shouted to one of his escort to turn back for help, then spurred his horse in the direction that the shot had come from. Galloping down the wide street towards the old Royal Jetty, he caught sight of men running in the direction of the dry docks; wheeling northward after them, along the road that skirted the arsenal and the artillery park, he ran down and captured a Negro named Troisballes, who was hauled off into the arsenal to be interrogated. Musketry fire had now broken out in several places in the town behind him and by the time that Barada arrived with a detachment of the National Guard armed groups were gathering in the streets.

Christophe, furious with rage and shock, swung his horse round and galloped back into the town, charging up one street and down the next, bursting down the half-built barricades and slashing at the dusky figures behind them. The musketry fire became heavy and one of his horsemen fell out of the saddle dead at his side. From the arsenal an orderly brought a message that Troisballes had broken down and revealed the password – 'patate' – and the names of the conspirators: among them the harbour master, Saintogne. While Christophe continued to ride round the town, supervising the arrest of the ringleaders, the bulk of the rebels, finding the resistance too strong for them and the streets filling with more and more of Christophe's troops, slipped out of town and made for the hills.

By dawn Le Cap was peaceful once more. But alarming news was coming in from the rest of the province: at L'Acul, Le Limbé and Port-Margot the field hands had risen and massacred the whites. The murders and burnings of 1791 were beginning again, as the first stages of Moyse's planned total extermination of the whites.

Taking with him a battalion of the 1st demi-brigade, a battalion of the 3rd and the dragoons of the National Guard, Christophe set off for L'Acul. He had got no farther than the Vaudreuil plantation when he came face to face with the advance guard of a party of rebels making for Le Cap.

Unlike the ill-armed slaves of 1791, these men had the weapons they had fought with during the wars against the British and the mulattos – "these are your liberty!" Sonthonax had shouted when he distributed muskets to the slaves he freed, and nobody had since dared take their arms away from them. The advance guard was not strong enough to withstand him and fled, but at Morne Rouge Christophe found himself opposed by the main body, marching in two columns, one across the Plaine du Nord and the other along the direct road from L'Acul. Christophe threw himself upon each in turn, attacking with such fury – for his wrath of the previous night had still not subsided – that those who remained alive and un-wounded ran in terror into the surrounding plantations where the dragoons could not pursue them.

The entire district of Le Limbé was in revolt. He found the military commander, Colonel Joseph Flaville, at his headquarters in the town and angrily demanded why he had not marched out into the countryside to protect the whites and suppress the rising. Flaville, equally angrily and with unconcealed hostility, answered that he lacked the resources – and that the people had a right to make their own decisions. Whether or not Flaville's troops were numerous enough to quell the rebels, they certainly outnumbered Christophe's, and now that he was in the town he was unable to plan or deploy. Inwardly raging, he withdrew from Le Limbé and hastened to Port-Margot.

The town was in the hands of the rebels, who were holding the military governor, Major Jolicoeur, as their prisoner. This time Christophe did not wait for parleys but led his men into the town at the double, infantry with bayonets fixed and the dragoons following and spreading through the streets, driving all before them. With Jolicoeur released, some of the rebels shot, and the remainder expelled from the town, Christophe added a detachment of the Port-Margot troops to his own and returned to Le Limbé, where Flaville had meanwhile openly declared for the insurgents.

In this sort of emergency, Christophe was as swift in action as Toussaint. He carried the town by storm, arrested Flaville, and sent him under escort to L'Acul to be taken on to Le Cap by sea, to avoid any chance of rescue en route. Barada had reported that he was completely in control at Le Cap and Christophe was able to establish his headquarters on the Fage plantation and set about restoring order to the rural districts.

Moyse, who had been directing the revolt from his headquarters at Fort-Liberté, received three separate pieces of bad news in rapid succession. First the failure of the night attempt to gain control of Le Cap; then the swift crushing of the outbreaks at Le Limbé and Port-Margot; and finally information that Dessalines, whom he had kept in the dark about the rebellion but whom he hoped would declare for him as soon as he received word that the North Province had gone up in flames, had instead scented failure and declared his loyalty for Toussaint, proving it by shooting dozens of suspects in the West Province and then moving his troops northwards to support the governor-general.

Moyse had to act quickly or lose by default. He rode to Le Cap, carefully avoiding contact with Christophe on the way, and, having immediately verified that all hope of taking the key city of the province was lost, showed to anyone who would look two letters that he claimed to have written to Toussaint, denouncing Flaville as unreliable. Loudly proclaiming that he would take the most energetic measures to suppress all seditious outbreaks, he assembled a party of white men who volunteered to attack the rebels at Le Dondon, one of the few remaining centres of serious resistance. His supporters there were astonished to see him arrive with two hundred of the detested caste that he had been urging them to murder, and still more surprised when he addressed them as rebels, had many of them shot and sent another dozen as prisoners to Toussaint at the Noé plantation.

Moyse collected some of his own troops and, gambling on the success of his deception, led them in the wake of the prisoners to the Noé plantation to claim his reward from Toussaint for having 'suppressed the revolt'. A further shock awaited him. On the road he was halted by one of Toussaint's officers with instructions that Moyse was to ride on alone. Otherwise he would be greeted with grapeshot.

In the great house at the plantation Toussaint met him with a volley of reproaches. In reply he stoutly protested his innocence, claiming that his enemies had bribed false witnesses to say that he had encouraged the revolt against Toussaint and Christophe. Toussaint listened, grew calmer and at last said that he believed his 'nephew' but that to give convincing proof of his loyalty Moyse must take a detachment of Toussaint's troops to Port-de-Paix and quell the revolt there. Moyse was delighted. He rode at the head of Toussaint's men down through the hills and into the port that lay opposite the old filibusters' island of Tortuga. To his surprise, he found the town quiet and with no signs of conflict. The military commander, Maurepas, who had received a message sent on ahead by Toussaint, arrested him, put him in fetters, and locked him up in an underground cell.

Toussaint rode down to Le Cap, pitilessly wielding the sword of retribution as he went. Any worker who had strayed from his plantation was lucky if he was not executed out of hand. The victims of Toussaint's wrath were reckoned in hundreds – some said in thousands. With terror going before him, he entered Le Cap on November 4, bringing forty of the leading rebels with him. The whole population of the town was summoned to the place d'Armes, where the 1st and 2nd demi-brigades were drawn up in a hollow square, with a squadron of Toussaint's personal guard behind them.

Suddenly there was the rumble of three cannon being dragged into the square, their gunners marching with lighted matches beside the touch-holes. The hubbub of voices was cut off abruptly; before the menace of the guns, the soldiers themselves were terror-striken, their bayoneted muskets quivering in their hands. In the silence that followed the first horrified gasp, Toussaint rode into the middle of the square unaccompanied, tense with fury, his dark face suffused with the crimson of still unassuaged revenge.

"Look at me!" he screamed. "This is the man who General Moyse said was a traitor to the country! This is the man who is the assassin of his brothers! This is the man who attempted to bring back slavery, who betrayed the Republic, who wanted to clamber to a throne over thousands of corpses!" As he shouted, the froth of his rage flecking his mouth, his eyes gleaming and bloodshot, he rode slowly round the square, still entirely alone, dominating soldiers and civilians alike with the magnitude of his frenzy.

"Today," he shrieked, "the guilty shall receive their punishment – and in a very few days General Moyse, my nephew, shall pay for taking up arms and conspiring against France, his country. And any man who takes up arms against her, even if he were my own son, shall suffer the same fate of traitors." He reined in his horse and darted his finger towards one of the officers, ordering him to step forward. As the man stood to attention before him, "Traitor!" he shouted, "scoundrel! shoot yourself!" The officer drew his pistol, cocked it, and blew out his own brains.

Toussaint continued to ride slowly round the square. At intervals his finger pointed, the designated victim stepped forward and shot himself. Such was the authority of the little man on horseback, so hypnotic the icy, macabre spell that lay over the parade ground that, as the shots continued to ring out and the lifeless bodies fell to the ground, not one of the men attempted to turn his pistol against his judge. More than three thousand soldiers and unnumbered thousands of civilians cowered before the rage of Toussaint.

When he had completed his tour of retribution, one side of the square opened and the prisoners were dragged in: Colonel Flaville, the informer Troisballes, some forty of the ringleaders, both military and civilian, each chained to another. They were led in front of the cannon while the troops behind them hurriedly moved to the flank. The gunners set their matches to the touch-holes; and the prisoners were cut to pieces with grapeshot. The explosion of the cannon-charges shook the onlookers from their trance. Taking to their heels, the civilians raced from the square. The soldiers were marched away and Toussaint rode off at the head of his personal guard, leaving the place d'Armes littered with the mutilated and still bleeding bodies of those who had plotted to overthrow him.

The next day, he went to Fort-Liberté, for more public executions; and then inland to Le Trou, where he is said to have put to death a thousand field hands captured during the rising in the northern plain. Having ordered Dessalines to take over the task of driving the field hands back to their labours with whip and bayonet, he rode back to Port-de-Paix, where he found that a court-martial presided over by the white officer, General Pageot, had returned a verdict that there was insufficient evidence against Moyse on a charge of treason and had acquitted him. Toussaint at once convened a new court, with himself presiding, arraigned Moyse on a charge of neglect of duty, declared him guilty and had him shot the same day.

III

Invasion

For two years Bonaparte had been First Consul; and for two years his anger against Toussaint had gathered head. He fretted in vain, for there was nothing he could do to chasten the impertinent Negro so long as the British navy maintained its blockade in the Atlantic. But in October 1801 France signed the preliminaries of the Treaty of Amiens with Britain, having in September of the previous year settled her differences with the United States in the Treaty of Mortefontaine.

There was no longer any impediment to Bonaparte's mounting a punitive expedition; and Toussaint was without allies. His relations with Britain had cooled, largely because of the Royal Navy's seizures of his shipping, which still sailed under the tricolour. With the induction of the southerner Jefferson as President in March 1801, United States policy hardened against the ex-slaves; Dr Stevens, now regarded as too favourably disposed towards Toussaint, was recalled and his replacement, Tobias Lear, was given the title of 'general commercial agent' instead of consul- general.

By the time that Vincent arrived in France to present to Bonaparte the draft of the constitution that had already been proclaimed, the dockyards were clamorous with the work of fitting out a great convoy and the victorious veterans of the Rhine and Italy were being equipped for a colonial adventure. Vincent, received by the First Consul in his office at the Tuileries, ventured to question the wisdom of the expedition, warning Bonaparte that an invading army would be resisted by the whole Black population, and that it might well be crippled by the climate and disease before its superior military skill could prevail. There was the likelihood, besides, that the British would try to place obstacles in its way, fearing that its real purpose was to attack Jamaica instead of Saint-Domingue.

"The cabinet of Saint James would have liked to oppose it," Bonaparte growled. "I let them know that if they did not agree I would grant Toussaint unlimited powers and recognise his independence. They've not said any more about it." Vincent persisted with his objection that European troops would not be able to support the island's climate, but he was ushered out of the room and, shortly afterwards, sent to cool his heels without promotion on Elba.

There is little doubt that France could have held the island simply by recognising Toussaint as governor-general for life and sending agents to preserve the links with the mother-country. To salve his wounded pride, Bonaparte was about to throw away France's most valuable colony, and with it the lives of more than 40,000 of his fellow-countrymen. To lead the expedition he chose his brother-in-law, General Leclerc, a dapper, fair-haired little man whose troops called him 'the blonde Bonaparte' because of his evident desire to ape the First Consul. At Bonaparte's command, and greatly against her will, Leclerc's wife accompanied him, moaning pitifully at having to leave her mansion in the rue de Courcelles and the excitement of Paris life and "live in exile among savages and snakes".

Pauline Leclerc was a pampered, vacuous creature. "It was," said one of her closest friends, "a positive calamity, after the first quarter of an hour's interview had exhausted the pleasure of surveying her really beautiful person, to have the burden of amusing, occupying and taking care of her." She had a beautiful body, the face of an idealised puffin, and a habit of promiscuity. She was also Bonaparte's favourite sister, a fact which disproves the accusation current at the time that he used the perils of Saint-Domingue to rid himself of the more aggressively republican – and successful – of his officers and men. If he had any motive beyond salving his *amour propre*, it was perhaps to provide employment and exercise for some of his crack troops during what he intended to be the brief interlude of the Peace of Amiens.

By October 28 the three squadrons that composed the expedition were ready: at Brest, commanded by Admiral Villaret-Joyeuse, fifteen French and Spanish ships of the line, six frigates, three corvettes and three other vessels, carrying a total of 7,000 soldiers; at Rochefort, under Admiral Latouche-Tréville, six ships of the line and ten other vessels, carrying 3,000 men; at Lorient, one ship of the line and three troopships, carrying 1,200 men. These were to rendezvous below Belle-Isle for the Atlantic crossing, and would be followed by more ships and troops in two convoys, from Flushing and Le Havre, and from Cadiz and Toulon.

Leclerc, who had been superintending the military preparations of the main force at Brest, returned to Paris, with his friend General Hardy, to fetch Pauline and their son Dermide, whom Bonaparte (further proof that he genuinely believed the dangers of the Saint-Dominican climate had been exaggerated) recommended that they should take with them, though the boy was only two and a half years old. Pauline, however, was not to be hurried. New dresses that she required as wife of the captain-general, new furniture that she would need as wife of the governor-general (for Toussaint was to be deprived of his post immediately), had still to be bought. It was well into the second week of November before they set off again for Brest, travelling by very short stages because Pauline suffered from carriage sickness; and it was not until November 28 that she was finally settled into her luxurious cabin in the *Océan*, the 120-gun flagship, entertaining senior officers and complaining in an interesting fashion of her migraines and vapours. Now, unfortunately, Admiral Villaret-Joyeuse decided that the winds were not sufficiently favourable. It was not until December 14 that the squadron finally sailed.

The weather was atrocious. With Pauline more miserable than ever and most of her admirers too seasick to care, the ships staggered through towering seas for a fortnight before joining up with the Lorient squadron below Belle-Isle. There was no sign of the Rochefort contingent and, after tossing queasily in the Bay of Biscay for another four days, Villaret-Joyeuse rightly concluded that Latouche-Tréville had gone on without him, and himself headed westward. Four hundred miles out from Brest they at last found fair winds and sunshine and on January 29 arrived at Samana Bay on the eastern side of the island, where Latouche-Tréville's squadron had been awaiting them for ten days.

Their arrival brought consternation. Watching them from the hills above the bay was Toussaint with his bodyguard. He had been visiting the former Spanish part of the island when word was brought to him of Latouche-Tréville's arrival and he rode north from Santo-Domingo to see for himself. Now, as he gazed on the 47 vessels gathering below him, his courage failed.

"We are lost!" he exclaimed. "All France has come to Saint-Domingue. She has been misled. She has come for vengeance."

The moment of hopelessness was quickly past; he determined to fight and he knew well what was the best rallying cry. "And they have come to enslave the Blacks!" he shouted. He wheeled and rode at breakneck speed across the island, along the northern coast and then down to Port-au-Prince, dictating messages at every halt and sending them off to his garrison commanders.

It was the size of the French armada, not the fact of its arrival, that had surprised him. He already knew by messages from France and news items in the British and American journals that he had failed to deflect Bonaparte's wrath by his assurances of loyalty to the republic at the time of Moyse's insurrection. "The Consular Government," *The Gentleman's Magazine* had reported in November, "is making preparations for sending a military force of 20,000 men to the island of Saint-Domingo for the purpose of reducing the Mulatto General Toussaint L'Ouverture to a due degree of subordination to the mother country, and preventing the erection there of a Negro Republick comprising a population of 500,000 souls which would endanger the existence of all the other West Indian islands, whether French or English." But 20,000 soldiers and the ships to transport them were a concept too big for Toussaint's mind – despite the warnings of Vincent and Christophe – and when he discussed the matter in December he spoke only of receiving 'envoys' from France.

Leclerc was in fact not at all ready to go into action with the force that had struck terror into Toussaint's heart. The expedition had been badly mounted and inefficiently supervised. Stores were inadequate and of poor quality. Men had been embarked haphazardly and units which were to fight together were distributed through different ships. Of the 20,000 men who should have composed the army, less than half had arrived, yet the general's instructions from Bonaparte did not permit him to wait for the stragglers.

The fleet sailed out of Samana Bay and along the northern coast of the island. When it arrived off Monte-Christi bay, at the boundary of the former Spanish and French territories, Leclerc insisted that Villaret-Joyeuse should anchor for a day while troops were ferried from one ship to another so that a detachment of 3,000 men could be formed for General Boudet to take through the Windward Passage and down the long sweep of the Bight of Léogane to Port-au-Prince. Leclerc would have preferred to use Boudet's troops for an immediate landing at Le Cap instead of those of General Hardy, which would be even more difficult to reform into their fighting units, but Villaret-Joyeuse, determined to assert his seniority at sea, replied that this contravened the First Consul's instructions and that he therefore could not permit his ships or men to cooperate. Leclerc gave way. He was delayed again by the need to form a division under General Rochambeau to take Fort-Liberté, and it was not until February 2 that he reached Le Cap, with the remaining fourteen ships of the line and nine frigates carrying 4,000 men.

Shortly after midday the fleet lay five miles off Le Cap. Although the wind was favourable, Leclerc gave no orders to enter the harbour. Some among his officers suggested that this was because of reluctance to expose his wife and child to danger; but it is more likely that he considered that it was impossible for his men to force their way ashore if Toussaint decided to oppose their landing. His information was that there were four thousand soldiers under Clervaux in the East, and eleven thousand under Dessalines in the West and South. Toussaint had been given sufficient time to bring many of these up to reinforce Christophe's five thousand in the North. Leclerc did not like the odds.

On shore Christophe was faced with an agonising decision. Le Cap, under his stern but energetic administration, had risen from the ashes of 1795 and was now almost as great as it had ever been. New buildings had sprung up along the beautiful wide streets, the flourishing plantations had brought new trade and bustle to the docks and business houses. On Sundays Christophe threw open his own house in the rue Royale to the city notables – the most brilliant and luxurious of the homes of all Toussaint's generals, furnished with the profits from the plantations that he rented from the state.

He had developed with authority and the years. Sturdy, good-looking, attentive, he received his guests with polished, almost pedantic manners, his old tempestuous temper well controlled. A French general, with no reason to paint a flattering portrait of him, reported to Bonaparte a little later that Christophe was "a man of some forty years, of unimpeachable morals. He is handsome in physique, chilly in manner, urbane in conversation. . . . There is much pride in his character. This pride has brought him enemies, but has won the respect of the greater part of his fellow-Blacks. . . . Although long accustomed to speak English, he speaks our language with ease and has distinguished manners."

This rich and successful man was now being called upon to destroy everything that he had earned and everything that he had built. The orders that he had received from Toussaint were that he was to prevent the French from landing. If they landed by force he was to retreat with his army intact into the mountains. But before doing so he was to set fire to Le Cap and everything in it.

The city had been in turmoil since daybreak, when the lookouts on the mountains first sighted the French fleet. This massive intervention from Europe had stirred up many of the old colour conflicts, the whites dreaming of the overthrow of Toussaint and his Black generals, whose rule they suddenly felt intolerable; the Blacks terrified by Toussaint's warning that the French had come to enslave them. Yet there were many cross-currents of loyalty and interest; many of the Blacks, including the mayor, César Télémaque, remained devoted to the French cause, while some of the whites, foreseeing that under Bonaparte the colony would be exploited as harshly and considerably more efficiently than it had been under the *ancien régime*, urged Christophe to resist. There seems little doubt that his own preference was for submission, to recognise the authority of the consulate and save the island from a renewal of past horrors. But his personal inclinations were subordinated to his obedience to Toussaint as his superior officer and his loyalty to him as a Black messiah.

At two in the afternoon, the watchers on shore saw a cutter stand out from the French fleet and make for the harbour, followed by two frigates. As the vessels approached Fort Picolet, guarding the harbour entrance, puffs of smoke could be seen drifting seaward and a few moments later there came the crack of gunfire. The fort's cannon had opened fire. The frigates hung hesitantly at the harbour mouth and then, their commanders noting that all the marker buoys had been removed from the channels, the two large vessels turned back towards the rest of the fleet while the cutter continued unmolested to the shore, where it hastily took up moorings at the first available jetty in the former *cale royale* at the foot of the rue du Conseil. Christophe ordered an armed guard to be placed on the cutter and then sent the port captain, Sangros, in a launch to the *Océan* with a message that he had dispatched a courier to Toussaint to inform him of the arrival of this great fleet, but that in the meantime he could not, without disobeying his orders, admit any warship to the port.

The launch that took Sangros to the French fleet returned to

Fort Picolet with Villaret-Joyeuse's aide-de-camp, Lebrun, bearing a letter to Christophe from Leclerc and proclamations to the people of Saint-Domingue from both Leclerc and Bonaparte. These, in French and Créole, had been printed on the *Océan's* presses during the voyage.

Christophe rode down to Fort Picolet through anxious crowds. When he had first heard of the French arrival in Samana Bay, before receiving Toussaint's message, he had given instructions for the streets to be swept and the barracks set in order, a sufficient indication of his willingness to receive Leclerc's troops peaceably. But the man who awaited him at the landing stage at Fort Picolet could scarcely have been more ill-chosen for his mission, for Lebrun was naturally arrogant in manner and took no pains to conceal his contempt for the crowd of Black soldiers around him and for their general who came to greet him. Christophe's pride, affronted by Lebrun's patronising manner, reacted even more sharply to the contents and tone of Leclerc's letter.

It is with indignation, citizen general [Leclerc wrote] that I learn that you refuse to receive the French squadron and the army under my command, on the pretext that you have received no orders from the Governor-general.

He warned that he had forces 'capable of overwhelming any rebels' and that if the forts and coastal batteries were not handed over he would land fifteen thousand men at daybreak the next morning.

Four thousand men are at this moment landing at Fort-Liberté and eight thousand at Port-Républicain.

You will find attached my proclamation which will inform you of the intentions of the French Government; but remember that, whatever good opinion your previous conduct may have inspired in me, I hold you responsible for everything that may occur.

Leclerc's message to the inhabitants urged them to read the First Consul's proclamation, which assured them that 'whatever may be your origin or your colour, you are all Frenchmen. You are all free and all equal in the sight of God and the Republic.' He ordered them to rally to the Captain-General: 'he brings you prosperity and peace. Rally to him; he who dares turn from him will be a traitor to his country and the wrath of the Republic will devour him as fire devours your dry sugar canes.'

Christophe's face was impassive as he read the letter and proclamations. When he had finished he told Lebrun that he still had no intention of taking a decision until he had received further instructions from Toussaint. He rode off, having ordered a carriage to take Lebrun to Government House to await Toussaint's reply – an arrangement that secretly delighted Lebrun, who had brought more copies of the pamphlet with him, and let them fall from the carriage as he drove through the town. He was impressed despite himself by the smart bearing and turn-out of the guard at Christophe's headquarters and a little put out of countenance when, almost immediately after his arrival, two white men approached Christophe with copies of the proclamation which they told him they had found in the street. They begged Christophe not to agree to Leclerc's demands but to meet force with force.

"The general comes with great marks of favour to bestow on you," Lebrun whispered to Christophe.

"I cannot listen to any proposals until I have the orders of the Governor-general," Christophe replied sharply. "These proclamations that you bring with you reek of despotism and tyranny. I intend to administer an oath to my soldiers, to pledge their lives to the defence of liberty." He sent Lebrun off to eat his dinner alone, attended by four silent Negroes who served him from silver dishes.

Christophe sat down to dictate a reply to Leclerc, refusing to hand over the forts or the town without orders from Toussaint.

I have sent one of my aides-de-camp to announce your arrival and that of the French army, but until his reply reaches me I cannot permit you to land. If you make use of the force with which you threaten me, I shall offer all the resistance worthy of a general officer; and if the struggle should be favourable to you, you shall not enter the town of Le Cap until it is in ashes, and even then I will oppose you.

You say that the French Government has sent to Saint-Domingue forces capable of vanquishing any rebels that may be found here; but it is you who have come to create them, among a people peaceful and obedient to France, by the hostile intentions that you express. . . .

As for losing your esteem, General, I assure you that I do not desire to merit it at the price that you put on it, since I should have to act contrary to my duty in order to obtain it.

He sent an officer down to the jetty with the letter. It would be some hours before he received any answer, for the wind was freshening and the squadron had tacked several miles out to sea. Meanwhile he issued orders for the defence of the town – and its destruction. Powder and shot were stacked in the artillery park and at the mortar battery on the quayside. Sacks of coal and iron gratings were carried out to the forts to provide the cannon with red-hot shot to be fired into the warships as they approached the harbour. To the horror of the inhabitants the news circulated that the senior artillery officer, a white man named Guilmond, was at the arsenal, supervising the manufacture of lances tipped with tow, with which the troops were to set fire to the town.

The mayor, Télémaque, led a deputation of citizens to Government House to beg Christophe to comply with Leclerc's ultimatum. Christophe repeated that as a soldier he had only one duty – to his superior officer, Toussaint. He added that he had no proof that the squadron lying off shore and wearing foreign colours (the Spanish vessels were flying their national flag) had in fact come from France. Pursuing this argument – too casuistic to be his own and in fact suggested in one of Toussaint's dispatches – he told the deputation that France would have found better means to make her wishes known, would, for instance, have sent representatives in a despatch-vessel, not an army in a fleet of warships. Then, dropping the pretence, he repeated that, if Leclerc persisted in trying to force a landing at Le Cap, the whole city would go up in flames before the squadron had cast anchor in the harbour.

Télémaque asked permission to lead a deputation to Leclerc to beg a postponement of the landings for forty-eight hours and thus allow Christophe time to receive a reply from Toussaint. This Christophe was only too ready to grant, hoping that some way would be found to spare his beautiful city. It was now past midnight and Télémaque went to the American agent's house to ask him to add his voice to that of the deputation when they set out the following morning. Lear, who had spent the day warning the American residents to be ready to take refuge in the merchant ships in the harbour, promised to speak forcefully to Leclerc. Despite Jefferson's coolness towards Toussaint, American trade with the island had increased steadily and there were at the moment no less than thirty-five American vessels in the harbour of Le Cap alone, among them the *Nelly*, a schooner which Captain John Rodgers, on temporary leave from the US Navy, had brought down from Baltimore in September.

By dawn a strong wind was blowing and it was not until two in the afternoon that the deputation ventured out to the flagship which, having been carried twenty miles out to sea during the night, had struggled back to a position four miles off shore. Leclerc received Télémaque and his companions coldly. He told them that he had no intention of modifying the demands in his letter to Christophe or the conditions implicit in the two proclamations, of which he handed more copies to the mayor. He warned him that the landings would begin half an hour after the deputation had returned to the shore.

The dejected civilians clambered into their boat, rocked the long way back to land and then hastened to Government House, tormented by the prospect of having their homes burned by Christophe or bombarded by Leclerc – and perhaps both at the same time. They implored Christophe to accede to Leclerc's demands. He again refused. As they begged and pleaded, they cast anxious glances through the windows. But there was no sign of sail, no sound of gunfire. As the minutes ticked by and dusk descended on the harbour it seemed that Christophe had successfully called the Frenchman's bluff.

In a sense he had. Leclerc had hoped, by exaggerating the size of his forces and those under Rochambeau and Boudet, to scare Christophe into surrender; but he had never intended to risk an opposed landing. He had given Rochambeau orders to feint southeast after landing at Fort-Liberté but then to swing westward behind the heights of Le Dondon and La Grande-Rivière and so come upon Le Cap from the rear. Leclerc would land at Port-François or the bay of L'Acul, less than ten miles to the west, and then strike back eastwards. The ships of the line he would leave facing Le Cap, for deception and to bombard the city while the two columns attacked from the landward side.

Leclerc was not the cleverest of Bonaparte's generals and he was certainly not the most lucky. He had sent boat parties ashore earlier in the day to bring back fishermen willing to pilot them round the coast and into the harbour, but they could not find any who would admit that they knew the coast at all. To cap this, when

he went aboard the frigate *Uranie* at seven that evening to lead the
remaining frigates, corvettes and armed sloops along the coast for
the landing under cover of night, the day's wind died away and the
vessels lay immobile in a dead calm. It was not until the following
morning that they were able to move – now destined for Port-
Margot twenty miles away.

The inhabitants of Le Cap spent a sleepless, mournful night and
at dawn – on the third day since the French fleet had been sighted –
the tree-shaded square in front of Government House was filled
with weeping women and children and old men, assembled by the
mayor in a last attempt to soften Christophe's heart. Stationed at
intervals along the streets were detachments of troops that
Christophe had brought in from the hinterland and armed labourers
who had come in from the plantations to defend the city and their
freedom. Tobias Lear, pushing his way through them at a very
early hour, obtained an interview with Christophe and, telling him
that he was making arrangements to embark all American citizens,
asked for permission to take with them any other white people who
wished to leave.

Christophe replied curtly that he was about to ride down to the
docks to instruct the officials to prevent any such thing. It was
evident that the colour-strife fomented by Leclerc's arrival had
begun to affect Christophe, despite his reputation as a friend of the
whites; but it was also plain that his orders were not being
stringently enforced, for Lear was able to pass off many French
women and children as American citizens and have them taken
aboard the ships. Christophe was confident that Leclerc had
backed down, but he continued to play his hand determinedly and at
midday he had all the available troops paraded on the place d'Armes
and there administered to them an oath of loyalty to Toussaint. He
then rode to the Town Hall to upbraid Télémaque for having
published the proclamations that he brought back from the *Océan*,
and to tell him that he was about to give orders for all non-
combatant civilians to leave the town and that he recommended
Télémaque and the town council to retire to Le Haut-du-Cap.

Suddenly the temper and the tempo of his actions changed – for
news arrived that Rochambeau had cannonaded his way ashore at
Fort-Liberté and had stormed the forts at Labouque and L'Anse at
bayonet point. The French had not been bluffing after all.
Christophe gave orders that all the white refugees should be
brought back from the American ships. He called in more field

hands from the plantations and issued the *lances à feu* to the squads whose duty it would be to fire the town. Télémaque, on hearing this, instructed all householders to lay in supplies of water, but by now most of the white inhabitants were making for the hills that sheltered Le Cap on the west.

The tension increased throughout the afternoon. At six o'clock one of the French men-o'-war, all of which had been on the move for several hours, tacked inshore towards the harbour. One of the guns at Fort Picolet fired a warning shot across its bows and received a broadside in reply. The cannonade that followed was the signal for the destruction of the town.

Christophe set the example. During the afternoon he had had barrels of tar brought into his house in the rue Royale and distributed through the rooms. As the sound of gunfire echoed up from the sea front he called in a squad of soldiers to broach the barrels and then himself threw the first torch to set the mansion and its magnificent furnishings ablaze. In every quarter of the town officers ran with parties of soldiers armed with flaming lances, methodically setting fire to house after house, while other squads, swinging the butts of their muskets, prevented their owners from trying to put them out. In those parts of the town not yet visited by this terrible plague of fire, people scurried to save what they could of their property before it was too late; and among them toiled Tobias Lear and Captain Rodgers, salvaging goods and urging American stragglers to hurry down to the harbour. Only one of them, a South Carolinian named Lancaster, of the firm of Lancaster and Richardson, insisted on remaining to protect his warehouse, and died in the flames.

By eleven o'clock the city resembled a vast funeral pyre, flames shooting through the roofs of houses and linking in great fiery arcs across the streets, the buildings themselves cracking and crumbling and rocking the earth with the shock of their collapse. At midnight the main powder magazine exploded with a terrifying roar that filled the sky with fire and smoke and burning débris. By dawn only one house in every ten remained unburned. Property worth one hundred million francs had been reduced to smouldering embers. The only living persons in the town were the looters, exhausted and drunk.

Tobias Lear, when the arsenal exploded and the looting began, found a boat whose captain was willing to take him out to the French fleet, where he intended to demand the dispatch of troops to protect American property. As they sailed past Fort Picolet, brightly lit by the flames from the burning town, they could see no sign of movement and none of the guns opened fire, from which Lear correctly deduced that the fort had been abandoned. He reported this to Villaret-Joyeuse, when, after daybreak, he caught up with the *Océan*, which was still beating about before the wind. The admiral assured him that he would take his squadron in immediately, but, despite the heart-rending spectacle of the crowds of fugitives moving agitatedly and helplessly about the slopes above the town, it was not until afternoon that Villaret-Joyeuse led his ships into the harbour – without a single shot being fired against them.

Westward, Leclerc finally managed to land with Hardy's division but, despite Rochambeau's rapid advance from Fort-Liberté, Christophe was able to get clear into the mountains with most of his troops, setting fire to the district of La Petite-Anse as he went. Hardy, starting his men on the twenty-mile march from L'Anse-à-Margot at five in the morning with nothing to eat or drink, soon found the column surrounded by armed Negroes, who eyed him with suspicion and fear. The general took his place at the head of his troops, ordered them to preserve the strictest discipline, and led them over the mountain roads through the Negro bands, whom he urged to return in peace to their plantations.

"Without firing a single cartridge," he wrote triumphantly to his wife, "I managed to get rid of three thousand savages who could have cut the throats of me and my troops in the mountains without my having either the time or the opportunity to escape." Arriving at Le Haut-du-Cap he found himself attacked by a mixed force of Negroes, mulattos and whites but here he had reached the plain and he was able to deploy his men and beat them off.

Leclerc had despatched another small detachment further westward which had no difficulty in capturing Port-de-Paix; Boudet's force took Port-au-Prince (renamed during the Revolution Port-Républicain) and in the South the Negro, Laplume, submitted with all his troops and was confirmed in his rank and command. The whole of the South, all the plain of the North, and most of the coast of the West were firmly in Leclerc's hands. He had brought with him Toussaint's son, Isaac, and his step-son, Placide, who had been educated in France, and he now sent them with their tutor to make contact with Toussaint. They carried with them a letter from Leclerc, offering to accept Toussaint's submission if he would publicly declare that the burning of Le Cap had not been done at his orders.

They also had a letter from Bonaparte in which the First Consul declared that he was "pleased to recognise and proclaim the great services that you have rendered to the French people. If their flag floats over Saint-Domingue, it is to you and the worthy Blacks that they owe this." He assured Toussaint that he appreciated that "in the circumstances in which you found yourself, surrounded by enemies while the mother country could neither help you nor send you provisions", Toussaint was justified in proposing a constitution that gave him extraordinary powers. He went on:

> But today, when circumstances are so happily altered, you will be the first to render homage to the sovereignty of the nation which counts you among its most illustrious citizens.

after warning him of the consequences of 'any contrary course of action', Bonaparte continued:

> What is there for you to desire? The freedom of the Blacks? You know that in all the countries where we have been, we have accorded it to those who did not have it. Respect, honours, fortune? After the services that you have rendered, and that you still intend to render, and with the special feelings that we have towards you, you need have no doubt about the respect, the fortune and the honours that await you.

2

Leclerc sent this letter to Toussaint on February 7, the day after his arrival at the Cape. He waited impatiently for a reply, for Bonaparte's secret instructions laid down that the first phase of the operation – the occupation of the coast towns and the preparation of the attack on the interior - should take no more than a fortnight. He would then move on to the second phase, that of crushing all organised resistance, leaving only scattered mopping-up operations for the third phase.

> In the first phase [said the secret instructions] only the rebellious Blacks will be disarmed; in the third phase they will

all be disarmed. During the first phase the demands will not be exacting; treat with Toussaint and promise him anything that he asks in order to get possession of the fortified positions and a foothold in the country. . . .

Unfortunately, everything had got off to a bad start, largely because of Christophe's obstinacy and defiance. The French troops had orders to deal gently with the Blacks and assure them that they came as friends not enemies, but time was ticking on and if, at the end of a fortnight, Leclerc had failed to persuade Toussaint to call off resistance, was he in fact in a position to carry war into the mountains?

This is the state of my forces [he wrote to the Minister of Marine on February 9]:

At Santo Domingo	400 men
At the Cape, Rochambeau's division	1,800 men
At the Cape, Hardy's division	1,800 men
At the Cape, Desfourneaux's division	1,400 men
At Port-de-Paix	500 men
At Port-au-Prince	2,800 men
To that must be added the marines	700 men
Total	9,400 men

Those are all the forces with which I am to enter into campaign within four days, if nothing arrives from Flushing, Cadiz, Toulon or Havre. I have, it is true, the sailors on board the ships of the squadron, but I think it would be risky to employ them, judging from the examples of insubordination and pillage that they provide every day. We are in a country where we must act as much by persuasion as by force. These people have been convinced that we have come to murder and burn them, and it is only by good conduct that we can destroy these impressions. . . .

He admitted that cultivation in the colony was of a very high standard, especially on the plantations that had been farmed out to the generals, but he was anxious about the immediate supply of food for his men, some of the stores carried by the fleet having been spoiled.

There are some victuals in the town rescued from the fire. The merchants at the Cape will not deliver them except at excessive prices and for cash; but I will contrive to get them somehow. There are a score of American vessels in the harbour, which also have some foodstuffs. They are Jews with whom it is impossible to deal; yet we shall certainly have to deal with them.

Adding together all my possible resources, I calculate that we shall be very lucky if we have enough food for two and a half months. I cannot rely on any business houses. These men are not French, they recognise no country except the United States. It is the United States that has brought the muskets, cannon, powder and all the other munitions of war here. It is they who have egged Toussaint on to resistance. I am personally convinced that the Americans plan to incite all the Antilles to independence, because they can then hope to have the exclusive commerce, as they have in Saint-Domingue. I should not regret it if England and France combined in threatening them. . . .

The two governments did not go as far as that but Talleyrand instructed the French *chargé d'affaires*, Pichon, to protest at the action of American merchants in supplying arms to the Blacks. "Remind the federal government of the goodwill that it has frequently shown over the affairs of Saint-Domingue and how all the colonial powers are interested in seeing peace and a stable government reestablished in that island. The troubles in Saint-Domingue would have spread to all nations who have a population of two colours."

During the week since he watched Leclerc's arrival from the heights above Samana Bay, Toussaint had been continuously on the move. After his westward dash to order Christophe to withstand any French attempts to land, he continued towards Port-de-Paix to give similar instructions to Maurepas. Returning, he was very nearly captured by the French column from L'Anse-à-Margot, for his was the mixed force that Hardy met and dispersed at Le Haut-du-Cap. He rode to the Bréda plantations (there were several, some now known by the names of Bréda's daughters, Mesdames d'Héricourt and de Noé), where he had worked as a slave and had since become master. There he collected money and reinforcements. Galloping over the mountains and down into the western plain, he made for Saint-Marc, halfway down the Bight of Léogane, and organised its resistance and devastation. He was on the point of continuing to Port-au-Prince – which, though he did not know it, had already fallen to General Boudet – when he received word from his wife that his sons and their tutor were waiting for him at Ennery, the plantation where he most frequently made his home.

The elder boy, Placide, was the natural child of a mulatto, Seraphin Clerc, and Suzanne-Simon Baptiste who, like Toussaint, was descended from the Arada tribe and was the sister of the slave who had given Toussaint his first smattering of education. Deserted by Clerc, Suzanne had set up house with Toussaint and, after the birth of Isaac, had married him. The Abbé Coisnon, who had come out from France with the boys on Bonaparte's orders, was their tutor at the Collège de la Marche in Paris. He brought with him the letters from Bonaparte and Leclerc. Toussaint set Bonaparte's letter aside for further reflection, but to Leclerc he replied that he had had no responsibility for Le Cap (an unworthy lie, loading all the blame on to Christophe's shoulders) and that he was willing to obey the orders of the French government as soon as Leclerc had shown him his letters of authority and had halted hostilities.

The elderly Abbé Coisnon returned to Le Cap with this message and on February 12 Leclerc wrote again, urging Toussaint to come and join him.

Have no worries about your personal fortune; it will be safe-guarded for you, since it has been only too well earned by your own efforts. As for your rank, you may rely upon the promises of General Bonaparte, whose letter you have in your hands.

From the solemn declaration of the First Consul, contained in his attached proclamation and in the letter that he sent to you, you need have no further anxiety about the liberty of your fellow citizens.

I await you, citizen general; come and confer with me frankly, with one of your comrades. To prove the sincerity of my intentions, I promise that during the next four days the division covering the Cape will not commit any hostile act. . . .

The value of this assurance, however, was diminished by the fact that elsewhere – and in those parts of the island where Toussaint most feared attack, since his position was already un-tenable in the northern plain – Leclerc refused to call off hostilities on the ground that it was too late to get counter-orders to the commanders. The truth was that neither man trusted the other, and with good reason.

> He is trying to play with me [Leclerc told the Minister of Marine on February 15]. I do not believe any of it. He is the most false and dissimulating man in the world. . . . He occupies Le Dondon, La Grand-Rivière, La Marmelade, Les Gonaïves, the district around Port-de-Paix, Le Gros Morne, the Mirebalais district – and I shall direct my attack against these points. . . . I have no means of transport. I am giving my men 6 days' ration of biscuit; after that we shall live on bananas and beef, which are not lacking in this country.

Leclerc's letter of February 12 reached Toussaint at Les Gonaïves. He answered that he did not trust the Frenchman sufficiently to go to him at Le Cap, but that he was willing to hand over his command to him in accordance with the First Consul's orders. He asked Leclerc to confide his plans to him and threatened that, in the meantime, if the French troops advanced, he would be forced to defend himself.

The laggard convoys from Toulon and Cadiz arrived at Le Cap on February 12 and 15, carrying nearly 4,000 men, and Leclerc brought the interchange to an end on February 17 by launching attacks against the positions that he had mentioned in his letter to the Ministry of Marine, at the same time publishing a proclamation that:

"General Toussaint and General Christophe are outlawed; all citizens are ordered to hunt them down and to treat them as rebels against the French Republic."

During the first two days of their advance, Leclerc's troops met with little resistance other than occasional ambushes from an enemy who was well acquainted with the ground and able to disappear into the bush or along the steep valleys after delivering a volley or two. But Christophe's pride and hot temper would not permit him to refuse pitched battle with his opponents. He determined to stand and fight – a decision that he knew was wrong.

The veteran French troops, tough and courageous, fought their way into the mountains over terrain which Leclerc declared to be worse that any he had seen in the Alps and drove towards the border of the North Province along the line of Saint-Raphaël, Le

Dondon, La Marmelade and Le Gros-Morne, aiming to sweep
down into Les Gonaïves, the first large town of the West Province.
Christophe, fighting with desperate fury in the front rank of his
mixed force of two thousand men, half of them regulars from the
1st, 2nd and 5th demi-brigades and the others newly-recruited
field hands, was driven from La Marmelade at the point of the
bayonet by Hardy's division. Threatened on one flank by Rochambeau and on the other by Desfourneaux, he fell back on Ennery,
still trying to stand between the French and Toussaint. It was
clear that neither the Black troops nor their generals had the skill
or experience to stand against Leclerc's men in the open field.

For a while it seemed as though the weather might come to
Toussaint's aid. After a deceptively temperate beginning ("the heat
is very bearable," Hardy wrote to his wife on February 15; "it is
true that we are still in what they call the rainy season, but it is
only like June in France"), the French found themselves pinned
down not by enemy fire but by rainstorms of a violence that they
had never encountered before. On February 20 all the French
columns were at a standstill, unable to cross the swollen mountain
torrents, halted by washed-out roads, wincing under the weight
and velocity of the increasing rain. But on the following day they
resumed their advance, driving Christophe from Ennery, while
behind him Toussaint marched eastward to confront Rochambeau
in the Ravin-à-Couleuvre and to try to preserve his line of retreat
to Saint-Marc.

The ravine, narrow, notched into a precipitous, brush-covered
mountainside, was ideal for defence. From the cover of the trees
and from barricades thrown across the road, Toussaint's men
fought furiously against the advancing Frenchmen, but after six
hours of hand-to-hand fighting they were thrown back, leaving 800
dead. Toussaint made for the river Ester, intending to continue to
Saint-Marc. On the way he learned that Dessalines had been driven
out of this coastal town by Boudet's forces and, after setting it on
fire, had made for La Petite-Rivière, inland on the Artibonite, the
long river that wound in many ragged loops north-westward below
the mountains of Cahos. Toussaint swung in that direction, hoping
to gather supplies and stores and rally his scattered forces at the
fort of La Crête-à-Pierrot on the heights above La Petite-Rivière.
He was followed by Christophe with the scanty remnant of the men
he had led from Le Cap. In the north-west, Maurepas had surrendered. All opposition to the French had ceased in the former

Spanish part of the island, and had never even begun in the South Province.

Yet Leclerc, reporting this on February 27, was far from bubbling with joy. He wanted stores, he wanted reinforcements, and he wanted money. If he was to make his fortune in this island where there was no loot because the enemy destroyed everything before he could lay his hands on it, then he must make it in cash. He intended to claim the mahogany concession on the vast deserted island of Gonave off Port-au-Prince, but there was no hope of turning that to profit until the colony was completely pacified.

He asked for 6,000 reinforcements immediately – he had lost 600 men killed, 1,500 wounded, 2,000 sick – and another 6,000 within three months. He complained that all his hospital supplies had been badly stowed and ruined; that inventories had been falsified and he was short of eleven thousand pairs of shoes; that he had not a single cooking pot or water bottle. He needed twenty thousand capes and coats to keep his men warm at night, and twenty thousand high-crowned hats to protect them from sunstroke by day. He wanted wine, flour, salt provisions, brandy, muskets. Most of all he wanted fifteen hundred thousand francs.

In addition to his other problems, Leclerc was faced with the difficulty of preserving order in the northern plain after his troops had moved up into the mountains and over into the West Province. Guerilla bands of plantation workers raided with fire and slashing knives right to the city walls of Le Cap and Fort-Liberté. Those who were captured received short shrift, though in this they were no worse off than prisoners taken on the battlefield. Captain Mends of HMS *Nereide*, who was entertained by the French fleet at Le Cap in March reported that 800 of Dessalines's soldiers "were taken and shot" and that during the fighting at Plaisance the French had "made six hundred prisoners who were all shot. . . . They shoot every one they catch. Two hundred were so executed the Morning we sailed. They are led to the Edge of a Pit, and made to kneel down with their backs to it, so that they fall backwards into it, when struck by the Ball; one who might be wounded only, in this manner, is equally covered with Earth, with those who more fortunately were killed outright."

Soon after his arrival at Le Cap, Villaret-Joyeuse had civilly informed his British counterpart, Sir John Duckworth, Rear-Admiral of the Red, commanding the Jamaica station, of the French squadron's dispositions and orders – a courtesy which provided him with the opportunity of asking Sir John to furnish him with supplies. Sir John, however, was forewarned. The British government had ordered the 83rd Regiment of Royal Artillery from Madeira to Jamaica, and had brought Sir John's squadron up to thirteen ships of the line – precautionary measures which "do not arise from any suspicion which they entertain of the ulterior views of France being different from those which have been professed by the Government of that country, but when so important an object may be at stake as the security of His Majesty's West Indian possessions, and particularly the island of Jamaica, they consider it their duty to prevent their being exposed to any possible danger arising from circumstances which they cannot anticipate." Or, as they put it to Sir John five or six weeks later: "Your future conduct toward all persons in authority under the French government should be regulated by a cautious regard to the protection and security of the valuable and extended possessions which are placed in your command."

The American government suspected that Bonaparte intended to pour men into Louisiana, ceded to him by Spain in 1800 under the Treaty of Ildefonso, to form a solid French barrier along the right bank of the Mississippi against any further westward expansion of the United States. Britain equally believed that Bonaparte, defeated in his attempt to reach India by way of Egypt, had turned his eyes to the Americas – but that his plan was to use Saint-Domingue as the base for operations against Jamaica and the other West Indian islands.

Sir John consequently expressed the greatest concern "that the reception your Excellency has met with has been of so hostile a nature, and in direct violation of that Duty which the Colonies owe to their Country." Sir John confessed that "it is most mortifying to my feelings to be so situated by the unexpected arrival of a very large sea and land force as to prevent me from the pleasure of holding any prospect of aid."

Having burnt whatever they could in the plains, all the Negro leaders were now in the mountains. Dessalines had taken up a position in the Cahos range when Toussaint arrived at La Crête-à-Pierrot, a fort that the British had built above La Petite-Rivière to command the road to the summits. Knowing that Leclerc would make for the Cahos as soon as he learned that the colony's treasure had been buried there, Toussaint sent word to Dessalines to take charge of La Crête-à-Pierrot while he himself struck back north-wards to join forces with Christophe.

He had not given up hope that by his presence and personality he could fan local insurrections into such flame that the French would be driven back into the towns. With six companies of grenadiers from the 4th colonial demi-brigade he slipped behind Leclerc's southward-marching columns and recaptured Ennery. There he found a copy of Leclerc's proclamation outlawing him and replied by issuing a proclamation of his own, outlawing Leclerc. He crossed over the mountains to San Miguel, in the Spanish sector, then up to Saint-Raphael and across to Le Dondon and La Marmelade, 'liberating' those towns without opposition, for Desfourneaux's division was too small to fulfill its task of policing the subjugated areas.

At La Marmelade he was halted by a message from Dessalines that one of Leclerc's columns had succeeded in reaching the treasure in the Cahos. Laden with booty, it was making its way down to Port-au-Prince. The others were laying siege to La Crête-à-Pierrot.

In a campaign so soon befouled by wanton atrocities on both sides – the six hundred Black prisoners shot in cold blood by Hardy's men at Plaisance were matched by eight hundred white men, women and children massacred by Dessalines's troops at Les Verrettes – it was startling for the French infantrymen arriving at La Crête-à-Pierrot to find themselves greeted with their own patriotic songs played by a military band – Toussaint, like Christophe, had a taste for martial music, and had been compelled to leave his bandsmen behind when he dashed to the north. The French were shortly startled in a less pleasant fashion when Dessalines, leading a sortie, slashed a way clean through their lines. He found it impossible to return to the fort, but within a few days Toussaint and Toussaint's kinsman, Charles Belair, marched up from north and south and the French were themselves encircled. Thus they remained for several days, like alternating circles on a target, black, white, black – until the garrison ran short of water and slipped through the French lines at night, leaving behind their wounded, some white artillerymen, part of Dessalines's baggage and all of Toussaint's bandsmen.

Christophe continued his guerilla forays in the north. Short of supplies and having lost all his heavy artillery, he was now reduced to the kind of warfare at which, in fact, the Blacks were superior to the French. Travelling light through a friendly countryside, by field tracks that the French did not know and would not have dared to use, his columns marched through the night, struck at dawn, and were away before the French could set their less mobile hunting parties on them. The more daring ventures Christophe led in person, on one occasion penetrating as far as the slopes of the Morne du Cap itself. The difficulties of dragging a cannon by side-tracks through the brush and up the moutain side – and of keeping up the spirits of his troops whose enthusiasm diminished as they ventured further and further into French-held territory – prevented him from taking up his position before the late afternoon. From the Morne he could look down across the ravine into the hospital and the prison and see French officers strolling in the courtyard of Government House, where he had ruled only two months before. Now he was an outlaw, with a band of tattered rebels and one 12-pounder.

He split his men into three parties, set them at intervals across the slope and, as the cool evening breeze began to blow towards the sea, aimed a twelve-pound ball at the group in the courtyard. The cannon-shot was accompanied by musketry fire from the other detachments. After firing a round or two, the cannon was dragged to a new position, while the infantrymen continued with their fire. The town fell into immediate confusion, the evening strollers scampering for cover, the troops trotting out of the barracks but finding it impossible to get across the ravine.

Convinced that this was an attack in force, the acting commandant sent urgent messages to Leclerc, asking for reinforcements. By morning Christophe and his men had returned to the mountains, while Leclerc, discouraged by the fiasco at La Crête-à-Pierrot and alarmed by continued reports of trouble in the occupied towns, ordered his troops to fall back on the coast. While Dessalines rallied stragglers at Fort-Marchand, Toussaint tracked Hardy northward, raiding his flanks as he crossed back over the heights from the West Province to the North, where Christophe was waiting to continue the harrying.

Leclerc's fortunes had soared and plummetted during the few weeks since his arrival. He had failed to crush all resistance and, though he held the towns and could establish cordons in the hills to protect these and some of the plantations, he faced the same eventual stalemate that had defeated the British. The four thousand troops from Flushing and Le Havre, so long delayed, appeared early in April, but scarcely served to keep his numbers constant. He had lost 1,500 men during the inconclusive march to La Crête-à-Pierrot and back, though he was careful to conceal this from Bonaparte, blaming his casualties on sickness rather than wounds – a lie that was shortly to be tragically realised.

Fortunately for him, it was at this moment that Toussaint began to lose heart. Through one of the French officers whom he had captured, he addressed a letter of submission to Bonaparte, sending it not through Leclerc but by way of Boudet, who had returned to Port-au-Prince. Boudet – as Toussaint had undoubtedly foreseen – forwarded the letter to Leclerc, and told Toussaint that he had done so. Toussaint was now able, without too great a loss of face, to suggest to Boudet that he should sound Leclerc on the possibility of a reconciliation. Meanwhile, Christophe reported that Leclerc had made approaches to him through General Hardy. Toussaint ordered him to continue the conversations, but did not reveal to Christophe or to any other of his generals that he was himself already trying to make contact with Leclerc through Boudet.

<h1 style="text-align:center">3</h1>

The first approach to Christophe came through an old acquaintance, a white planter named Wilton who had been given the rank of captain and appointed commandant of Christophe's former district at La Petite-Anse. Wilton signed and forwarded a letter that had been concocted by Hardy and Wilton's grandfather, Belin de Villeneuve, one of the oldest and richest of the returned planters in the North Province. Addressing Christophe as *"Mon cher compère"*, Wilton reproached him for having resisted Leclerc. He said that Leclerc had come merely to consolidate the order that Christophe had so capably established at Le Cap, and he reminded Christophe of the many occasions when he had said that he would be only too pleased to hand over the burdens of his office.

"Your intentions always seemed so pure to me, and your devotion to the French nation left me in no doubt as to what course you would pursue – but then, suddenly, at the appearance of the French fleet, you were no longer the same man." Christophe's friends, Wilton continued, were convinced that this unexpected change was attributable to bad advice from the other Black leaders. Leclerc was therefore ready to forgive him if he would join him with his troops.

They will be treated on the same footing as French soldiers and you and your family will be guaranteed everything that you may desire, especially if you decide to leave the colony – for that is the best thing you could do, in order not to be exposed to the hatred of those rebels against the French authority who may not wish to follow your example. You will be sure of a handsome fortune and you will be able to enjoy it under the protection of France in whatever country you care to choose. . . .

The letter was frank and direct enough to persuade Christophe of its honesty and, since time and adversity had moderated his rage, he was in a mood to listen. After reporting the approach to Toussaint he sent a friendly reply to Wilton, affirming that he had no wish to rebel but also warning that he would not submit unless he received assurances that slavery was not to be restored. "You above all people are in a position to know my devotion to the French nation. My feelings and intentions have not changed. I am still the same man: a sentinel set by my comrades at a post where it was my duty to watch over their freedom, dearer to them than existence itself. I was obliged to alert them to a blow which might have annihilated them. . . ."

He complained of Leclerc's refusal to understand that he was under orders from Toussaint and bound by duty to consult him before deviating from them. He accused Leclerc of being over-hasty in his use of force and Rochambeau of having attacked Fort-Liberté without warning, murdering its defenders. "After that sort of conduct, what might I not expect?" He ended by assuring Wilton that he was ready to consider submission. "There is no sacrifice I would not make for peace and for the welfare of my fellow citizens – if I can be sure that they will be free and happy."

Wilton passed Christophe's letter to Hardy, who replied immediately, superscribing his own letter "from General Hardy, commanding the Northern Divisions to General Christophe, commanding the cordon of the North" – a tactful and unforeseen mode of address to an outlaw. It was clear, he said, that Christophe had been misinformed by malicious persons "who have aroused in you a mistrust for the French Government and its representatives". But the conduct of those representatives since their arrival in Saint-Domingue, and their treatment of the rebel generals who had submitted to them – Clervaux, Toussaint's brother Paul, Maurepas and Laplume – should have convinced him that his suspicions were ill-founded.

> For twelve years, General, we have fought for liberty. Can you believe that after such great sacrifices we should make ourselves so vile in our own estimation as to undertake a task [the reintroduction of slavery] which would both destroy our achievements and tarnish our glory? . . . Until today we have fought you as enemies; tomorrow, if you so wish, we will embrace you as brothers. Send me your proposals, or tell me at what time you would like to come to the Vaudreuil plantation to present them in person. I shall be there. If we fail to agree, I give you my word of honour that after the meeting you will be free to return to your headquarters.

This letter, like Wilton's, was forthright and likely to impress Christophe; but in the meantime Leclerc had once more misjudged Christophe's pride and self-respect and had sent him a note which came near to wrecking the negotiations. "I will stand by the promises that have been made to you," he wrote, "but if you propose to submit to the Republic, bear in mind that a great service you could render her would be to provide the means of our laying hold of the person of General Toussaint."

Christophe replied to all three on April 21. To Wilton he wrote:

> The successful outcome of our correspondence depends only on General Leclerc. He has been good enough to write me a letter, but it is with repugnance that I find in it a proposal that I should dishonour myself with a monstrous act of cowardly treachery.

He minced words even less with Leclerc:

> You propose, citizen-general, that I should furnish you with the means of laying hold of General Toussaint Louverture. This would be perfidious treachery on my part, and the proposal, degrading to me, is in my eyes proof of your invincible reluctance to believe me capable of the slightest feelings of delicacy and honour. He is my superior officer and my friend. Is friendship compatible with such monstrous and despicable behaviour, citizen-general?

Although he was unable to read, and could write no more than his surname, Christophe dictated all important letters himself and it is his own voice which sounds the notes of authentic, if somewhat repetitive, injured pride in his reply to Hardy.

If General Leclerc, instead of proposing a perfidious dastardly action that would degrade me in his own eyes, had spoken to me as you have, in language compatible with the sentiments of honour and delicacy which he might at least have assumed me to have, I should have agreed to the meeting that you suggest – not at the Vaudreuil plantation but at La Petite-Anse or Le Cap. I am too favourably impressed by your own frankness and your word of honour not to agree to an interview at all, but it shall not be at the place you indicate but midway between our two lines. For this purpose I suggest the Montalibor plantation. If this is agreeable to you, inform me of the day and hour at which you will be there. I promise to be there.

The dignity that all observers had noted in Christophe's character is apparent throughout his dealings with Leclerc and the other Frenchmen. The Black head waiter, now risen to be leader of rebellious ex-slaves, speaks to these European generals as man to man, his standing never a moment inferior to theirs. But Leclerc's slight to his honour had aggravated his suspicions. In Leclerc's attitude he scented Bonaparte's own contempt for the Blacks, and to all three of his correspondents he emphasised the need for the French to make a clear statement of their intentions and a solemn declaration of their determination not to permit slavery to be reintroduced in the island.

We too, General, [he wrote to Hardy] have fought for twelve years for liberty, for those same rights, which, like you, we have purchased with our blood; and I have always been unwilling to believe that Frenchmen, after making such great sacrifices to obtain them for themselves, would one day come to take them away from a people who gloried in being part of that great nation. . . .

When Bonaparte established the Consulate he left undecided the status of the colonies, declaring that constitutions would be drawn up for them according to their needs. This, as Christophe and the other Black leaders realised only too well, left the way open for the reintroduction of slavery. Instead of assurances that they would be protected, the Blacks demanded definite legislation. "In the name of my country, in the name of the mother country," Christophe said in his letter to Leclerc, "I demand these salutary laws – and Saint-Domingue will be saved."

It was a demand that Leclerc could not ignore. Though he must have known that he was lying, he replied:

> This code is not yet in existence; I am working on it at this moment. The First Consul was unable to draw up a code for a country which he did not know and about which he had received contradictory reports. But I declare to you before the colony, and before the Supreme Being whose witness one does not invoke in vain, that the foundations of this code are liberty and equality, that all Blacks shall be free. . . . If this declaration does not satisfy you I shall take it as proof that you are unwilling to submit to the Republic. If it suffices, come to Le Haut-du-Cap tomorrow. I shall be there, and I assure you that if after an hour's discussion we have not arrived at agreement, you shall return to your troops. I give you my word as General-in-Chief.

Christophe met Leclerc at Le Haut-du-Cap at eleven am on April 25 and there accepted his terms and assurances. He handed over his line of fortified positions, disbanded the four or five thousand field hands who had rallied to him, and placed himself under the command of General Hardy with the 1,500 regular troops that remained with him.

Throughout the negotiations he had kept in touch with Toussaint and had repeatedly told the French that Toussaint was willing to submit as soon as he had their promise that freedom would be preserved. Then, as he wrote to Hardy, "General Toussaint Louverture himself, whom General Leclerc regards as no better than a criminal, but will not hesitate to throw himself with all our people into the arms of the Republic." And to Leclerc, in accepting the meeting at Le Haut-du-Cap, "I am flattered by the opinion you have formed of my loyalty, but I regret that you continue to believe that General Toussaint Louverture does not share that estimable quality. I think I am able to inform you that you are mistaken in that respect; I do not believe that I deceive myself when I warrant you that the mere confirmation of liberty and equality for all will bring him back into the arms of the Republic."

Immediately after his interview with Leclerc, Christophe wrote to Hardy, telling him of the instructions he had given for the implementation of his agreement with the general-in-chief, adding à propos of Toussaint: "I have myself just taken to that general the letter that the General-in-Chief gave me for him. I have reason, from the talk I have had with him, to hope for the return of tranquillity throughout the colony. He is replying to the General-in-Chief and will send his letter by one of his aides-de-camp."

Leclerc, in his letter to Toussaint, offered to incorporate all the other rebel generals and troops in the French army in their existing ranks, and to confirm Toussaint in the rank of lieutenant-general on condition that he resigned his command and retired to one of his plantations. Leclerc asked Toussaint to meet him at Le Cap to discuss the proposal.

Toussaint was now faced with the difficulty of breaking the news to the implacably white-hating Dessalines, whom he had told nothing of Christophe's negotiations with Leclerc nor of his own approach through Boudet. He had, indeed, continued to promise that the fight against the French would be carried on until victory or death. He rode down to Fort-Marchand, where Dessalines was recovering from an illness, and showed him Christophe's report on his meeting with Leclerc, complaining that Christophe had betrayed him.

Dessalines was not deceived. "I know him too well," he growled. "I would not for a moment do him the injustice of believing that he went to Le Cap without your orders. Behave honestly with me. Tell me frankly that you mean to treat with the French."

Toussaint produced Leclerc's letter, pretending that it had reached him only at the moment when he had left his headquarters and that he had not yet had time to read it. It was too obviously a device to avoid expressing an opinion on the proposals in the letter. Dessalines glared at him and snapped: "Impossible! You know what is in this letter. Who gave it to you?"

"Christophe," Toussaint replied.

"Then why didn't you arrest him and punish him for going to Le Cap without orders?" Dessalines shouted. He unfolded the paper and began to read it – then broke off in fury, screaming that he would hold Toussaint responsible for all the misfortunes he was about to bring upon the Blacks. Toussaint, still protesting that Christophe had acted without orders, swore that he would arrest him; and on this pretext he rode off.

He returned to his headquarters, where he learned that Leclerc had withdrawn the decree of outlawry against him on May 1. On May 6 he went to Le Cap, accompanied by his staff and an escort of three or four hundred cavalrymen who made his arrival more of a triumphal entry than an act of submission. As the cavalcade clattered into the place du Gouvernement the guns of the fortresses and warships boomed a salute. The escort wheeled and halted in line. Toussaint rode down their ranks and then, leaving them with swords drawn, entered Government House for his talk with Leclerc. His face was stern and there was cold fury in his greetings to the Negro generals – including his brother Paul – who had already submitted and were now presented with other members of Leclerc's staff.

The conversation with Leclerc was frigid, an exchange of reproaches during which Toussaint again denied that he had given orders for the burning of Le Cap, placing all the blame on Christophe. Since the talk was private, this brought no contradiction. When they rose, Toussaint accepted Leclerc's invitation to dine with him the following day and, accompanied by his body-guard, went off to spend the night in the town, which was illuminated in celebration of his return.

The dinner was not convivial. Toussaint refused all food and drink until the meal was nearly over. Then, cutting a piece of Gruyère from the middle of a cheese, he trimmed off all the sides and ate the small cube that remained, accompanying it with a glass of water from a carafe from which one of the other diners had already served himself. His evident fear of being poisoned may have been heightened by the cold reception given him by the French officers at the table. All of them had heard and resented the stories of the many white women who had granted this wizened Black man their favours in return for his patronage for their husbands and families, and news had recently filtered through from Port-au-Prince that General Boudet had found, in the false bottom of a captured box containing Toussaint's private papers, a hoard of letters, rings, keys, locks of hair and other gallant mementoes. These Boudet had ordered to be destroyed without examination, to avoid having to enforce Bonaparte's order that "white women who have prostituted themselves to Negroes, whatever their rank, shall be sent to Europe".

But if the presence of Toussaint aroused distaste among the white population, both military and civil, it was with frank horror that they observed Dessalines's entry into Le Cap a few days later. Unable to continue the struggle without Toussaint and Christophe, he had agreed to make his submission. His dark face flushed with unassuaged revenge, he glared defiantly at the crowds in the streets, the whites turning their backs in disgust, the Blacks bowing their heads and sometimes falling to their knees before this mighty and blood-drenched man. Leclerc appointed him commander of the district of Saint-Marc, where the violent, unpredictable creature showed himself as single-minded and cruel in the repression of all resistance as he had formerly been in organising and leading it.

Toussaint retired to the plantation at Ennery, near Les Gonaïves, taking with him most of his bodyguard, whom he disbanded in accordance with his promise to Leclerc, but retained as workers on the estate. Leclerc wrote on May 8 to Decrès, Minister of Marine and Colonies, telling him that he was satisfied that Toussaint would obey his orders "because he is convinced that if he does not carry them out I shall make him regret it. . . . I shall not lose a moment in restoring tranquillity and shall then have nothing to fear from any quarter in the colony. . . . As those of my reports which you publish also appear in the newspapers here, it is impolitic to put anything in which could destroy the ideas of liberty and equality that are on everybody's lips here."

He was worried lest indiscretion in France should give away his true intentions. "I beg you," he wrote to Bonaparte, "to forbid the publication in French newspapers of any jokes about the Blacks. It prejudices my operations here." He assured his brother-in-law that "if I have not yet carried out your instructions, it is because a suitable moment has not yet arisen. I am going to incorporate the colonial troops in my own. I shall send a great part of the officers and soldiers back to agriculture. I shall organise a good gendarmerie and when the time comes I shall act, but I must first have the 12,000 reinforcements for whom I have asked. . . . ."

He was aware that time was running out for him. He ought by now to have embarked on phase three of the secret instructions that Bonaparte had given him. He could not, because he lacked sufficient men. Yet every day that he waited, the strength of his army declined. In the marshes along the bay, eastward to La Petite-Anse and even below the quays of Le Cap itself, where the former quagmires had been filled in with loose stones, the mosquitos had been breeding, and with the summer came the remorseless, terrifying acceleration of death from the yellow fever they called 'the Siamese sickness'. Attributed, like malaria, to the 'bad air' of the coast and plains, the filthy and deadly mosquito-borne infection was worst in the large cities, Port-au-Prince and Le Cap. To conceal his losses and avoid panic, Leclerc had already given instructions that there were to be no more military funerals. The carts lumbered through the towns at midnight, collecting the day's dead left at the doors of their billets. The sickness struck as fiercely at his officers as at his men. Before the end of May Hardy was dead, and he was soon followed by other generals. Among the Blacks, long since immune to the disease, there were no casualties.

4

Leclerc's secret instructions from Bonaparte were lengthy and precise.

Win over Christophe, Clairveaux, Maurepas, Félix, Romain, Jasmin, etc., and all the other Blacks who have been favourable to the whites. In the first phase confirm them in their ranks and employment. In the third phase send them all to France with their ranks if they have served well during the second phase.

All the whites who have served under Toussaint and who during the incidents at Saint-Domingue have committed crimes are to be sent straight to Guiana.

All the Blacks who have behaved well, but whose rank does not permit them to be left on the island, are to be sent to Brest.

All the Blacks or mulattos who have behaved badly, of no matter what rank, are to be sent to the Mediterranean and landed at a port on the island of Corsica. . . .

Whatever happens, it seems necessary to disarm all Negroes during the third phase, no matter what side they are on, and send them back to agriculture.

All individuals who signed the Constitution must be sent to France during the third phase as prisoners, or free if they acted under constraint. . . .

Withdraw the colours of the national guard; present them with new ones and reorganise them. Reorganise the gendarmerie. Do not allow any Black to remain in the island if he has held a rank above captain. The island of Tortuga can serve as a depot for the Black prisoners. Ships of the line and frigates may serve the same purpose. . . .

No public instruction whatever shall be reestablished in Saint-Domingue and all the Créoles shall be required to send their children to France to be educated.

Fearful of Bonaparte's wrath if he dawdled, yet lacking the strength to take any firm, conclusive step, Leclerc began to blunder from one bad, weak decision to the next. Rigaud, Pétion and many of the other mulatto leaders whom Toussaint had driven from the island two years before had returned as officers in the French army, but Rochambeau, the commander of the West Province, who despised mulattos even more than Negroes, at once fell foul of them. His complaints, reinforced by Toussaint's jealous promptings that Rigaud was unreliable, led Leclerc to banish Rigaud once more from the island, thus depriving himself and France of one of their staunchest allies and snubbing a whole caste which, though small in numbers, was still often rich, usually well-educated, and – if only from self-interest and fear of the Blacks – preponderantly pro-French.

Leclerc's own health was not good, and was certainly not improved by the mounting gossip about Pauline's indiscretions. Le Cap was a wilderness of ruins when Leclerc entered it, the returned inhabitants living in tents or under tarpaulins rigged as roofs to the stone shells of their houses. Pauline spent the first two months of her stay in Saint-Domingue at Port-au-Prince – "boring herself to death", as Hardy reported; but at the end of his unsuccessful campaign against Toussaint, Leclerc brought her north and moved with her and his bodyguard to the Labattut plantation on the island of Tortuga, famous in previous centuries as the original home of the buccaneers. The setting was idyllic: cool breezes, orange blossom, the gentle swell and whisper of the sea, and, for an evening's entertainment, the Negro men and women losing themselves in the wild, lascivious abandon of the *chica*, while Madame la Générale observed them from her couch of banana leaves within a bower of frangipani and oleanders.

Leclerc decided that a change would be good for her. He set up a military hospital on the island and brought Pauline back to a house on the sea front at Le Cap. Later, when Government House was partially restored, he moved in there with her, and she found a fleeting interest in furnishing it with the contents of the many

crates that she had brought over in the *Océan*. Her boudoir she
dressed out in blue satin with silver fringes, her bedroom in white
and gold. On an altar-shaped table beside the bed an alabaster
figure of Silence held a candle in one hand and placed a finger to its
lips with the other. From a shell-shaped canopy a descending flight
of cupids held back the gold-trimmed curtains while pointing to the
large ornate looking glass that formed the tester. Here Pauline
reclined, receiving guests, regretting Paris and complaining with
every reason about the heat until Leclerc took over the Destaing
plantation on the heights above the town, where she recovered
some of her spirits.

It was an exotic background. The troops in the interior had
orders to send back rare animals which were eventually destined
for the menagerie in the Paris Jardin des Plantes. Trees were hauled
intact to one of the courtyards, replanted and then roofed over with
sails from the marine stores, making a vast cage in which parrots
and monkeys could disport themselves for Pauline's entertainment.
Within the great house the general's lady held court again,
receiving, among others, a young American, Mary Hassal, whose
sister was married to a French officer.

She was in a room darkened by Venetian blinds, lying on a
sofa, from which she half rose to receive me, [Miss Hassal
wrote to Aaron Burr]. She amused General Boyer, who sat at
her feet, by letting her slipper fall continually, which he respect-
fully put on as often as it fell. She is small, fair, with blue eyes
and flaxen hair. Her face is expressive of sweetness but without
spirit. She has a voluptuous mouth and is rendered interesting
by an air of languor which spreads itself over her whole frame.
. . . She hates reading, and though passionately fond of music
plays no instrument. . . . She can do nothing but dance.

Her admirers were legion. "*Le vent brulant qui allait souffler pour
la mort soufflait avec non moins d'energie pour l'amour,*"* her
husband's secretary wrote of that torrid summer. Fréron, one of her
earliest lovers, from whom Bonaparte had saved her by the
forced marriage to Leclerc, and who had come out with the expedition as a civilian in search of a fortune, died under the wind's
scorching breath. Another, General Humbert, was so indiscreet in

---

* The scorching wind which was going to blow for death was blowing no less
fiercely for love.

his admiration that the petty, harassed Leclerc ordered him back to France with an adverse confidential report. More and more, Leclerc's dispatches took on a querulous note and his suspicions and criticisms of those around him increased.

My position grows daily worse [he wrote to Bonaparte on June 6]. Toussaint is untrustworthy, as I had expected.

His suspicions had been further aroused by the interception of two letters from Toussaint to one of his former aides-de-camp, Fontaine, in which Toussaint had asked "how many trips are made to La Fossette [the town cemetery] each night?" and expressed his happiness that "Providence [the town hospital] is at last coming to our aid." On June 5 Leclerc ordered General Brunet, commanding the French troops at Les Gonaïves, to arrest Toussaint by stealth.

Brunet wrote to Toussaint on June 7.
We have some matters to discuss, my dear general, which it is not possible to deal with by letter but which an hour's conference would settle. [Toussaint had complained that French troops in the neighbourhood of Ennery had been pillaging his plantation.] Were I not overwhelmed with work and petty problems, I should have brought you my reply today, but since I cannot get away for a few days, will you come here, if you have recovered from your indisposition? And let it be tomorrow, since one should never be laggard in good works. You may not find in my simple quarters all the refinements that I would wish to provide for your reception, but you will find the candour of a man of honour who desires nothing but the prosperity of the colony and your personal happiness.
If Madame Toussaint, whose acquaintance I should very much like to make, would care to accompany you, I should be most happy. If she is in need of horses I will send mine. I repeat, general, that you will never find a more sincere friend than I. . . .
PS. Your servant who is on his way to Port-Républicain called here this morning; he has continued his journey with his pass in order.

In fact, Toussaint's servant had been arrested, but he was unaware of this when he went off in the late afternoon of June 7 for his interview with the candid, honourable General Brunet. He arrived at Brunet's headquarters on the Georges plantation at eight and was taken directly to the general's study. Brunet greeted him and excused himself for a moment. As soon as he had left the room one of Leclerc's aides-de-camp, Major Ferrari, entered with a squad of grenadiers who seized Toussaint, tied his hands and hustled him down to the harbour at Les Gonaïves, where he was put aboard the frigate *Créole*. In the meantime, the local commander at Ennery had taken 100 men up to the plantation to arrest Madame Toussaint and the remainder of the family and bring them down to Les Gonaïves to be held on another frigate, *La Guerrière*.

The shameful operation went off with a speed and simplicity that astonished Leclerc. Neither Dessalines, who had not forgiven him his surrender to the French, nor Christophe, who was disillusioned by his constant double-dealing, made any move to save Toussaint, and a few small risings in the countryside were put down without difficulty. When it heard the news of the little Black upstart's arrest, the white world breathed a sigh of relief. Leclerc, however, was still conscious of the threat to his authority of the thousands of Black soldiers who had been disbanded and sent back to the plantations but who had retained their arms. Until he had taken their weapons from them he was unable to make any serious inroads on their liberty. He begged Decrès for men and money.

Do something for us, and do not leave us abandoned as you have done up to now.

His pleas were not to be heard — at least not until it was too late. For the moment his brother-in-law's eyes were fixed on another prize. "My intention, citizen minister," Bonaparte wrote to Decrès on June 4, "is that we shall take possession of Louisiana with the least possible delay; that this expedition shall be carried out in the greatest secrecy; and that it shall appear to be destined for Saint-Domingue."

Leclerc was left to his own devices and began to exhibit a talent for bungling stupidity that was rare even in a professional soldier. Although the island remained under martial law, he was advised that the formation of some sort of consultative body would help to dispel fears about French intentions. He appointed a provisional assembly of twenty-two members, nominated by himself and his generals, and explained in a public announcement that he had decided against a popularly-elected deliberative assembly because he "knew too well the evils of gatherings of that nature". It was not surprising that the majority of the members proved to be among the most reactionary of the planters; Christophe, one of the few coloured representatives, discovered that the only men of liberal views were two of the officials who had come out with the expeditionary force: the prefect-designate, Bénézech, and the *commissaire de justice*, Despéroux, both of whom shortly died of yellow fever.

The colonist-members, who had learnt nothing and forgotten nothing, were soon encouraged by Leclerc's ineptitude to indulge in dreams of regaining their former power and privileges. One of them went so far as to introduce a motion proposing the return to slavery of all Negroes who had not been free before 1794. It was greeted with approving shouts of "No slavery, no colony!" – a lobbying slogan that the *colons* had made great use of in Paris.

Christophe sprang to the rostrum to denounce the bad faith and wild folly of such suggestions. "The men who make them," he shouted, "are the most dangerous enemies of the French interest; for my part, and in the name of the Blacks, I say: 'No liberty, no colony!'" He was boiling with rage and indignation. The assembly, unconvinced by his arguments but impressed by his fury, rejected the motion and Christophe hurried off to Government House, where he repeated his harangue to Leclerc.

The majority of these men [he said, referring to his fellow members of the assembly] fought against us under the British flag. They now have the audacity to proclaim their liberticidal doctrines under a republican government. Take care, citizen general! Instead of preserving peace, these gentlemen are rekindling the fires of civil war. And in particular beware of General Rochambeau: he is the implacable enemy of the mulattos and consequently of the Blacks, and his behaviour will infallibly lead to their taking up arms against the Government.

The force of his anger and the fact, which even Leclerc could appreciate, that the open advocacy of slavery on the advisory council was not calculated to promote peace in a country whose population was three-quarters composed of ex-slaves, induced the captain-general to dissolve the council and return to governing by edict, putting military commanders in charge of local as well as central affairs. Thus protected by the military machine against any untoward encounters with reality, his spirits rose and the letter that he sent to Bonaparte on June 24 was quite hopeful in tone.

The South is already disarmed. Dessalines is now disarming the West. Within a fortnight Maurepas, Christophe and Clairvaux will disarm the North. Once the North is disarmed, if my reinforcements have arrived, I shall end the job here and Saint-Domingue will be French for all time.

He was equally optimistic in his dispatch to Decrès on July 6. "The South and West are almost disarmed; the North will begin to be so within a week. The gendarmerie is being organised and, as soon as the disarming is complete and the gendarmerie in position, I shall strike the final blows."

On June 24 it was "within a fortnight", and on July 6 "within a week"; but on July 12 "I have not yet been able to order the disarming of the North. . . . I am forced to be very circumspect. . . . For a week past there have been illicit gatherings in the plain and even in the town. . . . The aim of the plot is to massacre the Europeans. . . . I am pressing on with the organisation of the gendarmerie and with disarming. I shall not be easy until these two operations are concluded."

By July 18 the hesitancies and doubts had disappeared. "The state of the colony is good; the disarmament of the Blacks is proceeding without fuss; a few brigands have taken refuge in the mountains, but they are isolated and dare not approach our posts." But on July 23 the tune changed again: "I have this moment learned of a disturbing incident. The disarming on Tortuga has been carried out badly; the Blacks have risen and have burned some plantations. . . . A similar insurrection has occurred at Port-de-Paix. I have no details and it is impossible for me to send European troops, they drop dead en route."

Despite all the signs of trouble to come Leclerc, through arrogance, fear or sheer stupidity, continued to issue new ordinances which delighted the reactionary *colons* and confirmed the suspicions of the Blacks. He banned the sale of small properties, thus preventing them from acquiring land. He forbade the marriage of Blacks domiciled on different plantations. He prohibited any change of name or addition to names – a senseless irritation to most ex-slaves who were accustomed to add to their Christian names that of their master or the plantation on which they were born or some real or pretended attribute (as Toussaint had adopted first the plantation name of Bréda and then the messianic name of L'Ouverture).

Soon afterwards astonishing news began to filter from Paris – news that finally destroyed the image of the Republic as the bestower and guardian of liberty. On May 20 Bonaparte had the Corps Législatif pass a law maintaining slavery in those colonies that had been captured by the British and returned under the Treaty of Amiens. In June he reintroduced the slave trade. On July 2 he restored another of the laws of the *ancien régime*, under which mulattos and Negroes were forbidden to enter France without special permission.

Saint-Domingue was not named in the treaty, since it had never been completely conquered by the British, but Leclerc was instructed to reintroduce slavery at his own discretion, although the Minister of Marine foresaw that "we may encounter new difficulties if we precipitately overthrow that idol of Liberty which has caused so much blood to flow up to now". Indeed, the general feeling of unease was spreading markedly. The risings reported by Leclerc were led by 'brigands' who had never made their submission to the French: Janvier Thomas, Auguste and Samedi Smith in the South, Lamour de la Rance and Lafortune in the West, Scylla, Mavougou, Va-Malheureux and Petit-Noël in the North; but they were being joined by men deserting from the colonial regiments whose loyalty to their officers was not strong enough to overcome their horror at the prospect of renewed slavery.

From the men to their officers, this prickly fear passed on. Christophe, invited to a banquet at Government House, brought a detachment of troops and ordered them to stand by to defend him if he were the victim of a surprise attack. At table a French officer filled his glass with wine. Christophe, who seldom drank, had the glass removed untouched and called for another. It had no sooner been set before him than the Frenchman, with mock politeness, filled it again. Christophe's self-control suddenly snapped.

"Listen, little white man!" he rapped out, "if I had drunk the wine you poured for me, I should have had a great mind to go on and drink your blood – and your general's too!"

There was silence at the table – and then uproar, in which Leclerc could be heard agitatedly ordering the duty officer to call out the guard.

"It is no use calling out your soldiers," Christophe thundered. "Mine are already standing to arms. I can make you my prisoner at a word. But if you think I would betray you then you do not understand me. I am obedient to you as I was to Toussaint. If he had told me to throw this island into the sea, I would have done all I could to carry out the order. I know how to obey and I know how to command." While he spoke, the grievances and fears crowded to his mind. "Respect for promises and treaties! The safety of our persons! The sacred duties of hospitality," he raged on. "Have not your cruel policies violated all of these? Prison, exile, torture and death – these have been the rewards of those whose blood has been shed for our liberty!"

In an ecstasy of fury he apostrophised his dead and absent comrades. "You are no longer beside me, friends, soldiers, heroes of our mountains! And you Toussaint! the pride of our race, the terror of our enemies; you whose genius led us from slavery to liberty, you whose hand adorned peace with virtue, you whose glory fills the universe! – they have cast you into fetters like the meanest criminal!"

With eyes gleaming, he rounded on Leclerc once more, while the rest of the guests sat open-mouthed. "But what is there in common between you and Toussaint? Your name means nothing to us – except that on the 18th of Brumaire [when Bonaparte seized power by overthrowing the Directory] you turned your parricidal weapons against the representatives of your country. And doubtless it was as a reward for that deed that the Consul gave you the governorship of Saint-Domingue." He strode out of the room, called for his escort, and galloped back to his headquarters.

There was nothing that Leclerc could do. On August 2 he reported to Decrès that the districts of Plaisance, Gros-Morne, Port-de-Paix, Saint-Louis and Le Borgne were in revolt. Four days later:

> The insurrection is spreading. Sickness continues and will last until the 1st of Vendémiaire [September 23] according to all reports from the inhabitants. . . . My hospitals are crammed full and I do not know how to cope with the expense that they entail . . . All the Blacks are convinced by letters that have arrived from France, by the law restoring the slave trade, and by General Richepanse's decrees re-establishing slavery in La Guadeloupe, that we intend to make them slaves, and I cannot

disarm them without long and stubborn fighting. These men will not surrender.

The tenuous threads of good sense and moderation were snapping throughout the colony. In the West, the coarse, brutal Rochambeau continued to persecute the mulattos. In the wilder districts the bizarre, savage Dessalines ravaged villages and plantations in pursuit of 'brigands'. The brigands retorted with the traditional horrors of burning their prisoners to death over slow fires, or binding them between two planks and sawing them in half. And at Le Cap the bewildered Leclerc emitted the continuous high-pitched whine that is the distinctive call of military commanders.

My position is becoming embarrassing and may become bad [he reported to Bonaparte on August 6]. The first attacks have driven the rebels from the points they occupied, but they have redeployed in other cantons. In this insurrection there is real fanaticism; these men let themselves be killed rather than surrender. . . . I begged you, citizen consul, not to do anything that might cause them to have misgivings about their liberty, until the moment when I was ready to deal with them. . . .

By August 9 he was more optimistic. Transports had come with reinforcements whom he planned to combine with his colonial troops and launch against the rebels "at all points" on the following day. He was well pleased with Dessalines, Christophe and Maurepas, "the only three who have any influence", and added that Bonaparte might judge their dependence on him by the fact that "Christophe and Dessalines have asked me not to leave them here when I return to France". It was likely that their wish would be granted, for by late October "I hope to be able to send to France or elsewhere all those who are a nuisance to me here. . . . The more services the Blacks render me now, the less I shall need to keep them when the sickness is past."

As he was signing the letter, news came in of more trouble, and he added a postscript in his own hand: "I have just heard of a bloody battle that General Boyer has been engaged in at Le Gros-Morne. The rebels have been exterminated; fifty prisoners have been hanged. The men die with unbelievable fanaticism; they laugh at death. It is the same with the women. . . . ."

He was still planning for a future in which he would have

beaten down resistance, reduced the Blacks to slavery and re-established the old profitable commerce with France.

   I am reckoning on restricting foreign trade to one port only – the Môle, for instance – where consignments will be discharged and then broken up for distribution by our national coastal vessels. Thus none but the French will be able to be consignees. But I cannot take these measures yet without damming up the spring from which flows the future prosperity of the colony. I am letting the Americans sow, and I shall have the French gather in the harvest. . . ."

By August 25 he had collected 20,000 muskets from the disarmed Blacks and estimated that there were as many more hidden on the plantations. At this point General Charles Belair turned 'brigand'. A man of intelligence and restraint, related to Toussaint and widely believed to be the leader he chose to succeed him after Moyse's death, Belair attracted many waverers to his standard in the mountains of the West Province. His defection was followed by that of senior officers in the North: Sans-Souci, who commanded the district of La Grande-Rivière, and Capoix, colonel of the 9th colonial demi-brigade.

   Dessalines captured Belair by a trick and sent him back to the coast for court-martial. He was then ordered to join Christophe in a two-pronged attack against Sans-Souci and his fellow rebels in the mountains of the North. The attack was only partially success-ful; and the time had arrived when a partial success was in fact a serious setback for Leclerc, compelled to throw each new batch of reinforcements into battle immediately they landed, before they succumbed to sickness. He confessed to Bonaparte that he was forced to remain on the defensive in the Plaine-du-Cap until he received more supporting troops. Bonaparte had recently con-gratulated him on his success in duping Toussaint and had added: "we await with impatience the arrival of Christophe and Dessa-lines". Leclerc assured him that he had not forgotten his instruc-tions:

   Maurepas is a dangerous rascal. . . . I am not strong enough to arrest him at present, because his arrest would pro-duce an insurrection in his district and I have enough of that sort of thing at the moment. . . . Dessalines is the butcher of the

Blacks. I have all the odious measures carried out by him. . . .
Laplume, Clervaux and Paul Louverture are three imbeciles
whom I can get rid of at any time. That will be as soon as I
can. . . . Vernet is a cowardly rogue; I shall get rid of him at
once. Charles Belair will be tried and shot. . . . [As for
Christophe] he has maltreated [the Blacks] to such a point that
he is execrated and I shall send him to you without fearing that
his departure will produce the slightest insurrection.

Despite his outbursts against Leclerc and the consulate,
Christophe was still devoted to France and still regarded it as the
France of the Revolution. Like Toussaint he realised that the
Blacks of Saint-Domingue would never be in full control of their
destinies until they were as well educated as the whites (though he
did not know that education was precisely what Bonaparte intended to deny them), and like Toussaint before him he leaped at
the proposal that his eight-year-old son should go to France with
General Boudet, who was being sent back to make a confidential
report to Bonaparte.

It was at this time that he met General Pamphile de Lacroix, the
new commander of Fort-Liberté. Lacroix, coming from the comparatively peaceful Spanish sector and impressed by the tension and
anxiety of the French part of the island, asked Christophe why unrest was continuing to spread.

You are young and a European [Christophe answered]. You
have done all your service in the armies of the Continent and
you have consequently no preconceived ideas about slavery, so
I can speak to you frankly. The rebellion increases because distrust is greater than ever.

If you had skin of our colour, perhaps you would not even be
as trustful as I am, for I have confided my son Ferdinand to
General Boudet to have him brought up in France. I do not
believe the brigands who began the insurrection are of any
importance. The danger lies not with them but in the general
mood of the Blacks – they are afraid because they have heard of
the decree of 30 Floréal [maintaining slavery in the colonies
given back under the Treaty of Amiens]. They are frightened
when they see the First Consul restoring the old laws in the
other colonies. They are fearful lest the careless words that they
hear [from the white colonists] on all sides here will reach

France and suggest to the government the idea of similarly depriving the Blacks of Saint-Domingue of their freedom.

Christophe added that he was himself convinced of the sincerity of the French, otherwise he would not have remained with them, and that there were still many Blacks like himself who supported them. Lacroix then asked him a little maliciously why, having failed to make contact with the rebel Sans-Souci during his recent campaign in the mountains, Christophe had not yet found a Black sufficiently loyal to betray Sans-Souci's position to him. Christophe reddened and answered angrily:

If Sans-Souci had been a true soldier I flatter myself that I should have got at him, but he is a cowardly and cruel brigand who doesn't hesitate to kill anybody whom his suspicions light on. He runs whenever he chooses and protects his retreat by leaving devastation behind him.

Then, since he was seldom able to restrain himself from total frankness, Christophe paused, considered what he had just said, and added:

He is acting a great deal more sensibly than we did at the time of your landing. Then, if our system of resistance had been not to fight but to retreat and play upon the fears of the field hands you would never have got at us. Old Toussaint never left off saying that, but nobody would listen to him. We had weapons – our vanity in making use of them was our downfall. These new rebels seem to intend to follow Toussaint's plan. If they stick to it we shall have difficulty in overcoming them.

But although Christophe was unable to find rebels willing to betray Sans-Souci to him, it was clear that he was in touch with some considerable figures among them, for just before Boudet sailed for France with young Ferdinand, Christophe sent out to their ship supplies of fruit, vegetables and cattle, all of which had long vanished from the beleaguered Cape and were obtainable only from the rebel-controlled interior.

The First of Vendémiaire, the first day of the new year in the republican calendar, came and went – but without any of the promised abatement in the rate of sickness. Leclerc was now losing between 100 and 120 men a day. On 4 Vendémiaire (September 26) he wrote to Bonaparte: "The month of Fructidor cost me more than 4,000. . . . Today they tell me that [the sickness] may continue until the end of Brumaire [October 22]. If that is so, and it continues at the same intensity, the colony is lost."

He was beginning to suspect that Dessalines was ready to join the rebels.

A month ago when I sent him on raids, he destroyed the weapons that he found. Today he no longer destroys them and no longer maltreats the Blacks as he used to do. . . .

No general commanding an army has ever found himself in a more trying situation. The troops that arrived a month ago no longer exist. Rebels carry out attacks in the plain every day; they burn and the sound of firing can be heard at Le Cap. It is impossible for me to take the offensive. . . .

Two days later, Christophe said goodbye to his son and Boudet at Le Cap and, on the way back to his headquarters at Saint-Michel, halted at Le Haut-du-Cap to talk with the commander, Clervaux, and his second-in-command, Colonel Pétion. Both were mulattos. Clervaux was still uncommitted but Pétion, who had defended Jacmel for Rigaud against Dessalines and Christophe, was now plotting with Dessalines to turn against the French. Pétion took Christophe on one side and said to him: "You were wrong to send your son to France. Bring him back – you still have time. It looks as if great things may be about to happen." Christophe, unwilling to be drawn, answered, "The air is full of blood and there is mourning on every face. I have spoken harsh truths to General Boudet – if the whites persist in their ways they will lose everything." Then, neither man wishing to commit himself further, they shook hands and parted.

On October 7 Leclerc sent yet another special emissary with a confidential letter to Bonaparte – the third in less than three weeks. At Le Cap alone he was still losing fifty or sixty men a day from yellow fever, probably a hundred and thirty a day in the colony as a whole. His colonial troops were deserting "by companies" and of his white troops he had only 921 men fit for duty and 759 convalescent out of a nominal strength of fifteen battalions.

Here is my opinion on this country: We must destroy all the Negroes in the mountains, men and women, retaining only children under twelve years old; destroy half of those in the plains; and not leave in the colony a single coloured man who has worn an epaulet. . . . If you are to be master of Saint-Domingue you must, without a day's delay, send me 12,000 men. . . . You must send me immediately ten millions [of francs] in cash, and not in any other form. Your constant refusal of money has contributed not a little to the worsening of my position here. . . . I know the French Government cannot make the same pecuniary sacrifices as the English Government, but there is a mean between parsimony and prodigality without which a general can do nothing.

He was a sick man, often falling asleep as he worked with his secretary, Norvins, in his bedroom, where a desk had been slipped under the mosquito net instead of his bed, and where the papers in front of them grew limp with their sweat in the oppressive, unrelenting heat. He wanted to send Pauline back to France with their child, but she refused to go unless he gave her a hundred thousand francs. "My sister Murat has a carriage of her own," she complained. "She writes to me about it herself, to infuriate me, chattering about fêtes and balls and everything that Bonaparte is doing for her. That's why I must have a hundred thousand francs, so that I can have a more beautiful carriage than she has and so that she can see me finely dressed at the Tuileries."

She failed to get the money and, in her inconstant way, soon decided that she was happier in Saint-Domingue in any case. "My sister Murat has a carriage – like all the bourgeois women of Paris. She's no better off than any of them. Whereas here I reign – like Joséphine. I am the first lady in the land. . . ."

Though Leclerc continually spoke of taking a strong line with his Black generals, his only decisions were to kill more prisoners, to use more indiscriminate violence against both Blacks and mulattos. It was a policy of intimidation and terrorism imposed either too late or too soon. As Lacroix remarked: "Although they deal the final blow to insurrection and destroy its roots when it has been crushed [such measures] can become the breeding ground of rebellion when they are employed immoderately and prematurely."

The growing accord between mulattos and Blacks, so strikingly illustrated in the secret alliance between Pétion and Dessalines, sprang from the mulattos' suspicion that they had as much to fear from Bonaparte as did the former slaves; that he did not recognise any distinction between brown and black. Early in October 1802 the arrival of the frigate *Cocade* at Le Cap provided the spark for this tinder. She carried on board her a number of Blacks who were being taken to forced labour in France because they had caused trouble in La Guadeloupe. During the night several of them leaped overboard and succeeded in swimming ashore, where they gave details of the repressive measures that General Richepanse had introduced – including a story that some mulattos had already been put up for sale as slaves.

On October 9 Clervaux was present at a reception given by Pauline Leclerc. Too much wine, or the goading presence of Bonaparte's sister, produced a remarkable and untypically violent outburst from him. "I was free before all this," he shouted. "Nothing has changed for me, except that my colour is no longer despised. And if ever I thought there was a question of restoring slavery, I would turn brigand at once!"

His outburst, like Christophe's earlier one, passed without retribution. Leclerc, though he was present, had neither the power nor the personality to deal with these unruly generals. Clervaux, himself not a very strong character, returned to Le Haut-du-Cap and a few days later found himself precipitated into rebellion by his own second-in-command. During the night of October 13, Colonel Pétion gave orders for the guns of Le Haut-du-Cap to be spiked and their white artillerymen to be disarmed and sent back to Le Cap. He then called Clervaux, who had been asleep, told him that the insurrection had taken place, the French authorities at Le Cap now had word of it, and the only thing to do was to march upon the city and take it.

Clervaux, enraged and terrified at the same time, lost his head completely. Without pausing to dress, he leaped on a horse and made off into the mountains. It was several hours before he could be brought back and his quarrel with Pétion patched up, and in those hours the rebels lost their chance of driving the French out of the colony, for Leclerc had been given just enough time to organise his defence. With the handful of European troops who were fit for duty and the twelve hundred men of the National Guard he disarmed the Negroes of the colonial regiments and confined them in ships in the harbour, many of which had lain idle for months, their crews too depleted by yellow fever to put out to sea. He posted a small garrison at Le Haut-du-Cap, which had been deserted while the mutineers regrouped, and awaited the attack, which came soon after midnight.

Clervaux, Pétion and the local 'brigand' leader, Petit-Noël, now had a combined force of between five and six thousand men, made up of Clervaux's men of the 10th, 13th and part of the 6th demi-brigade, Petit-Noël's irregulars, and a sprinkling of field hands who had been encouraged by the new defection to join in. With terri-fying screams they threw themselves at the hastily-organised defences of Le Haut-du-Cap and, since the defenders lacked artillery, soon drove them back by force of numbers on to a planta-tion half a mile away, leaving the main road to Le Cap open. But now lack of discipline caused further delays. Scattering over the countryside to fire the neighbouring fortifications and plantations, they took another two days to regroup for their attack and to drag their cannon into position on the slopes above the town.

On the morning of October 16 the square in front of Government House was filled with terror-stricken women and children, demand-ing to be put aboard the ships in the harbour, while every man who could carry a sword or fire a musket was allotted a post on the town fortifications or on guard at the hospitals and stores. Leclerc, as he mounted his horse to lead his troops out on the Haut-du-Cap road, paused to say to Norvins: "I entrust you with my wife and child; I am leaving you these four sergeants and this cannon. If I am beaten you will receive the order to embark my wife, my son, and all who are with them."

Pauline, whose many frailties did not include faintheartedness, was chatting gaily as she led the way back to her private apartments and, when some of the colonists' wives pushed their way in and begged her to take them out to a ship with her, she retorted sharply: "You are afraid to die. But I am Bonaparté's sister and I am afraid of nothing!"

"You do not know these monsters!" the terrified women protested.

"I shall be dead when they get to me," Pauline replied, "and so will my son." She turned to Norvins and continued: "You promise to kill both of us, do you not?"

Outside the city, the rebels were advancing against Leclerc's tiny force, whom they outnumbered by at least three to one. From the slopes their cannon opened fire on Fort Jeantot, the only remaining strongpoint in their path, while their infantry, some armed only with the knives that they had brought with them from the plantations, came chanting along the road from Le Haut-du-Cap. Their columns stretched into the distance and across the fields on either side. Leclerc sent a messenger back to Government House to order Norvins to take Pauline down to the docks and put her aboard a ship. Pauline refused to move and the messenger returned to report to Leclerc the failure of his mission.

The wave of rebels advanced to Fort Jeantot, curled round it, then broke and retreated. A second wave formed and, with howls of vengeance which were heard inside the town and echoed in screams of despair, the rebels threw themselves against the fort once more. An aide-de-camp galloped up to Government House and shouted to Norvins: "The General-in-chief orders you to embark Mme Leclerc and their son, by force if necessary, and the rest of you with her. Send back the boats."

Norvins ordered the four sergeants to pick up the armchair in which Pauline was seated. A grenadier sat the three-year-old Dermide on his shoulders. Escorted by Norvins and other members of the clerical staff, drawn swords in their hands, Madame la Générale began a strange progress down the long, straight rue Notre Dame towards the docks. "I don't care," she said to Norvins. "I will not go aboard." And then again: "I will not." And finally she burst into uncontrollable giggles: "We're just like a Mardi Gras masquerade!" she exclaimed and then, looking at the serious faces on either side of her, rocked from side to side with renewed laughter.

The second tide of rebels advanced and, like the first one, collapsed. The fire from the French infantry and from Fort Jeantot was rapid and exact. The rebels had discovered too late that the only undamaged guns they had saved from Le Haut-du-Cap were 18-pounders – in which their twelve-pound cannon balls were useless. They came on for the third time and now, as they hesitated once more in front of the fort, the cavalry of the National Guard came wheeling round the flank of Leclerc's infantry and in a fury of thudding hooves and whirling sabres drove them into panic-stricken flight. Leclerc's third messenger found Pauline at the dockside, still arguing that she would not set foot on the lighter. "Victory!" he cried. "The general has completely routed the Blacks. He begs you, madame, to return to Government House where he will shortly join you."

5

Christophe had made no move. He increasingly distrusted Bonaparte, but his lingering respect for the Republic – as well as his

compelling sense of discipline and loyalty – prompted him to support Leclerc. There was, too, the uncertainty of his reception if he
went over to the rebels, who, with the exception of Clervaux and
Pétion, were his bitter enemies. He remained thus hesitant and uncommitted until the night before the rebels launched their attack on
Le Cap. Then news reached him at his headquarters on the Saint-
Michel plantation, on the road that ran southeast from Le Cap to
La Petite-Anse, of the latest and most cold-blooded of the French
atrocities. The Black troops shut up in the ships in the harbour at
Le Cap – between one thousand and twelve hundred soldiers with,
it was said, civilian men, women and children – had, on Leclerc's
orders, been bayonetted and their bodies thrown into the sea.

Christophe summoned Colonel Boyé, the senior French officer
of his staff. "I am sending you back to your general," he said,
speaking quietly at first but his voice quickly rising. "Tell him that
he is impudent, ignorant and dishonourable. Tell him that I scorn
the millions of francs and the honours that he has offered me to
abandon the cause of my brothers. As for you, colonel, if it were not
for my respect for the law of nations, you would never see Le Cap
again." As Christophe shouted the last words, Boyé saw the
general's bodyguard raise their sabres. He stood motionless, un-
flinchingly waiting to be cut down. Christophe, always quick to
admire courage, ordered him to be given a battalion as escort
through the rebel territory as far as the outposts of Le Cap. At the
same time he paraded the remainder of his men – the 1st, 2nd and
5th colonial demi-brigades – and marched them off to join the
rebels, who had just suffered their defeat at Fort Jeantot.

They were camped in confusion inside and around the little town
of Le Haut-du-Cap. Leaving his troops on the outskirts, Christophe
rode on with some of his bodyguard, seeking Clervaux or Pétion,
but the news of his arrival brought Petit-Noël instead, accompanied
by a large body of his own men and noisily denouncing Christophe
as a traitor and a murderer. Christophe drew a pistol from his
saddle holster and cocked it. Petit-Noël, his eyes blazing, leaped
from his horse and ran at him, sabre in hand, shouting: "There are
no Frenchmen to help him now – we two will fight it out!"

Fortunately for Christophe, Clervaux and Pétion hurried on to
the scene at this moment and managed to separate the two men,
while their soldiers of the 13th demi-brigade put themselves
between Petit-Noël's followers and those of Christophe's troops
who had been alerted by the bodyguard and were advancing at the

double with bayonets fixed. The din of shouting and mutual threats continued for several minutes, until Pétion at last managed to make himself heard. Pointing towards Le Cap, he asked Petit-Noël and Christophe if they intended to continue quarrelling among themselves, to the benefit of nobody but the whites? The noise subsided for a moment, but then broke out again, Petit-Noël repeating that Christophe was a traitor and Christophe replying that he would not ally himself or his men with bandits who were fighting only for loot and not for the principles of liberty and equality. Seeing that Christophe's troops were now all in position and outnumbered his own men, Petit-Noël drew off, threatening to settle the quarrel later. He parted company with the main body, led by Clervaux and Pétion, and joined forces with the lesser bandit chieftains – Cagnet, Labruni and Grand-Boucan.

Although dissension among the rebels gave Leclerc time to consolidate his forces, concentrating the remainder of his men at Saint-Marc and Port-au-Prince in the West Province, and at Môle Saint-Nicolas and Le Cap in the North, his position was now as bad as that of the British four years before. On November 2 he died of yellow fever. His final words were a criticism of the French government and its treatment of him, but it is likely that he at last realised how much his defeat was due to his own weak arrogance and ineffective double-dealing. Pauline, who accompanied his body back to France, wept bitterly and cut off all her hair to lay beside him in the cedar coffin. "She knows, of course," commented Bonaparte, "that cropping will make it grow twice as luxuriantly."

The West Province, once held in complete subjection by Dessalines and Rochambeau, was now overrun by the rebels. Dessalines, after his last conference with Pétion at Le Haut-du-Cap, rode through Plaisance, Gros-Morne, Les Gonaïves and across to La Petite-Rivière, conferring with rebels and with still loyal local commanders and concerting the general rising which was now imminent. On 17 October news came of the defection of Pétion's troops at Le Haut-du-Cap. Horsemen careered from one plantation to another, giving the pre-arranged signal of three pistol shots. The field hands dropped their tools and ran for their hidden weapons – the captured stocks that Dessalines had unaccountably 'lost' during recent months. Dessalines himself swooped on the fortress at Crête-à-Pierrot, stripped it of arms and ammunition which he sent to be used in the siege of Saint-Marc, and then went northwards to link with Clervaux, Christophe and Pétion.

These three were short of ammunition, food, money and even soldiers, for their troops had begun to desert and go home or join the better-organised brigands. Pétion approached Sans-Souci, the colonel who had deserted some months before and was believed to have accumulated a store of six thousand pounds of gunpowder at his camp at La Grande-Rivière, and asked for some to be lent to him. Sans-Souci, who dreamed of becoming the leader of the whole insurrection, curtly refused, saying that he had risked his life to get it and had been the first to take up arms against the French. Pétion finally succeeded in borrowing a thousand pounds of powder from Toussaint-Brave, who had remained at Fort-Liberté with his Black troops after the French evacuation. With these new supplies Christophe fought his way through the crossroads at Le Limbé, which a party of French troops had reoccupied, and up into the mountains, followed by Clervaux and Pétion, whose aim was to make for their native West Province or perhaps even the South, since the mulattos were stronger there.

As they climbed higher up the steep mountain roads, seeking a place where they could regroup and organise their resources, they found their way blocked by Sans-Souci at the head of 5,000 well-armed men. He had pondered over his recent conversation with Pétion and had decided that it was time for him to demand recognition as commander-in-chief of all the rebel forces. He asked for a parley with Pétion at which he put this proposal to him, revealing at the same time that he intended to separate Christophe from his troops and kill him, because he still supported the French in his heart. Pétion placated him by acknowledging him as his superior officer and by accepting from him confirmation in the rank of brigadier. He then implored him not to excite quarrels or settle personal vendettas at a moment when mulattos and Blacks had at last joined forces against the whites. To this Sans-Souci replied: "So you oppose my putting Christophe to death, general – well, you will repent it later."

Christophe had remained apart, but he could well guess the sort of proposals that Sans-Souci would put to Pétion and saw from their faces the direction that the conversation was taking. Followed by his guides he rode up to Sans-Souci and demanded to be recognised as his military superior, swinging his sabre and shouting that he would slice off Sans-Souci's head if he did not instantly

I. "*After the fire of 1793—which destroyed the Auberge de la Couronne—and the departure of most of the white population, he was appointed a captain of infantry.*" The earliest known portrait of Henry Christophe.

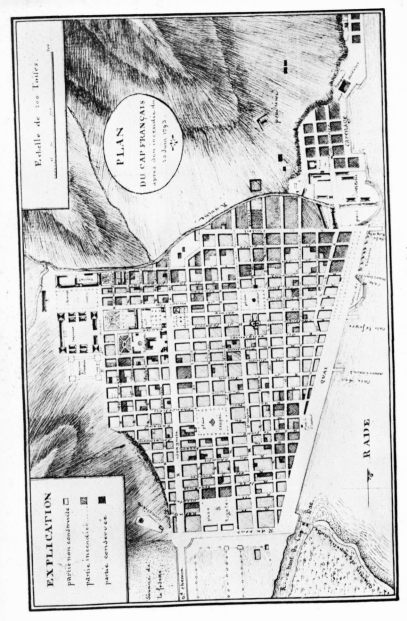

II. Cap-François, from a manuscript Histoire de la révolution de Saint-Domingue (*n.a.f.* 4372) in the *Bibliothèque Nationale, Paris.* The lighter shading indicates buildings destroyed, the heavier shading those still standing, after the fire of 1793.

III. *"Captain Marcus Rainsford . . . was denounced as an Englishman, charged with spying, and condemned to death by a court-martial over which Christophe presided with gravity and consideration." Rainsford's own sketch of the trial.*

IVa. "Short, thin, protuberant-jawed . . . Toussaint would have been a figure of fun—except for the swiftly darting eye, the inexhaustible energy, the confidence and ruthlessness with which he enforced his commands."

IVb. "Neither the Black troops nor their generals had the skill or experience to stand against Leclerc's men in the open field." A contemporary sketch of the fighting in Saint-Domingue, showing both sides wearing French uniform.

promise obedience. The fury and authority in his voice were so compelling that Sans-Souci reined his horse back and stutteringly acknowledged him as *'mon général'*. The incident fizzled out in threatening looks and muttered complaints. Pétion, having received Sans-Souci's word that he would not offer any further hindrance to Christophe, continued south to the Artibonite with the 13th demi-brigade. Sans-Souci returned to La Grande-Rivière. Clervaux remained with Christophe, and together they settled their men into camps in the mountains of Vallière and La Mina, where Dessalines found them and was recognised by them as commander-in-chief.

Despite Leclerc's repeated requests, Bonaparte had not sent him a suitable deputy. The command therefore devolved on the senior lieutenant-general, Rochambeau, a man whom Leclerc had described as "a brave soldier and good fighter, but without an ounce of tact or political sense, no moral strength and easily led". At Port-au-Prince, as military governor of the West Province, he had distinguished himself by converting his headquarters into a harem and by devising a new way of disposing of mulattos and Negroes: he had them taken out in barges, battened under hatches, and suffocated with burning sulphur.

He arrived at Le Cap on November 17 to find it under attack by Dessalines, who sent two strong columns under Christophe and Clervaux against the Cliquet plantation and Le Haut-du-Cap while two others attacked on the east and west flanks against La Petite-Anse and Fort Picolet. Christophe, capturing Cliquet and Leclerc's old headquarters on the Destaing plantation, was finally stopped at the Gorge de la Providence by the batteries of two blockhouses which his troops failed to storm. The rebels withdrew into the depths of the plain and on November 19 Rochambeau and the citizens of Le Cap were enheartened by the arrival of reinforcements from Europe. Rochambeau promptly sent some of them to recapture Port-de-Paix and Fort-Liberté, successful, vigorous actions which looked well in his despatches but, by spreading his forces as thinly as they were before, condemned him to continue on the defensive.

He celebrated his success by dealing with Maurepas. This Black general, commanding the district of Port-de-Paix, remained loyal when Clervaux and Christophe went over to the rebels; but Leclerc brought him to Le Cap for security's sake. Rochambeau had him taken out with his family to the warship *Duguay-Trouin* for execution. He was tied to the mast and his cocked hat perched derisively on his head. His wife and children were forced to watch while the ship's carpenter nailed his epaulets to his shoulders. When he had been tortured enough, he and his family and their companions were bayonetted and thrown into the sea. With Rochambeau's assumption of supreme command, bestial cruelty had become an open instrument of French policy.

After the abortive attack on Le Cap, Dessalines decided to return to the West, to clear that province of the French. Before he left, Christophe conferred with him on the problem of Sans-Souci and the other brigands who refused to accept Dessalines as commander-in-chief, each nursing his own ambitions. Christophe was convinced that the Blacks would never prevail until they matched the French in discipline and unity and he now promised Dessalines that he would bring Sans-Souci to heel. He did it in a way which proved that, though he lacked Dessalines's savage and often unmotivated ferocity, he could equal him in ruthless perfidy.

He sent a placatory message to Sans-Souci, setting out his conviction that the success of the Black cause depended on unity and asking if Sans-Souci would agree to meet him and give him the benefit of his advice on how best to achieve this. Sans-Souci, supposing this to be a veiled offer to meet his demands, readily accepted Christophe's suggestion of a rendezvous at the deserted Grandpré plantation and, uncharacteristically allowing his enthusiasm to get the better of his caution, took only his principal lieutenants and a small escort with him. There was silence as they rode up the tree-lined avenue to the great house; the orchard and kitchen garden were as overgrown as the fields and not a soul stirred in the long rows of slave-barracks at the rear. They dismounted and clattered into the soiled, empty, echoing rooms, splintered and blackened by countless raids and lootings. They did not have to wait long. Suddenly the neglected garden was full of Christophe's troops and they realised that they had walked into a trap. Only one man, Major Charles Pierre, was granted his life by Christophe; the remainder were bayonetted to death.

With a semblance of unity thus uncompromisingly imposed, Christophe and Clervaux went down to L'Arcahaye for a conference of the generals of all three provinces. It lasted for four days, with Dessalines presiding at each session. On the final day, they all rose to acclaim Dessalines as generalissimo and to swear to die rather than live under French rule. As always during the past decade, they fought under the same flag as their white opponents, and it was still a tricolour that draped the table at which Dessalines sat. When he rose to his feet to acknowledge the cheers of his generals, he snatched the flag from the table and ripped it into three places. The white piece from the middle he crumpled and threw to the ground; the blue and red pieces he waved above his head. Later that day, his wife's goddaughter, Catherine Flon, sewed the two sections together, the blue above the red, and the flag of Haiti was born.

Although there was now a national flag, true unity was still far away. On his return to the North, Christophe marched with 2,000 men against the Frenchman, Lacroix, who had recaptured Laxavon, Ouanaminthe and Fort-Liberté. He was badly beaten and himself wounded during a French cavalry charge in which he lost three hundred men. In his retreat to Grandpré he was not only pursued by the French but also harried on the flanks by the men who had formerly served under Sans-Souci. It seemed as if his treacherous murder of Sans-Souci had turned the whole province against him. In the mountains of Vallière his orders were disregarded. At Le Dondon his old opponent, Petit-Noël, refused to recognise his authority or that of Dessalines. As the fires of resentment swept along the mountain crests, Christophe found that even his regular troops were beginning to desert him. He fell back on Clervaux's headquarters at La Marmelade, but Petit-Noël drove him and Clervaux out and over the mountains down to Les Gonaïves.

Returning triumphantly to Le Dondon, Petit-Noël found Paul Louverture, Toussaint's brother, waiting to plead with him for unity. With the memory of the days when they had put down all risings against the French still flaming in his mind, Petit-Noël angrily refused to consider reconciliation with Christophe or with Dessalines, whom he sneeringly referred to as "the commander-in-chief of the Artibonite planters". His indignation became so violent that Louverture decided to make for safety at Les Gonaïves with Christophe and Clervaux. He had underestimated Petit-Noël's rage: he was not many miles on the road from Le Dondon when some of Petit-Noël's men overtook him and cut off his head.

Nobody was now capable of negotiating peace between the warring chief and factions; but there was still one man capable of imposing it. Dessalines marched northwards at the head of a strong force. He attacked Le Dondon with three columns simultaneously and drove Petit-Noël out of the town, then chased him into the mountains, captured him and put him to death. The speed and severity with which he struck brought the lesser leaders flocking to offer their submission. But they could not conceal their hatred of Christophe and, to avoid further trouble, Dessalines moved him permanently to Les Gonaïves, while Clervaux was transferred to the Artibonite.

The unsuccessful attacks on Le Cap and Christophe's defeat by Lacroix had shown the Black leaders that, as in Toussaint's time, they were still unable to meet French troops in pitched battles. Dessalines decided to concentrate most of his attacks in the West and South, where Rochambeau's persecutions of the mulattos had brought many allies, and to reorganise and train his troops and build up his supplies, leaving the brigand chieftains to carry on guerilla warfare in the North.

Rochambeau, unable to bring his enemy to battle yet also prevented from establishing strong points in the interior because of the constant raids and ambushes, decided to copy the Jamaican planters who had used 100 Cuban man-hunting bloodhounds in putting down the Maroon rising of 1795. He imported several couples from Havana, where dogs were bred specially to track down runaway slaves, intending to use them to smell out ambushes, but they proved to be unsatisfactory. They were difficult to control (the British had engaged expert handlers, as well as dogs) and their operational range was less than that of a trained infantryman. Rochambeau, whose mind was ingenious in evil, decided to use them instead as a new form of punishment, a new instrument of torture. The dogs should be used not to track the rebels down, but to tear them to pieces after they were captured.

The training of the animals was offered as a spectacle for privileged guests and first tried out in an arena constructed on the Charrier plantation near Le Haut-du-Cap. Four couple of dogs were to be set upon a Negro who was stripped naked and whose hands were tied behind his back.

> After being excited, the animals were loosed and flung themselves ferociously on their prey [one eye witness wrote]. His flesh torn in shreds, the Negro fell to the ground. . . . Suddenly the dogs halted, formed a circle round their victim, stiffened their forelegs, and began to bay. The exercise had failed – for this is the way these animals behave when they are overcome by fear. . . .

One might have expected this lack of success to discourage the executioners, but that would be to misjudge the characters of the monsters who presided over these ceremonies. They picked up the Negro, now covered with bites, untied his hands and gave him a hunting crop. With a bayonet in his back, he was forced to advance on the dogs to get himself devoured by them. . . . The dogs, more humane than the humans, fell back and then ran yelping away. . . . The victim was carried off to hospital . . . and reprieved.

Despite the failure of this experiment, there were others held in the presence of distinguished audiences, which included women as well as men. At one staged in an arena built in front of Government House at Le Cap, Rochambeau's chief-of-staff offered one of his young Negro servants as a victim. As at the Charrier plantation, the dogs were so intimidated by their prey, despite the fact that he was naked and tied to a post, that they did no more than gather in a circle, snarling at him. The chief-of-staff, blushing with annoyance and embarrassment, jumped into the arena, drew his sword, and ripped up his servant's belly, whereupon the dogs gathered sufficient courage to leap upon the Black and tear him to pieces.

The monstrous inhumanities practised by Black and white alike were as futile as they were horrible. Hatred beyond normal human limits bred a superhuman contempt for the most atrocious pain. The eye witness of the blooding of the dogs at the Charrier plantation – himself no Negrophile but a planter and confirmed partisan of slavery – described "a new punishment which they said would succeed in intimidating the Blacks".

Three Black deserters [he continued] were recaptured in the act of setting fire to a house; they had, in addition, disembowelled a pregnant woman and torn out the eyes of one of our soldiers with a bullet extractor. They were condemned to be burned alive.

On the place Saint-Louis, at Le Cap, at the right hand corner of the well, a pyre was built and covered with *bagasse* (the fibrous residue of sugar cane); three stakes set in a triangle, with a sliding collar on each, held the three Negroes back to back, facing the onlookers.

The centre of the pyre was lighted and the flames quickly reached the two men who were down wind. In less than two minutes their bodies swelled up, the skin split, the fat, dripping from their flesh, gave fresh life to the flames that devoured them. Their arms and legs contracted, and, after some terrible screams, a white froth came from their mouths, cavernous sounds from their chests – and all was ended. The silence of death reigned over the crowd, which was witnessing this sort of torment for the first time.

The third Negro, however, an eighteen-year-old, had been shielded from the flames. He could not see his comrades, but he heard their cries. These, far from intimidating him, stimulated him, and he shouted in Créole: *Zautes, pas connait mouri; guettez comment yo mouri!* (You don't know how to die – watch how I die!) By a superhuman effort, turning his neck in the collar, he faced the stake, sat down, placed his legs in the fire and allowed himself to be burned, motionless, without betraying any anguish, without allowing the slightest groan to be heard, without uttering the faintest cry. . . .

The same insane hatred marked the actions of the leaders on each side. Rochambeau, having made five hundred prisoners in one battle against Dessalines, ordered them to be put to death. Dessalines had his men erect five hundred gallows during the night and, in full sight of the French lines, hanged five hundred Frenchmen at dawn. Rochambeau again economised his ammunition by sending Black prisoners out to sea to be drowned instead of shot. The skipper of the barge that took them out, pinioned ready to be thrown overboard, fancied himself as a wit and, when challenged by the sentries at Fort Picolet, would invariably reply, "I'm just off to soak some cod." They had sandbags tied around their necks as sinkers; when the bags or the ropes rotted, the corpses rose to the surface and floated inshore.

Senseless evil was matched by insensate heroism.

I have seen them marching against a redoubt, [wrote one Frenchman] in a tight column, raked by grapeshot from four cannon, and never taking a step backwards. The more of them fell, the more it seemed to stimulate the courage of the others; and they came on singing, for Negroes sing everywhere and make songs about everything. This was the hero's song: *Grenadiers, à l'assaut! Ça qui mouri zaffaire à yo, Qu'y a point* *papa, Qu'y a point maman! Grenadiers, à l'assaut! Ça qui mouri zaffaire à yo!**

Three times these brave men, their weapons at the shoulder, advanced without firing a shot; and, thrown back each time, they did not retire until three-quarters of their number were strewn upon the glacis. You could form no idea of this cold courage without having seen it. . . . That black rectangular mass, marching to death, singing, under a magnificent sun, stayed long in my memory; and even today, more than forty years later, the impressive, grandiose picture returns as vividly to my imagination as in those first moments.

But blind courage was not enough against military skill. Bonaparte, at last awakened to the necessity of repairing the blunders he had made, decided to provide substantial reinforcements. The survivors of Leclerc's men would be immune to fever for at least five years. By husbanding his resources, gradually building up his strength, Rochambeau might in time achieve Leclerc's dream of destroying most of the Black population.

Unluckily for him, the uneasy peace in Europe did not last. On May 16, 1803, war between France and Britain began again, and with it came the end of all French hopes of holding Saint-Domingue. The realisation may have provided some bitter consolation for Toussaint, held prisoner at the fortress of Jouy, shivering in a damp cell at the beginning of another insipid alpine summer, and now within a few weeks of death from consumption and pneumonia.

Rochambeau, who took twelve thousand men down to Port-au-Prince in March to deal with the troubles in the West and South (and, it was said, to renew acquaintance with the ladies of his harem), received orders from Bonaparte to return at once to Le Cap. From July onwards the British blockade was reestablished and the rebels, scenting the kill, pressed back the French troops now devoid of all hope of reinforcement. Their triumphant, menacing fires lit the hills and plains around the French-occupied towns, whose inhabitants cowered in fear of bestial torture and rape to come.

As soon as the news of the renewal of war reached Dessalines he wrote to Lieutenant-General Nugent, Governor of Jamaica, offering preferential terms to British merchants if Nugent would give

* See p. 23.

him military supplies and support against the French. This was a matter on which Nugent had not yet had instructions from White-hall and, as Admiral Duckworth pointed out to the Admiralty, "the Lieut.-General, like me, felt the greater embarrassment in promoting the views of the Blacks against the Whites". They agreed between them to offer Dessalines enough arms and ammunition to drive the French army out of Saint-Domingue on condition that he gave the British two ports to be used as trading posts, allowed them to occupy the fortified bases of Môle Saint-Nicolas and Tiburon, and promised protection of white civilians and restitution of property to white owners.

Captain James Walker of the *Vanguard* and Hugh Cathcart, the Jamaican trader who had formerly been British agent at Port-au-Prince, presented these proposals to Dessalines and Christophe – whom Dessalines had promoted to lieutenant-general – at Les Gonaïves, on Monday, August 28. Dessalines gave assurances that he would protect white inhabitants, though he said that he could not answer for the consequences if towns had to be taken by assault (a traditional and not outrageous reservation, within a decade of Badajos). The reinstatement of white planters in their estates he rejected as "too strong a dose", since many of the whites who had been helping the French – with a view to reducing the Blacks to slavery again – were the same men to whom Toussaint had given their plantations back after they had deserted once before and fought for the British.

He said he would never trust them, recalling the meetings of Leclerc's advisory council, at which some colonists had suggested "extirpating the Negroes in toto should they find it impracticable to reduce them to slavery . . . and to form another population by importation from Africa. . . . . Himself and his generals had come to the determination . . . that in future the whites should be confined to the different towns in the colony – that the soil should be exclusively possessed by the natives (Blacks and mulattos)."

This was the first open statement of the rebels' new resolution: to make the colony not only independent but also exclusively coloured, barring all whites from office and from the ownership of land. For this reason Dessalines flatly refused even to consider the proposal that the British navy should be given the use of Môle Saint-Nicolas and Tiburon.

The French suspected, and frequently openly alleged, that the British government betrayed the Treaty of Amiens by supplying

the rebels with arms and ammunition. It seems clear from Cathcart's confidential reports to Duckworth that there was no truth in
this, though weapons may well have been sold to them by British
and American merchants. Earlier, when a member of Leclerc's
staff had complained to a British officer that there were British
markings on muskets captured from the rebels, the Briton had
replied:

> Good heavens, don't you know we're a nation of merchants?
> Those muskets probably left Kingston, Jamaica, in an armed
> convoy guarded by our fleet and carrying our troops to fight
> against Toussaint. Our traders could sell only muskets from our
> own factories; it was a good opportunity; and I understand that
> Toussaint bought fifteen or twenty thousand of them – to use
> against us. We always combine business with politics.

On this occasion, however, since the truce was over and
Dessalines had impressed both Cathcart and Walker with his
willingness to cooperate with the British, Walker agreed to let him
have ten barrels of gunpowder and forty muskets – which he had
taken from a French prize – so that Christophe could attack a
group of a thousand 'Congos' in the mountains, who were sending
supplies to Rochambeau at Le Cap. 'Congo', still a term of dis-
paragement, was now used by the rebels who had formerly been in
the French army to describe those who had from the earliest days
been members of irregular bands.

Shortly afterwards Dessalines sent a message to "the Admiral
commanding His Britannic Majesty's forces cruising off the Cape",
telling him that Clervaux was attacking the Congos, Christophe
was marching on Le Cap, and that Dessalines himself would begin
the siege of Port-au-Prince within a few days. "If it should please
you to order one of the vessels under your command to cruise off
that town, Your Excellency would be rendering my army a signal
service for which I should be particularly grateful." The Royal
Navy cooperated closely, the British ships blockading the ports to
prevent supplies getting in and gleaning where the rebels reaped,
waiting for the fall of each town to seize the escaping vessels and
troops and escort them to Jamaica. Captain Walker took off the
French garrison from Saint-Marc in September. On October 5
Port-au-Prince fell. On October 12 Brunet and the Negro general
Laplume surrendered Les Cayes, capital of the South Province, to
Captain Cumberland of the *Pique*. On November 11, with 20,000

men against Rochambeau's 5,000, Christophe established himself on the heights commanding the Plaine du Cap while Dessalines advanced via Le Limbé.

Rochambeau went to meet them at the head of his men. As always in pitched battles, the Blacks suffered very heavy casualties and had little in the way of artillery to reply to the fire from the French fortified positions. The fighting continued all day and was halted only by a tempest of rain that fell in such torrents that it was impossible to see. The storm continued almost without abatement for three weeks, battering and soaking the flagging morale of the French troops who had been reduced to eating their horses, mules, donkeys, even Rochambeau's imported Negro-hunting dogs. The civilian population of Le Cap, sullen under Rochambeau's brutal-ities and exactions (one of them had recently been shot out of hand for not producing a large sum of money that the general demanded from him and that he did not possess) had lost all heart for the fight.

On November 19 Rochambeau capitulated to Dessalines, agree-ing to hand over the forts and artillery undamaged within ten days provided he and his troops were allowed to embark on the ships in the harbour with all their baggage and the honours of war. On November 22 Dessalines, Christophe and Clervaux signed a pro-clamation promising justice to all men of good will, including former white property-owners – a reversal of the policy announced to Walker and Cathcart only a few weeks before.

Rochambeau sent his chief-of-staff to open negotiations with Captain Loring, commanding the British squadron patrolling off the Cape. He secretly hoped that the weather, continuing bad, would drive the British away for long enough for his own ships to get clear, but Loring was tenacious. Negotiations dragged on until November 30, when Loring was surprised to see the blue and red flag of the rebels hoisted on Fort Picolet. Captain Bligh, whom Loring sent into the harbour to speak with Dessalines and discover what was going on, was intercepted by a French naval attaché and taken aboard the frigate *La Surveillante*, where he found Rocham-beau at last ready to come to terms. He had embarked his troops five days before, hoping to slip out of harbour during a squall, but a head-on wind had prevented them from moving. Dessalines, tired of waiting, had entered the town that morning and threatened to sink the French ships with red-hot shot if they did not leave the harbour at once.

Bligh went ashore to inform Dessalines that the French were now British prisoners, and shortly afterwards the wind changed sufficiently for the vessels to leave: three frigates and seventeen smaller ships carrying 8,000 men, firing a token broadside and lowering their colours as they went. At Jamaica the ships were sold as prizes and the men interned in prison hulks. Rochambeau's infamous conduct was well enough known for Duckworth to refuse to meet him. As Christmas approached the Governor of Jamaica grew apprehensive that the high spirits of the season and an excess of drink might prompt some of the Negroes to lynch the Frenchman. He was sent to England in the *Révolutionnaire* and remained a prisoner there until he was exchanged in 1811. Two years later he was killed at the battle of Leipzig.

IV

Independence

1

The twelve-year struggle was over. What had begun as a protest against cruelty, and continued as a fight for liberty, had ended with independence. The land still shuddered with the terror that had gripped it and the horrors it had seen. The white world that sighed with relief when Toussaint was kidnapped now found itself confronted by an entirely new nation of Blacks, victors of the greatest slave revolt in history.

Dessalines summoned his generals to Les Gonaïves to renew the oaths they had taken a year before at L'Arcahaye and to confirm him as governor-general of the state to which they restored the ancient Carib name of Haiti – the land of the mountains. On January 1, 1804, they swore "to each other, to posterity and to the entire universe, to renounce France for ever and to die rather than live under her domination" – and proudly dated their declaration "the 1st day of the independence of Haiti". The generals returned to their commands – Christophe in the North, Pétion in the West and Geffrard in the South, while Dessalines occupied himself with drawing up regulations for uniforms and badges of rank, and ordered a capital city to be built at Fort Marchand on his favourite plantation and to be named Dessalines.

There were French soldiers in the former Spanish part of the island and isolated bands of unsubmitted brigands in the South – notably one led by Jean-Baptiste Perrier, who called himself Goman. To deal with them Dessalines still had need of arms and ammunition and for these he turned to the British once more. Captain Cumberland sold him the weapons the French had surrendered to him at Les Cayes, receiving sugar and coffee in payment, which he sold in Jamaica and distributed among his crew as prize money. Captain Loring similarly sold the 5,000 muskets that he had taken from Rochambeau's men at Le Cap, though Dessalines grumbled that they should have come to him free under the terms of the capitulation.

All this was viewed with great misgiving by Edward Corbet, the agent whom the Governor of Jamaica sent to try to renew the Maitland-Toussaint agreement with Dessalines. When Dessalines refused, Corbet protested that the arms the British were supplying might well be turned against their own compatriots. But it was soon apparent that Dessalines's immediate victims were to be the remaining French colonists. Many of these, remembering how well Christophe and Toussaint had treated them after the first French exodus, remained behind. Dessalines, in breach of his assurances to the British and the proclamation that he issued before the fall of Le Cap, and on the pretext that they were aiding the brigands, began to massacre the whites in all the towns of the South.

On March 16 Captain Perkins of the *Tartar* went ashore at Jérémie to investigate these reports, and the following day wrote to Admiral Duckworth:

I am informed that on the 29th of last month, which was the day following our departure from Jérémie, General Dessalines had a muster of the white Inhabitants then remaining in the place which amounted to almost 450 men, women and children. When they had collected together he gave orders for their property of every description to be taken from them, and then instantly put to death. In the course of three days 308 were murdered, the remainder have been hid away in different places. The strictest search was made for them and some few found, when they instantly shared the same fate. I have only heard of seven lives that this monster (for his cruelties declare him such) Dessalines has spared, and then through the earnest prayers and entreaties of a vast number of Black men who possess some feelings of Humanity.

I assure you that it is horrid to view the streets in different places stained with the Blood of these unfortunate people, whose bodies are now left exposed to view by the river and sea side. In hauling the seine the evening we came to our anchor several bodies got entangled in it, in fact such scenes of cruelty and devastation have been committed as is impossible to imagine or my pen describe. On Dessalines's departure from Jérémie for Port-au-Prince he was followed by 25 mules loaded with plate

and other valuables all Plunder in Jérémie and I understand it
was not equal to what he collected in Aux Cayes, the greater
part of which was found buried underground.

PS I forgot to mention I am informed Dessalines stands in
great fear of the English and will be very cautious offering any
umbrage.

In this same evil mood Dessalines returned to Port-au-Prince
and continued his terrible revenge.

On General Dessalines's return, [Captain Perkins reported to
Duckworth in April] he ordered all the white men then remaining in the town to be immediately put to death. The order was
executed without the least ceremony – the Black soldiers being
at liberty to satisfy their inclinations in the most barbarous
manner, they having a thirst for the blood of these unfortunate
people.

Some they shot having tied them from 15 to 20 together.
Some they pricked to death with their bayonets, and others they
tortured in such a manner too horrid to be described. In the span
of 8 days no less than 800 were actually murdered by these
assassins and their bodies thrown into the bogs and marshes to
rot away.

The White women are spared provided they consent to live
with the Black men as their wives, but should they refuse they
would instantly be put to death or sent to the mountains to work
on the plantations. I have been informed of eleven that were
murdered for not consenting to the embraces of the Black Brutes
– one a beautiful young lady who after being forced by Col
Germaine (a Negro) and twenty-five of his men to satisfy their
brutish desires was afterwards pricked to death with their
bayonets. Even the mulatto women are in danger of their lives
and particularly those who have lived with White men, being
promised the same fate if they do not consent to live with the
Black officers.

Perkins believed that fifty white men had escaped and were still
hidden in the town, despite searches by the troops, and that
Dessalines had collected plunder to the value of a million dollars.

On Monday the 25th March, Dessalines left Port-au-Prince
for Cap-François, there being at that place 1800 to 2000 white

people whom he is determined shall fall a sacrifice to his vengeance; in fact he thinks nothing of being the executioner himself, for he ordered a man to be brought to his chamber, and
while in conversation stabbed him with his poniard to his heart.
The immense treasure that has been collected at different places
is deposited in the mountains where they cannot be surprised
and where they are creating strong fortifications and magazines
for the reception of ammunition which is plentifully supplied
them of every description by the Americans.

I am actually told [Captain Perkins concluded somewhat wist-
fully] that American schooners lately arrived at one of their
ports with gunpowder which was sold for four dollars per lb.

Christophe had sent Bunel, Toussaint's former treasurer, to
negotiate in the United States for the purchase of ships and ammunition. He was firmly convinced that Haiti needed the help of white
men to recover from the effects of continuous war and to re-establish
its agriculture and commerce. On this point he came into head-on
conflict with Dessalines, newly arrived at the Cape and thirsting
for more blood, and the two men quarrelled so violently that a
report reached Jamaica that Christophe had taken up arms against
the commander-in-chief. In the end he managed to persuade
Dessalines that no foreigners other than Frenchmen should be
harmed and set guards on their houses. He also pleaded successfully for the lives of those Frenchmen who had dealt honestly with
the Blacks and those – notably priests and surgeons – who had
served with them. Nonetheless, nine-tenths of the white French
population perished in 'the night of horrors' of April 20.

At short intervals [one American resident wrote] [we] heard
the pick-axe thundering at the door of some devoted neighbour,
and soon forcing it. Piercing shrieks almost immediately ensued
and these were followed by an expressive silence. The next
minute the military party was heard proceeding to some other
house to renew their work of death. . . .

A proclamation was published in the newspaper, stating that
the vengeance due to the crimes of the French had been sufficiently executed and inviting all who had escaped the massacre
to appear on the parade, and receive tickets of protection, after
which, it was declared, they might depend on perfect security. As
the massacre had been expected, many hundreds had contrived to

secrete themselves; most of whom now came forth from their hiding places and appeared on the parade. But instead of receiving the promised tickets of protection, they were instantly led away to the place of execution and shot. . . .

Télémaque [the mayor] who had supported Leclerc and another officer expressed their horror at such scenes; and were punished by being compelled to hang with their own hands, two Frenchmen then in the fort.

His bloody work concluded, Dessalines published another declaration, pulsating with his own savage enthusiasm, condemning Toussaint for his leniency, praising himself for his ruthlessness:

The day of vengeance has come and the implacable enemies of the rights of man have received the fitting punishment for their crimes. . . .

Like the torrent that bursts its banks and shatters everything in its path, the fury of your vengeance has dashed down all that resisted its impetuous career. Perish all tyrants of innocence, all oppressors of mankind! . . .

We have repaid these cannibals war for war, crime for crime, outrage for outrage. Yes, I have saved my country, I have avenged America! This avowal before heaven and éarth is my pride and my glory! What do I care for the opinion of my contemporaries or of future generations? I have done my duty; I approve of myself; that suffices me. . . .

There had been panic as well as the primitive lust for revenge in his massacring of the whites. He feared that they would turn against him if the French came again, and it was this return of the French that was to haunt Haiti for the next decade. Already the generals had made plans to withstand the invasion that they expected Bonaparte to launch. This time they would follow Toussaint's advice to the letter, destroying the towns, laying waste the plains and the foothills, and retreating to the mountains where Dessalines had transferred most of the heavy guns from the coastal batteries and where the mountain sides within range of the guns were planted with yams and bananas to provide food for the garrisons.

Tremble, usurping tyrants, scourges of the New World, our daggers are sharpened, your punishment is at hand! Sixty

thousand armed men, tempered in war, obedient to my commands, burn to offer fresh sacrifices to the shades of their
murdered brothers. If any nation is mad or bold enough to
attack me, let it come! . . . I await them with firm foot and
tranquil eye. Willingly shall I abandon to them the coast and the
sites where towns once existed; but woe to those who approach
too closely to the mountains! Better would it have been for them
to have been swallowed up in the depths of the sea than torn to
pieces at the furious hands of the children of Haiti! . . .

Once more he affirmed the oath that had been taken at L'Arcahaye
(and ignored in the conciliatory proclamation before the entry into
Le Cap):

> Generals, officers, and soldiers, unlike he who preceded me,
> ex-general Toussaint Louverture, I have been faithful to the
> promise that I made you when I took arms against tyranny, and
> as long as I live I shall keep my oath. Never shall a *colon* or a
> European set foot on this soil with the title of master or owner.
> That resolution shall henceforth form the fundamental basis of
> our constitution. . . .

The extravagances of his language struck an answering note in
many hearts. The violent racial consciousness bred from years of
hatred and atrocity was expressed in the ordinance that all citizens
of the new state should be known as *Noirs*, irrespective of their
shades of colour. In drawing up the Act of Independence itself, one
of the committee, amid wild applause, had shouted: "To set out
this declaration we need the skin of a white man for parchment, his
skull as an inkhorn, his blood for ink, and a bayonet for a
pen!"

In July Dessalines learned that the senate in Paris had offered the
title of Emperor to Bonaparte. Determined not to be outranked
by a Frenchman, he drew up a proposal that he should be nominated
Emperor of Haiti and on August 14 circulated it among his generals
for their signatures. On September 2 he was formally acclaimed as
Jean-Jacques the First, Emperor of Haiti. The coronation, performed by Father Corneille Brelle, a Breton missionary who had
been one of Toussaint's chaplains, took place at Le Cap on October
8 – seven weeks before Napoléon's at Notre Dame. It was accompanied by much gunfire and parading of troops and simulated in the

principal towns of the other provinces. On New Year's Day, when the first anniversary of the declaration of independence was celebrated in the rising new capital of Dessalines (formerly Fort Marchand) the troops knelt to present arms to the emperor.

One of Dessalines's first actions as governor-general had been to design new uniforms for his soldiers. These were now beginning to be issued, two thousand of them having been supplied by a Baltimore firm. The Americans were rapidly re-establishing themselves in the market from which Leclerc had evicted them. They had, according to a complaint lodged by the French vice-consul in Philadelphia, entertained Dessalines's officers at a banquet at Les Cayes at the very moment when Frenchmen were being massacred in the city. Others had been sending out American Negroes as recruits for Dessalines's army, shiploads of arms and ammunition and even, it was alleged, six hundred white specialist armourers and munitions workers. For all these services they were paid in coffee, cotton, timber and even – for Dessalines's hoard of silver was considerable – in dollars.

The island had been so ravaged – and the expectancy of a French return was so strong – that even the families of the most influential people were living gypsy existences, sleeping on camp beds in derelict hovels, bereft of furniture and short of food and clothing. On November 11, 1804, Christophe's wife sent him a letter from Les Gonaïves. She had gone there after the coronation with her friend, Madame Dessalines, in readiness for the New Year celebrations, and was camping on the sea shore.

Madame Henry Christophe, to her dear spouse,

It is with true pleasure, my dear friend, that I avail myself of this favourable opportunity to inform you that we all enjoy perfect health, with the exception of Victor* who is a little restless; I think it is his teeth; and I hope it will amount to nothing. I have been without your dear news for several days; if you knew the satisfaction that I feel when I receive them, you would send them to me every day. I beg you to have the laundry-woman hurry with my linen, for I and the children are on the point of being without any and you know that it is difficult to get washing done here. When it is ready, oblige me by giving orders for it to be sent to me at once. The sugar that you told me to expect has not yet arrived; this delay grieves us very much,

* Their youngest son, born March 3, 1804.

since we had awaited it impatiently, and especially Madame
Dessalines, who is expecting her mirrors by the same boat on
which you loaded the sugar. She and her young ladies charge me
with sending you their best wishes.

Our children join me in wishing you good health and em-
bracing you from the bottom of our heart.

Your affectionate spouse,

Madame Christophe.

So long as the British navy patrolled from Jamaica up through
the Windward Passage and out into the Atlantic, Dessalines was
safe from a French invasion by sea, but there still remained several
thousand white and coloured troops in the Spanish part of the island,
commanded by General Ferrand. In March 1805 Dessalines
launched an attack in four columns across the frontier, three of
them under his command in the south and centre while Christophe
advanced from Le Cap along the northern coast and then down to
the city of Santo-Domingo. The Negroes of this part of the island
had led comparatively easy lives under their indolent Spanish
masters and showed little enthusiasm in welcoming their ferocious
liberator – though their apathy rapidly dissolved at the impact of
his cruel and unpredictable temper. Burning and looting his way
through increasingly hostile territory, Dessalines arrived before
Santo-Domingo on March 6 and was joined by Christophe the next
day.

It was a week before the army was fully deployed along both
banks of the Ozana river and when Dessalines finally opened his
attack on the city he discovered that it was well fortified and the
French, with their Spanish and coloured auxiliaries, ready to put
up an obstinate resistance. A fortnight later, the garrison received
reinforcements from the north-east of the island, brought round by
sea. Dessalines, unquiet at leaving the West long unprotected (he
had stripped the garrisons to make up his army of twenty thousand
men) called off the siege and returned to his headquarters in the
new capital at Marchand, setting fire to towns, slaughtering the
unwary, and carrying off livestock as he went.

Christophe went back to Le Cap, where he celebrated his
patronal festival – July 15, the feast of Saint Henry the Emperor
as well as Saint Swithin – with parades and speeches. Dessalines
arrived during the evening and stayed for a fortnight, so that the
civic authorities had the opportunity of repeating the celebrations

on July 25 – appropriately the feast of both Saint James and Saint
Christopher. There were parades in the morning, speeches in the
afternoon, and in the evening a banquet and ball at which the
emperor entertained the principal citizens. Dancing was Dessalines's passion, second only to bloodletting. He was accompanied
everywhere by his dancing master, but despite much practice he
remained a clumsy performer, exploding in moments of excitement
into wild capering.

He was pleased with his reception at Le Cap. Three days later
he appointed Christophe commander-in-chief of the Haitian army,
an honour for which he seemed destined since the beginning of the
year. His name had immediately followed Dessalines's in the list of
signatures of the declaration of independence; he had commanded
the northern column in the attack on Santo-Domingo despite the
presence of Clervaux, who was his senior; and Clervaux's recent
death of fever at La Marmelade had opened the way to his appointment without friction. Since Dessalines was empowered to name
his successor as emperor, Christophe's appointment gave him in
the public eye the status of heir-apparent. His enemies – those
who remembered his close cooperation with the French, or had not
forgiven him for murdering Sans-Souci – were silent or, like
Yayou, Sans-Souci's former lieutenant, were transferred by
Dessalines to the South.

Although Dessalines was not yet in his fifties, the question of his
succession was already exercising the minds of the senior generals
and officials. It was evident that he was incapable of administering
the new nation and, indeed, when not fighting, showed little
interest in anything but dissipation. The fiasco of the recent expedition to Santo-Domingo had done a great deal to diminish his
credit; his policy of making his subjects work by beatings,
bayonettings and decimation had not changed; and a large part of
the fruits of this labour was diverted to swelling his personal fortune, which he squandered on twenty mistresses, each of whom
enjoyed a regular and handsome allowance from the imperial
purse.

The brilliant soldier had proved to be a bad emperor, and it was
in many people's minds to get rid of him. To what extent Christophe led the plotting is not clear. His sense of discipline and
respect for his seniors fought against his contempt for Dessalines.
"That jumping jackass," he said of him at the ball on July 25, and
to see the scorn with which the onlookers sniggered behind their

hands at the emperor's antics was an affront to his dignity and pride of race. He had been at odds with Dessalines over the massacre of the whites. He knew that Dessalines disapproved of his inclusion of both white and mulatto advisors in the group of administrators that he had formed at Le Cap and with whom he discussed events in the world outside and the future of his own troubled country, using their learning and experience to supplement his own lack of education.

In August he sent a schooner laden with flour to the principal ports of the West and the South, ostensibly to barter its cargo for sugar and coffee. But besides flour the schooner carried one of his confidential agents, Bruno Blanchet, who had conversations at Jérémie with General Férou, at Les Cayes with General Geffrard, and, on the return journey, at Port-au-Prince with General Pétion. The talks were secret, their purpose obscure – a tentative sounding of the generals' attitude towards the emperor. All of them were suspicious, none went further than agreeing that he was not entirely satisfied with the existing government. If Christophe intended recruiting allies in a plot against Dessalines, the attempt was a failure.

Rumour of Christophe's criticism reached Dessalines's ears, and in September he ordered his adjutant, Captain Dupuy, to summon him to Marchand where, he announced, he intended to kill him as soon as he arrived. This was no meaningless phrase, he had before now plunged a dagger into a man while talking to him, and his guards were trained to cut a man down instantly if the emperor fingered his snuffbox in a certain way. Dupuy, having obtained Dessalines's signature to the order, very courageously scribbled on a scrap of paper "Reply that you are sick" and folded this into the letter before handing it to the trooper of the Imperial Guides who took it to Le Cap. Christophe did as he had been advised, and the emperor forgot the whole affair, turning his wrath against Pétion and Geffrard instead.

He recognised Pétion's intelligence and influence with his caste and planned to gain his allegiance by marrying him to one of his many illegitimate children, a young woman named Célimène. The proposal put Pétion in a quandary: he was attached to the woman with whom he was already living and by whom he had recently had a daughter, and he had been told that Célimène had already been the mistress of one of Toussaint Louverture's nephews. After much hesitation he asked to be excused the honour. Dessalines, believing that he had rejected Célimène because she was a Negress, never forgave him.

Geffrard he suspected partly because he commanded the South, traditionally a mulatto stronghold, and partly because he had shown signs of resentment when Dessalines had sent him a harsh rebuke by mouth of a junior officer. He now became convinced that Pétion and Geffrard were plotting to bring Rigaud back to displace him, and during the second anniversary ball at the Imperial Palace at Marchand on January 1, 1806, he left the festivities and went to his study, where he summoned Christophe, Christophe's former lieutenant, General Paul Romain, and Colonel Pierre Toussaint, governor of the Saint-Marc district. To them he declared his conviction that Pétion and Geffrard were planning to proclaim Rigaud ruler of Haiti, in the interests of France. He proposed that the two mulatto generals should be murdered that night.

The situation was difficult. Still heated by his capering at the ball, the emperor was likely to fly into a rage if crossed; on the other hand, Christophe had no desire to see him begin a purge which might not stop until thousands had been smelled out and sacrificed, and which could precipitate an explosion in which Rigaud and the mulattos might well return to power. He suggested that the time might not be ripe; that both generals seemed to have strong backing from the troops and civil population of their provinces; that it might be advisable, in order to avoid the possibility of civil war, to keep them under surveillance and wait for proof. Romain and Toussaint expressed the same opinion and Dessalines, after staring at them for several seconds, hurried out of the room and back to the dance floor, where he resumed his cavortings.

Both Christophe and Pierre Toussaint sent a word of warning to Pétion and Geffrard, and the two mulattos asked for an audience, in which they complained that the emperor was treating them coldly. When Dessalines poured out his misgivings about their relationship with Rigaud, they replied that they had never dreamed of supplanting the emperor. Dessalines at last assured them that his trust in them was unchanged – which was true enough, since he had none – and they returned to the West and South in an atmosphere of uneasy peace, determined to canvass support among their subordinate officers.

Dessalines played into their hands with a series of unpopular measures that culminated in a bad-tempered tour of the South during the course of which he stirred up more fear and hatred.

Geffrard died suddenly in May and word went round that he had been poisoned by the emperor. Dessalines denied this – "when God took Geffrard he was in more of a hurry than I was" – but he had Geffrard's papers impounded, seeking criminal correspondence with Christophe, against whom his distrust had now turned once more. Captain Dupuy, who conducted the investigation, assured the emperor that he had found nothing, whereupon Dessalines lost himself once more in the pleasures of the dance and the embrace of his mistress of the moment, Euphémie Daguilh.

The period of quiet was brief. He ran out of money and discovered that it was no longer flowing into the treasury as freely as before. He summoned to Les Cayes an accountant whom he had already used to investigate irregularities in the public finances of the West Province and ordered him to hold a similar inquiry in the South. The news struck terror into the hearts of the prominent citizens of the region, for almost all of them had paid their taxes by promissory notes which they had no intention of honouring.

Dessalines left Les Cayes on September 8 after ordering the local garrisons to search every ship coming into their ports and, if they found André Rigaud, to "chop off his head" on the spot. He was passing through one of his periods of hysteria, suspecting everybody, talking interminably of blood and destruction. The mother of one of the officers of his personal guard having offended him, he ordered the son to have her beaten in public. Hearing of a quarrel between two members of his staff he ordered them to fight a duel to the death; he attended to see that his orders were carried out and forced them to fire shot after shot until, after twelve exchanges, one of them fell mortally wounded. It was almost with pleasure that he received news on October 13 of an army revolt at Les Cayes, precipitated by grievances over pay. When he set out to deal with it on October 15 he declared with eager anticipation: "I will have my horse walk in blood up to his breastplate."

Leaving General Vernet, the finance minister, in command at Marchand and sending a warning note to Christophe, he set off with his staff and personal bodyguard. Two battalions of the 4th demi-brigade were to follow him. He reached L'Arcahaye the next day and ordered three companies of light infantry and three of grenadiers from the 3rd demi-brigade to set out at once for Port-au-Prince, nearly thirty miles away. They were not to enter the town but to halt by the Saint-Martin plantation at the Pont-Rouge, so called because of its red painted guard rails.

It was Dessalines's intention to leave L'Arcahaye in the morning, ride down to Pont-Rouge, where the infantrymen would be rested from their previous day's march, and lead them into Port-au-Prince, impressing any potential rebels among the citizens with this display of force, before continuing to the South with reinforcements from the Port-au-Prince garrison. What he did not know was that the revolt had spread up from Les Cayes to Port-au-Prince and that Pétion and other generals of the West Province were already in league with those of the South. Equally ignorant were Colonel Thomas Jean and Major Gédéon, who commanded the six companies of grenadiers and *chasseurs*. Perhaps because of anxiety not to be overtaken by the emperor, the march discipline of their men was deplorable; they hurried along in disorganised batches, the senior officers riding at the rear to round up the stragglers. As the soldiers trotted forward, the field hands came to the side of the road and shouted slogans of liberty, reproaching them for serving the tyrant Dessalines. At Pont-Rouge they were met by a group of rebel officers who harangued them and persuaded them not to halt but to continue into the town.

When Thomas Jean and Gédéon rode up to Pont-Rouge they suddenly discovered that they were among strange troops, who arrested them and took them to Pétion. Pétion invited the two officers to join him. Thomas Jean hesitated and was at once marched away under close arrest. Gédéon agreed and was awarded a colonelcy and Thomas Jean's former command. An officer from the 21st demi-brigade of the same build as Gédéon – a plump man – was given Gédéon's busby and scarlet trousers and sent to join the troops of the 15th demi-brigade waiting at Pont-Rouge. (Dessalines, for purposes of morale and deception, had retained the former numbering of the demi-brigades, each of which was in principle composed of 1,600 men. In fact, the army was not as large as he pretended – a piece of information relayed to London by Robert Sutherland, a British trader in Port-au-Prince, who was given a contract to supply the army with buttons and from this was able to calculate that its strength was not more than twenty thousand.)

By five o'clock the following morning – the hour at which Dessalines was to leave L'Arcahaye – the trap was fully set. It is indicative of the hatred that he had managed to arouse in his subjects that as he rode closer to Port-au-Prince and the number of field hands who had knowledge of the ambush grew greater with every mile, not one of them offered a word of warning. From a distance he saw the troops drawn up for inspection at the Pont-Rouge and in front of them the scarlet-pantalooned, busby-topped, corpulent figure of the officer whom he took to be Gédéon. As he rode unconcernedly forward, he was astonished to hear an aide-de-camp, Colonel Leger, who had served for a time with the 15th demi-brigade, suddenly exclaim: "But, Sire, these troops are from the South!"

"Impossible!" said Dessalines. "How could they be?"

Concealed behind the bushes at the side of the road were three or four of the rebel generals. It was one of these who now shouted "Halt!" and then, to the troops, "Form a circle!" Men dashed from the undergrowth to block the Arcahaye road, others pressed in from the sides. Dessalines screamed, "They have betrayed me!"

In the presence of hundreds of mutinous soldiers his fierce courage did not desert him. Raising his riding crop, he began to slash at the upturned faces around him. Though their officers continually shouted "Open fire!" not one of the men dared to raise his musket. The emperor drew his pistol from the holster and shot one of the soldiers, then wheeled his horse to force his way back up the road. Only at this moment did one young soldier summon up enough courage to fire – not at the terrible person of the emperor, but at his horse.

The animal fell, trapping Dessalines's leg – and with his cry of "Help!" to his aides the spell was broken. The dreadful figure, human at last, lay thrashing defencelessly on the ground. Within a second it was riddled with bullets. Then the generals hurled themselves on it with dagger-thrusts and sabre-cuts and more pistol shots. The soldiers cut off the fingers to steal the rings and stripped off the clothing for the sake of the gold lace. The body was dragged for more than a mile into the city, kicked and slashed and stoned by passers-by, and left in the place d'Armes to suffer whatever more indignities came to the minds of the citizens of Port-au-Prince, so suddenly emboldened in the presence of their emperor whose face was no longer recognisable. He found only one mourner, a Black woman, long insane, named Défilée, who sat on the ground beside him weeping until soldiers came to take him to the city cemetery and bury him without a monument. For a long time after, she went each day to scatter wild flowers on the grave of the brave monster who had won Haiti her independence.

2

News of the rebellion and Dessalines's death reached Christophe from several sources. On October 13, before the assassination, some of the mutinous officers in the South wrote to tell him that they had taken arms against the emperor and "we proclaim you joyously and unanimously the Supreme Head of this island under whatever title it may please you to adopt" – but there is no certainty that it ever reached him. Both Vernet at Marchand and Pierre Toussaint at Saint-Marc sent him the news and he wrote at once to General Romain, his old comrade and friend, telling him that "it is with tears of blood that I inform you that I have just learned . . . that HM the Emperor has been assassinated."

Whether his grief was deep is doubtful; he had discussed Dessalines's deposition, and deposition with such a man in such a situation could scarcely stop short of death. It is possible that he was incensed at the plot having been carried out by others without his knowledge. He must also have been concerned about his own position: as commander-in-chief, was he to be done away with as well as his master? He ordered Romain to "report to me here, as soon as you receive this".

To Dessalines's widow, a gentle woman and an old friend, he offered his sympathy and asked if she felt herself in danger at Marchand – if so, he would send an escort to bring her to join his wife on their plantation at Millot, a dozen miles outside Le Cap. He suspected that the prominent part played by Pétion and other mulattos might indicate the renewal of the old bitter strife between Black and part-Black and he accused them of dividing the country "on the eve of general pacification in Europe when we should be thinking of nothing but completing our defences and preparing to meet the enemy. Very guilty men have played a part in this business."

However, on October 23 he received a copy of a proclamation by Pétion, Gérin (who had taken over Geffrard's command in the South) and other rebel leaders, signed at Port-au-Prince on "October 16, 1806, the 3rd year of Independence and 1st of True Liberty", denouncing Dessalines's crimes and declaring that "the people and the army, whose instruments we are, proclaim General Henry Christophe *chef provisoire* of the Haitian Government, until such time as the Constitution, in conferring his august title officially upon him, shall have established his designation."

Christophe summoned the civil and military officials of the North Province to Millot, where he drew up a declaration which he gave them to sign. It praised the army of the South for its courage and energy in combating "the tyranny beneath which we groaned" and confirmed that "like them, we feel we cannot better ensure the welfare of our country than by handing to General Christophe the reins of government . . . [which] upon our lively entreaties, he has accepted." Typically, one of his first official acts was to issue a proclamation to all neutral nations, offering protection to their merchants and urging them to trade with Haiti.

He ordered elections to be held throughout the country on November 20 and the appointed representatives to meet at Port-au-Prince on the 30th to draw up the new constitution and, among other things, provide him with a title, though it was commonly accepted that he should be called President. As his personal representative he sent a mulatto merchant, Juste Hugonin, to Port-au-Prince: Hugonin hid a shrewd brain behind a talent for buffoonery which he frequently exercised in the Christophe ménage with such tricks as crawling under the dinner table and making Christophe leap out of his chair by scratching his ankle and yapping like a dog. Christophe's tolerant attitude to whites and mulattos frequently stood him in good stead; on this occasion, Hugonin's mixed blood enabled him to discover what the mulatto faction was planning and to send full reports to Christophe at Le Cap.

Christophe's earlier notion that the assassination of Dessalines was the first move in a mulatto plot to take over control of the country was soon confirmed. Hugonin discovered that their intention was to elect Christophe as President of the Republic with only vestigial powers, while giving all the real authority to the President of the Assembly – to which post Pétion would be appointed. To ensure that the constitution was drawn up on these lines, they packed the Assembly with their own supporters. Hugonin reported that fourteen extra representatives had presented themselves from constituencies created overnight by the mulattos and had thus converted Christophe's probable majority of six to a minority of eight. Christophe's protests were ignored and on December 22 Hugonin warned him that the Assembly, meeting in the parish church of Port-au-Prince under the chairmanship of the senior delegate, César Télémaque, was about to make its decision. "The constitution will be the sergeant and you the corporal," he wrote.

Christophe acted at once. He issued a proclamation to his

troops, denouncing Pétion and his associates as "rebels against authority who seek to establish a constitution that will put power in their hands and deliver to them the control of finance and places. The commander-in-chief orders you to march to preserve your rights and to maintain your liberty. Once these scoundrels have attained their ends, they will not leave you even the right to complain." He led his army swiftly to Saint-Marc, where he learned that the Constituent Assembly had ignored his protests and had elected Pétion as President of the Assembly in accordance with the mulatto plan. It had also elected Christophe to the presidency of the Republic, an appointment which he was now in the odd position of rejecting by force of arms.

Pétion's troops were dispersed through the province and Christophe was advancing with such speed that it was not possible for Gérin to send help from the South in time. Pétion consequently decided not to risk being surrounded and besieged in Port-au-Prince but to meet Christophe in the field and defeat him by superior tactics. His training in the French army had left him with a very poor opinion of the self-taught Negro generals who had gained promotion in Toussaint's wars. "Christophe has not enough military ability to command a platoon," he once said.

He established advanced fortified positions on the road leading north and settled down to await, with quiet confidence, the arrival of Christophe whom he knew to have left L'Arcahaye. The day wore on but brought neither the sound of gunfire nor any message from the forward positions, which were sited on the Lerebours plantation under the command of the owner, Louis Lerebours. Pétion eventually sent one of his senior officers, General Bonnet, to investigate, and Bonnet, riding up the road towards Lerebours, suddenly became aware of long files of men moving in the opposite direction through the trees on either side. From their hats he recognized them as Christophe's soldiers. Guided by one of the Lerebours field hands they had taken winding paths through the plantation and had come in at the rear of Pétion's forward positions, cutting his forces in half. Within minutes a great panic had seized the defenders, the roads and fields were crowded with fleeing men and the rout was not halted until all who were able had found refuge inside the walls of Port-au-Prince.

Pétion was not among these fortunate ones. Finding it impossible to get back to the city by land, he was forced to make his re-entry by sea, discovering when he did so that a hastily-summoned council of war had decided to abandon Port-au-Prince and retreat southwards to link up with Gérin's army. Christophe's troops, however, continued to advance so swiftly that Pétion's men were unable to leave the city without running the risk of being massacred. They manned the batteries on the walls and held off Christophe's attacks for two days, by which time reinforcements had arrived from the South. Christophe retired to L'Arcahaye, organised his frontier defences there and then went back to Le Cap.

The third anniversary of the declaration of liberty had been spent in civil war and the island was now worse divided than ever. The French still held the former Spanish part, while the former French colony was now split roughly along the line of the Artibonite River with Pétion using the style of President of the Assembly of the Republic of Haiti on the south side of it, and Christophe still calling himself simply Commander-in-chief of the Army of the Empire of Haiti on the north.

It was under this title that he wrote at the end of January 1807 to Vice-Admiral James Richard Dacres, who had succeeded Duckworth in command of the Jamaica station on March 1, 1805:

> Pétion and other factious people who revolted with him have settled with the French Government to send emissaries to create a Revolt at Jamaica, in the same manner that the agent Roume did formerly. Their plan is to introduce them into the island from American or Danish vessels which are carrying on the Contraband Trade with the south. . . . On account of the friendship which I have always professed to the British Government, I think it is my duty to forewarn your Excellency, that you may take proper measures to counteract their baneful projects. I think the best mode would be for your Excellency to order a Blockade of all the sea ports occupied by the Rebels, from Jacmel down to Port-au-Prince. . . .

The letter was entrusted to Christophe's confidential messenger, a Black named Thomas Richardson, who was empowered to give the Governor of Jamaica more details of the plot.

By this time, Christophe had been outlawed by the government set up in Port-au-Prince and the presidency had been declared vacant. He replied by summoning his own assembly in the North Province and having himself elected President of the State of Haiti on February 17, 1807; the assembly also approved a constitution, drawn up by Christophe, which appointed him generalissimo of the land and sea forces for life. In response to this, the Southern senate elected Pétion President of the Republic of Haiti for a term of four years on March 9, 1807, an honour which compelled Pétion to ask for several important alterations to the constitution.

Christophe's disingenuous plea for a blockade of Pétion's ports met with no response from the governor and the admiral in Jamaica, but the idea of making use of the British navy was not his alone. On April 13, 1807, Robert Sutherland, the British merchant who had so smartly calculated the size of Dessalines's army from the number of buttons supplied, wrote to a friend in London, informing him that "the British Flag has been received by General Pétion with marked respect. You would no doubt have heard of the Division that has taken place in the island. His Imperial Majesty General Christophe is suspected by the existing government of this quarter as being favourable with Bonaparte and they state that he wishes to be proclaimed Emperor of the Western world." This suggestion that Christophe was friendly with the French was, as Sutherland undoubtedly well knew, a downright lie. He was already conducting raids into the French (formerly Spanish) part of the island, in contrast to Pétion, who was making friendly approaches to General Ferrand.

Sutherland continued that Pétion was writing to William Windham (the minister for the colonies who had in fact resigned with the rest of Grenville's administration in the previous month) and "I trust the right honble secretary will state in his reply the necessity there will be for the Haitian government to be punctual in their engagements with British merchants. In the course of this month there be upwards of five million pounds of coffee sent to England in British bottoms, which has during the last two months been exchanging for British manufactory, and if His Majesty's Minister would only open the trade between this island and British America and would occasionally permit British bottoms to go to America for flour, we should soon drive all the Americans from this island, and the British would have the exclusive Trade of this valuable colony."

Ten days later, on April 23, Sutherland wrote again, complaining that he was unable to get his ships past the French privateers, that "unless the Admiral on the Jamaica station gives us some protection the French cruisers will ultimately benefit by this Trade" and that "there is no doubt but General Christophe who has got the

North part of this island, has had lately frequent and friendly communications with the French general Ferrand who commands the Spanish city of St Domingo. It is worthy of remark that General Christophe has got his family (two sons) in France under the immediate charge of Talleyrand."

It was only one son, an unhappy young hostage who was shortly to die in a French hospital; but Sutherland had staked his fortune on Pétion and was prepared to support him even more substantially than with words and misrepresentations. Towards the end of May some of Pétion's partisans seized towns along the northern peninsula and Pétion sent a division by sea from Port-au-Prince to reinforce them. Among the vessels that transported them was Sutherland's armed merchantman, the *Lord Duncan*, with Sutherland himself aboard. The convoy never reached its objective for, on the way up the coast, the general in command, Bazelais, learned that Christophe had withdrawn most of the garrison from Les Gonaïves to resist a threatened attack by Pétion against Saint-Marc. Bazelais, unable to sail past such a tempting prize, landed his men, pillaged the place, and sent the loot back to Port-au-Prince. For Sutherland, the holds of the *Lord Duncan* crammed with sugar and coffee, the voyage had been more than worthwhile.

Christophe was in bed with fever at his headquarters at Saint-Marc when a messenger from Les Gonaïves was brought into his bedroom by his orderly-officer, Saint-Georges, to report the loss of the town. His face streaming with sweat and his eyes mad with fever, Christophe fumbled beneath his pillow, pulled out a pistol and fired it at the bearer of such bad news. His shaking hand betrayed him and the bullet struck Saint-Georges, killing him on the spot. A week later, recovered from the illness and directing the attack with which he successfully recaptured Les Gonaïves, he repeatedly called for Saint-Georges, quite unaware that he had killed him, but the incident remained in the minds of those around him, proof that their new master could be as uncontrolled in rage as Dessalines.

He returned to Le Cap on June 20, but was not allowed to rest. Pétion, repeating the manoeuvre that had gone astray through Bazelais's cupidity, sent another thousand men to land at Port-de-Paix and threaten Christophe in the northern peninsula, while assembling the bulk of his army for a decisive thrust upwards through Saint-Marc. Christophe, confronted with the threat at

Port-de-Paix only sixty miles from his capital, set off from Le Cap with half his army and Pétion prepared to strike.

Once more the situation was startlingly changed by a reversal of allegiance that nobody could have predicted. General Yayou – one of Pétion's principal collaborators in the murder of Dessalines and, as a former associate of Sans-Souci, one of Christophe's bitterest enemies – confronted the troops who were about to march northwards and, in an impassioned speech, urged them to desert Pétion and join the army of the North. His rhetoric failed to convince them and he was forced to clap spurs to his horse and gallop off the parade ground, whence he continued riding, hotly pursued by Pétion's cavalry, until he reached Jacmel, commanded by General Ambroise Magloire, another of Christophe's secret supporters. But his defection delayed Pétion's northward advance, giving Christophe time to retake Port-de-Paix. Christophe returned to Le Cap, where he celebrated his wife's feast-day, August 25, with an order of the day to the army, requiring his soldiers and by implication all citizens, to address him as 'Monseigneur'.

He also informed them that he had received a dispatch from London stating that "the British Government recognises His Excellency the President Henry Christophe as the chief of the Government of Haiti, and it is determined to contribute its aid to establish its supremacy". This heartening but completely fictitious piece of news came from Jean-Gabriel Peltier, a French refugee and pro-Bourbon pamphleteer who had appointed himself as Christophe's London agent. Peltier enjoyed the distinction of having been sued for libel in the British courts by Bonaparte during the Peace of Amiens, because of offensive articles in *Paris*, a magazine which he published from London at ten-day intervals. The Court of King's Bench found him guilty, but sentenced him only to a fine which was at once covered by public subscriptions. He was a tricky, unreliable but persistent canvasser of favours and had first shown an interest in Haiti during Dessalines's reign. On the emperor's death he made approaches to Pétion through Robert Sutherland, asking to be allowed to represent Haiti in Britain. But he soon realised that Christophe's policy was more likely to be acceptable to the British government and by June 1807 he had decided to support him.

Christophe paid Peltier in sugar and coffee, from which the Frenchman was said to make £8,000 a year. In return, Peltier was expected to do a great deal of lobbying and correspondence, for Christophe was indefatigable in seeking opportunities to form

V. "Dessalines had his men erect five hundred gallows during the night and, in full sight of the French lines, hanged five hundred Frenchmen at dawn." A sketch by Captain Marcus Rainsford.

V Ia. "*Wilberforce was the missionary, eager to bring the light of the true Protestant religion and the high moral principles of Kensington Gore to the interesting but inferior Negroes of Haiti.*"

V Ib. "*Clarkson, on the other hand, filled the role of colleague and collaborator, showing from the earliest days a genuine excitement and sincerity in setting about obtaining public recognition of complete equality for the Haitians—as human beings and as a nation.*"

VII. Citadel-Henry. "This was the ultimate impregnable stronghold to which the King would retreat with his personal guard and continue the fight against the worst that the white man could send against him."

VIII. "Christophe carried a stout silver-knobbed cane . . . as he stalked about the streets, dressed in imitation of his model monarch, George III, in a severely plain jacket with no decoration other than the gold star of the Order of Saint-Henry."

links with the British Government in the hope of winning recognition as the legitimate ruler of Haiti. When Britain abolished the slave trade and her warships were ordered to seize all slavers as prize vessels Christophe offered to buy any slaves they were carrying and make them free citizens of Haiti. He suggested that the navy should cooperate with him in driving the French out of the Spanish part of the island: "should two English frigates be ordered to cruise off Santo-Domingo and cut off all supplies the Americans pour in, General Christophe would soon be in possession of it."

It was not unreasonable for Christophe to expect a sympathetic reception for his overtures. Britain's prominent part in the abolition of the slave trade made her the natural ally of Christophe's state of Haiti, whose inhabitants were principally ex-slave Blacks. Reactionary France, on the other hand, would more naturally lean towards the former free Blacks and mulattos who supported Pétion's Republic: a bitter commentary on Bonaparte's perversion of the ideals of the great revolution. It was unfortunate for Christophe that, though the Britain of Clarkson and Wilberforce wished him well, her government could not afford to expose the West Indian colonies to the contagion of liberty.

In early October 1807 Peltier was joined by Thomas Richardson, the envoy whom Christophe had sent to the governor of Jamaica in the spring. Peltier, who lived at 7 Duke Street, Portland Place, found Richardson lodgings nearby at 21 Great Castle Street and together they bombarded Castlereagh with pleas and petitions. They urged him to prevent all trade with Pétion: "by that means General Ferrand at Santo-Domingo receives ammunition etc." They begged for recognition of Christophe:

From that day . . . since there will be no longer any fear of rebellion in the interior, and no anxiety in respect of France, the Haitian army will be reduced by three-quarters, commerce will be trebled, and England will find in Haiti, whenever she requires, ten thousand auxiliaries to attack, if need be, Cuba, or Puerto Rico.

My lord, during this week alone seven vessels are leaving for Haiti. You will soon have 100 of your vessels in the roadsteads of that island, a million properties and 3,000 of your subjects to protect. It is not possible, without committing a great imprudence, to abandon all that to the hazard of events. There is no point on the globe where you have the hope and perspective of such advantageous and extensive trade. . . .

The note of warning, almost indeed a threat, was sounded again towards the end of the letter. Although, as they assured Castlereagh, it was far from their thoughts to use language other than that of deference and respect in addressing His Majesty's ministers, they begged him to consider whether "General Christophe, who as an Englishman by birth and as head of a wealthy state has both dignity and pride, may not after too long a delay consider himself entitled to feel affronted and close his ports to British vessels." Castlereagh was unmoved.

A few weeks later, Richardson quarrelled with Peltier. The cause of their falling-out was a report in *The Times* of November 27 of Christophe's proclamation to the army on August 25. Richardson realised that Peltier had been sending false information to Christophe, claiming for himself the credit of having won recognition from the British government. (The statement was taken seriously in France, where *Le Moniteur* caustically remarked, "that the Brigands who massacred the Whites at Copenhagen should ally themselves with the Brigands who massacred the Whites at Saint-Domingo will not surprise anybody.") Richardson asked Castlereagh for a decision on the points he put to him, and to "honour me with an officielle answer . . . as no other person whatever are charged with affairs of the President but me only." He pleaded that the answer should not be long delayed "as I propose to depart for Haiti in the ship *Roskeus* in five weeks at furthest".

3

When he did leave for Haiti, in the final days of 1807, Richardson had nothing more substantial than assurances of lively interest to take back with him to Christophe. The ship that he travelled in – her true name was *The Young Roscius* – was commanded and owned by Captain Thomas Goodall, a man in his early thirties who, as a midshipman, had married Charlotte Stanton, the daughter of the manager of several midland theatres. On coming to London with her husband, Miss Stanton achieved considerable success as an actress. The young couple took lodgings in Covent Garden and then as their family grew – they eventually had eight children – moved to Sussex Square.

Goodall, finding it difficult to support them all on naval pay, took to the merchant service. During his last visit to Le Cap in *The Young Roscius* – named as a tribute to his wife's profession

– he had been approached by Christophe with a proposal which would take him back into the fighting services again, and with a rank far higher than midshipman. Like most blue-water vessels, *The Young Roscius* was armed against privateers. Christophe's suggestion was that Goodall should have the armament increased, sell her to the State of Haiti, and continue in command as an officer in the Haitian navy.

When he returned to London in October, Goodall carried out the rearmament and borrowed enough money to buy a second ship, the brig *Hopewell*, which he also armed heavily. The two vessels, loaded with cargo which included new state carriages for Christophe and his wife, sailed from London late in December, called at Portsmouth to take on additional crew and then set sail for Haiti. It was a rough passage. Off Ushant the heavy seas caused the cargo to shift and some of the new guns had to be jettisoned from *The Young Roscius*. But both vessels eventually arrived safely at Le Cap, where Christophe delightedly appointed Goodall vice-admiral of the Haitian navy and commander-in-chief of its only squadron.

The Young Roscius, mounting ten eighteen-pound carronades and four brass long-eights, was renamed the *Foudroyant* and given 150 Haitian soldiers and sailors in addition to those of her British crew who wished to continue to serve in her. Captain John McCulloch, who had come out as master of the *Hopewell*, was appointed rear-admiral and took over the command of the *Foudroyant* while Goodall returned to Britain to find yet another vessel for the fleet, promising Christophe that it should be nothing less than a 36-gun frigate. Captain McCulloch, unhappily, did not long enjoy his promotion. His first sortie in the *Foudroyant* was to Jean Rabel, a town on the north peninsula still occupied by Pétion's troops. Two armed Southern schooners lay at anchor under the forts. McCulloch fearlessly sailed his brig into the harbour, emptied a broadside into one schooner, which blew up, and then led a boarding party to capture the other; but in the moment of victory he was killed by a musket shot.

McCulloch's body was taken back to Le Cap, where Christophe ordered a state funeral for the first of the British mercenaries to fall in his service. In the church of Notre Dame, still ravaged by the fire of 1802 and open to the sky, the regimental bands played solemn music as companies of soldiers marched in to the beat of muffled drums. Minute guns, that had been firing since dawn, accompanied the massed trumpets and the choir. The service closed with 'God Save the King' and the coffin was carried to the military cemetery to the brisk strains of 'Rule Britannia'. McCulloch was succeeded by Captain Pearce, a former sub-lieutenant in the Royal Navy, but Pearce was soon posted ashore to train new crews and succeeded by a junior officer, who in April 1808 fell in with HMS *Daedalus* while patrolling the Bight of Léogane with two armed schooners that had recently been added to Christophe's navy.

The Admiralty, though it had recently abolished running the gauntlet as a form of punishment, was still wedded to the cat o'nine tails and considered five hundred lashes a reasonable maximum; it also allowed individual commanders a free hand in disciplining their crews, with whips, canes and rope's ends. His Britannic Majesty's vessels consequently suffered from a paucity of recruits, a fair number of post-court-martial fatalities, and an excess of deserters. In addition to press-ganging merchant seamen it had begun intercepting vessels of all nations and searching them for naval runaways – a practice which was to contribute materially to the outbreak of war between Britain and the United States in 1812, and which now led to the first brush with Christophe.

Captain Warren of the *Daedalus* discovered seventeen English-men among the crew of the *Foudroyant*. These were taken back to Jamaica for service in the Royal Navy after the Haitian soldiers and sailors had been landed at Les Gonaïves. As for the *Foudroyant* itself, Admiral Dacres reported that "anticipating the wishes of their Lordships to avoid as much as possible any interference with the Blacks of St Domingo, that might occasion an enmity between us, especially while the Government think fit to permit British vessels to trade to their ports by licence, I have suffered this vessel to depart and return to Cape François." But he added that if the new vessel that Goodall was reported to have gone to fetch from London "be fallen in with at sea bound for Cape François, I shall order her to be detained for adjudication [as a prize] unless she should be furnished with a special licence for the purpose."

Since February 1806 American vessels had been forbidden by Act of Congress to trade with Saint-Domingue (though Dacres reported to the Admiralty that he had proof that Sutherland was falsifying British licences to help American merchants to evade the regulations). The result had been an increase in the British trade. Peltier submitted a note to Castlereagh in March 1808 showing that in fourteen months up to December 1807, at least eighty ships totalling 24,000 tons and manned by 2,400 seamen, had taken

British goods from London, Liverpool, Whitehaven, Bristol, Guernsey and other ports to Haiti. Many were small private ventures, such as *The Young Roscius*, but there were some large shipowners – George Geddes and Co., for instance – who had a dozen vessels in the trade.

What Peltier did not mention was that the firm of George Geddes was doing most of its business with Pétion's part of the island – its agent there was the energetic Robert Sutherland – and, because of the opportunities provided by Pétion's *laisser-faire* attitude, there was probably more British trade with the South than with the North. To stimulate this, and to gain recognition for himself, Pétion sent one of his senators, Théodat Trichet, to London in the summer of 1808. Trichet was taken under the wing of J. Staniforth, of the firm of Staniforth and Blunt, 15 New Bond Street, who wrote to Castlereagh from his home in George Street, Hanover Square, assuring him that Pétion's claims were far more weighty than Christophe's: he controlled the South Province of 120,000 inhabitants, the West of 180,000 and 40,000 of the North's total of 170,000; and twenty of the army's original twenty-eight regiments had sided with him.

The claims were exaggerated: Christophe was still in control of a large part of the West Province, and the regiments that Pétion counted in his list included several that were under strength or existed only on paper. But it was true that Pétion held a dangerously large part of the north peninsula and was able to arm and provision his troops through the magnificent harbour at Môle Saint-Nicolas. It was therefore with unaffected joy that Christophe greeted the return to Le Cap of his vice-admiral, Thomas Goodall, on September 26 in the corvette *Lord Mulgrave*, a very fast sailer pierced for 22 guns, though with only 18 mounted. It was not the 36-gun frigate that Goodall had boasted he would bring back, but it was certainly a handsome vessel. Christophe went aboard at once, to a salute of twenty-one guns, and inspected the newest and largest ship in his fleet. He was still beaming with satisfaction when he returned to shore and the *Lord Mulgrave* began to discharge the cargo for which Goodall had received his Board of Trade licence to take the ship to Haiti.

That the cargo was largely an excuse to obtain the licence and was by no means a full load was shown by the fact that the holds were completely cleared within a day and Goodall was able to take on an extra complement of sixty sailors and forty soldiers on the

28th. On the 29th the British master, mate and several other sea-men, who had known nothing of Goodall's intention to sell the ship and did not wish to serve under Christophe, were discharged. On October 1, Admiral Goodall sailed from Le Cap in his flagship, the *Lord Mulgrave*, wearing the Union Jack at the poop and the black and red of the State of Haiti at the main (the blue and red having been taken by the Republic) followed by the rest of the entire fleet: the brig *Foudroyant*, formerly *The Young Roscius*, 14 guns, 132 men; and the two schooners, *Avant-Garde* and *Province du Nord*, each of 7 guns and 65 men. The *Hopewell* had been put out of action during Goodall's absence.

They headed westward for Port-de-Paix, which had long been under severe pressure from Pétion's troops by land and was block-aded by armed merchantmen supplied to him by Sutherland and other British and American traders. At the sight of Goodall's squadron, Pétion's ships under Admiral Panayoti turned away to the west. Goodall's force chased them as far as Jean Rabel Point and then returned to Port-de-Paix to join the citizens in their celebra-tion of the raising of the blockade and the release of a brig and two schooners which had been penned in the port.

Flushed with success and the unstinted tipple poured into them by the grateful populace, the victorious mariners rolled back to their ships and boisterously resumed the pursuit of the enemy. Their enthusiasm carried them along the coast and right into the harbour of Môle Saint-Nicolas, where the four vessels tacked hazardously from side to side until the shore batteries opened fire and the drunken crews, at last realising where they were, headed smartly for the harbour mouth and back to Port-de-Paix.

It was, nevertheless, a famous victory, and one that dismayed the Jamaican merchants who saw the strengthening of the northern fleet as a threat to their trade with the South. It was they who were the first to warn Vice-Admiral Rowley, Dacres's successor at Port Royal, that Goodall had joined Christophe with the *Lord Mulgrave*; and Rowley issued confidential instructions to his captains that "in the event of any such ship making her appearance in the Bight of Léogane, you will examine her very strictly and take care that she does not violate the conditions of any licence which may have been granted to her under His Majesty's signet and sign manual for the purposes of Trade."

The first Royal Navy ship to get on to Goodall's track was the sloop *Sappho*, patrolling the north coast from Cap Saint-Nicolas to

Samana in search of privateers. She entered Môle Saint-Nicolas in the second week of October and there her captain, Commander W. Charlton, heard from the general of the southern forces the story of the strange behaviour of the *Lord Mulgrave* and her three attendant vessels a few days earlier. The general also told him that his most recent information was that the ships were at Port-de-Paix.

At daylight on the following morning [Commander Charlton reported] we weighed and stood to sea, beating to windward under the land the whole of the day, and in the evening a few minutes before sunset, being abreast of Jean Rabel, distant two leagues, we discovered from our masthead four sail coming down before the wind, and shortly after could plainly make them out to be a Ship, Brig and two Schooners, steering directly for us. I, therefore, as soon as dark, being close in under the land, tacked and laid our head off shore under the two topsails waiting their approach, having previously cleared for action; at 8 pm they were right astern of us, distant about a quarter of a mile.

Charlton and the crew of his single-masted, lightly-armed sloop, were confronted with four ships carrying a total of fifty-six guns.

An hour before daylight we bore up under easy sail, and as the day broke discerned the four sail laying to under our lee, when they likewise bore up and immediately made sail, which we did also in pursuit of them, and continued in chase running down past the Cape [Saint-Nicolas], and at a quarter past 9 am we discovered two more strange sail in the S.W. quarter, standing in towards us which proved to be His Majesty's Ship *Daedalus* and Brig *Pert*, who fetched in near enough to cut off the retreat of the flying squadron, and at 10 o'clock after firing many guns we brought the whole of them to.

From this point the captain of the *Daedalus* took charge, and Charlton concluded his report with a pardonable flourish:

I trust I may be permitted in justice to my officers and ship's company to say that, from the moment of our discovering the squadron until our bringing the whole of them to, expecting almost momentarily to be alone with them, they conducted themselves in the most cool and steady manner possible, and I am assured that had there been occasion for further hostile measures than were used, they would have displayed a rigid attention to the observation of the late gallant Admiral Lord Nelson, prior to the action of Traffalgar.

The captain of the *Daedalus*, after interrogating Admiral Goodall, decided that the *Lord Mulgrave* should be sent to Port Royal with a prize crew, and that Goodall and his British officers should go with her. The remainder of the *Lord Mulgrave's* crew were transferred to the three other Haitian vessels, which were allowed to return to Port-de-Paix. While *Sappho* convoyed her prize to Port Royal and *Daedalus* resumed her patrol, Commander Hall of the *Pert* was sent on the ungrateful errand of informing Christophe of the capture of his flagship and his vice-admiral.

The president was in a towering rage. "Are you trying to make a fool of me?" he shouted at Commander Hall. "First you capture my ship – then you have the impertinence to come and tell me what you have done!" As Hall continued with his account, Christophe's fury was diverted to Captain Warren, whom he incorrectly assumed to be still in command of the *Daedalus*. He broke off the interview, summoned a secretary, and dictated a long and indignant letter to Admiral Rowley.

My actions against those who have rebelled against legitimate authority have been paralysed by this officer; the first time by the detention of the brig *Foudroyant* at the moment when that brig was about to take several of Pétion's ships; and now in almost similar circumstances when the corvette *Lord Mulgrave*, charged with an important mission against the same rebels, was about to fulfil it.

The line of conduct pursued by Captain Warren on this occasion clearly demonstrates that he was acting less against the corvette that he seized than against the Government to which she belongs and, as the declared protector of the rebels, each time that my Forces are in a position to bring them down he intervenes to make a diversion in their favour; and he wages single-handed war against a friendly government which has never ceased giving proofs of its attachment to HM's subjects, protection to all the English traders established in its ports, and help in all cases where such help was needed. . . .

I am therefore sending to your Excellency Monsieur Simon,

Brigadier-General of the Haitian Armies, to claim in the name of the Government the State Corvette *Lord Mulgrave*, illicitly detained by HM Frigate *Daedalus*, Captain Warren, and further to beg your Excellency to order the cessation of this Captain's vexatious actions. . . .

General Simon was accompanied by Harmer Gaskell, one of the British merchants resident at the Cape, carrying an urgent "Memorial and Representation of their case" signed by himself and sixteen of his colleagues. They described the distressing situation in which they found themselves placed by the capture of the *Lord Mulgrave*, "as the whole of our persons and property in this place are held responsible for the same" and pointed out that the ships of Christophe's navy performed a useful service to British vessels by keeping away French privateers. Contrary winds, however, held up the ship on which General Simon and Mr Gaskell were travelling and they did not arrive at Jamaica until October 26.

Meanwhile, Admiral Rowley had spent a very worried week, trying to decide where his duty lay. As soon as the *Sappho* arrived at Port Royal on October 18, Commander Charlton applied for the *Lord Mulgrave* to be condemned as a prize. At the same time Goodall sent Admiral Rowley a letter complaining that "conveying a letter on his Majesty's Service to a Squadron of his ships whom I bore down on to deliver it, the *Lord Mulgrave* belonging to General Christophe was by them seized and brought to this Port."

If I had considered the Service I was in as illegal, I might have avoided them; but after having interviews with Gentlemen high in office when in England, I considered myself as acting properly, and it was generally known in England that the ship was intended to be sold in Haiti. I did sell her to the President. She was regularly cleared out at London with a King's licence for Haiti, having considerable cargo of British Manufactured Goods on board, *not contraband*, and 80 tons of Provisions for His Majesty's Navy at Antigua.

There is at Cape François, and other ports under the Government of the President, large quantities of British Property. I hope your Excellency will take into consideration the trying situation to which it may be exposed, should the ship not be restored.

Goodall had indeed been carrying a letter addressed to the commander of any Royal Naval vessel that he might meet, informing him of the capture of two British vessels by privateers and containing an offer by Christophe that as soon as his squadron had completed its present task of dealing with Pétion's ships in the Bight of Léogane, he would put it, together with 800 soldiers from Le Cap, at the disposal of the British for an attack on the privateers' nest at Samana. This offer appeared to be genuine, for it was repeated to the commander of the *Flying Fish* then moored in Le Cap roads, to whose press-gang Goodall had handed over those British members of his crew who were "fit for service", i.e., those who refused to volunteer for duty on the *Lord Mulgrave*. The suggestion that Goodall was in such a hurry to deliver his message that he had deliberately sought out the *Daedalus* and *Pert* scarcely agreed with the known fact that he had for more than twelve hours been doing his utmost to elude the *Sappho*: but his reference to the reprisals that Christophe might take from the British merchants at the Cape disquieted Rowley even though he had not yet received their memorial.

On October 20, the Advocate-General, Mr William Ross, to whom Commander Charlton's proctor had submitted the case, advised that "a question of greater delicacy and importance has, I believe, seldom occurred, since almost every point would depend upon decisions relating to the British Government's attitude towards the two rival governments of Haiti." Officially, the Advocate-General had no doubt, Haiti was merely an enemy colony in revolt against its own government; but in practice it had in certain respects been recognised by the British government as independent. If it were still an enemy colony, then the *Lord Mulgrave* was a legal prize and Goodall a traitor who had taken service with His Majesty's enemies. If it were an independent state, the ship was not liable to seizure, but Goodall should still have been aware that, by taking service with Christophe, he would be called on to molest British vessels trading with Pétion. The Advocate-General accordingly recommended "that the most prompt measures should be taken to send the *Lord Mulgrave* to England, with Mr Goodall and two or three of his principal officers, under the charge of a Prize Master."

This course of action did not recommend itself to the admiral. It meant a delay of several months and also entailed the risk that the *Lord Mulgrave* might be lost by storms or captured by the French. Rowley would then find himself held responsible for the loss, by the Admiralty and the ships' companies of the *Sappho*, *Daedalus* and

Pert if she were eventually adjudged an enemy vessel, and by Christophe if she were not. "Considering the violent disposition of General Christophe, I was not without apprehension that in consequence of the detention of this ship he would resort to violent measures against the persons and property of his Majesty's subjects trading in that part of St Domingo acknowledging his authority." The admiral consequently sent the papers to King's House, to the Governor of Jamaica, the Duke of Manchester, with a request for his opinion.

The duke sent him in return an extract from the secret instructions that he had received when given his appointment. This stated that "the contending Parties between the Black Chiefs of St Domingo seem by late accounts to be so nearly balanced, and their alternate successes and defeats so frequent, that no judgement can be here formed with regard to the form of Government in which that Island will ultimately repose. The two Heads of the contending Parties, Christophe and Pétion, have equally sent overtures for the effectuating an alliance with His Majesty; but it has hitherto been thought expedient to decline any engagement with either or to depart from the strictest neutrality. I am to instruct your Grace to follow this line of caution; you will take care that no supplies of ammunition or arms shall be sent from the Island of Jamaica and that all persons trading thither do abstain from taking part with either Chieftain, confining themselves to their duties as Traders and doing nothing which shall make them forfeit the good will of either, or subject His Majesty's Government to any responsibility. . . ."

This, beyond informing Rowley that Goodall's activities were unlikely to please the government, gave him no help. He made a new bundle of the papers, added the Duke of Manchester's letter and his enclosure, and sent them all off, on October 21, to Henry John Hinchcliffe, asking for his opinion.

Mr Hinchcliffe, who was the judge of the Vice-Admiralty Court, excused himself from pronouncing on the case before it ever came into court, but added:

I cannot conceive that His Majesty's Ministers should intend to sanction so extraordinary a measure as the equipment of this vessel in England for the use of Christophe, to be directly employed against Pétion, nor to suffer . . . that either party should be authorized to engage in their service adventurers of any nation with vessels of such force as that which Mr Goodall appears to command.

Mr Hinchcliffe agreed with the Advocate-General that the best plan was to send the ship, with Mr Goodall and his officers, back to England.

On October 22, Rowley received a letter from Goodall, who had been allowed to return to his quarters on the *Lord Mulgrave*, appealing to him to hand the ship back to Christophe and asking that:

> Your Excellency might take into consideration that General Christophe is an Englishman, and Pétion a decided Frenchman. That the former is devoted to the Flag he was born under, and never had a greater gratification than when he could be of Service to it, and see in his ports His Majesty's Ships, where they are treated with hospitality and magnificence.
>
> For God's sake, for the sake of humanity, let me entreat your Excellency to restore the Ship.

It is difficult to believe that Goodall had more loyalty to Christophe or his cause than any other mercenary, but the letter impressed Admiral Rowley sufficiently for him to ask the Advocate-General to study the case once more and again give an opinion on whether the *Lord Mulgrave* was liable for seizure. Mr Ross replied on October 23 that "if this vessel is to be considered as merely the property of Christophe . . . I am strongly inclined to think there is not that complete hostile character affixed to the present Establishment at Haiti, in relation to the British Government, as can afford any strong ground to expect that a vessel, proved to belong to Christophe, would incur condemnation in the Vice-Admiralty Court."

Pressed to say straight out whether Rowley might return her to Christophe or not, he said: "It being suggested that circumstances may render it inexpedient to send the *Lord Mulgrave* to England, there does not occur any impediment to the restoration of the vessel – at the same time it may be proper to remark that Mr Goodall should not be permitted to accompany her, but should be put in a situation to answer to the British Government for his conduct."

With a sigh of relief, Admiral Rowley put Goodall and his five

British officers on board HM sloop *Raven*, with orders to its captain, Commander Grant, to take them to England "to be dealt with as His Majesty's Government may be pleased to direct, they having been found in arms in the service of General Christophe, and you are to take particular care that they do not escape, and that they are not allowed to have communication with any persons from the shore without my authority." Commander Charlton and his crew, deprived of the share of the prize-money that they had hoped for, had the mortifying task of escorting the *Lord Mulgrave* back to Le Cap, taking with them General Simon and Mr Gaskell who had just arrived at Port Royal on a mission that was no longer necessary.

The weary Admiral Rowley, reporting all these events to the Admiralty, concluded his letter: "as I have not hitherto been furnished with any instructions, with respect to the manner in which it is the intention of His Majesty's Government the Parties contending for supreme authority in St Domingo should be treated, I request that their Lordships will be pleased to transmit to me, by the earliest conveyance, such as they may think necessary for my future guidance."

Goodall arrived at Plymouth in January 1809, and was held prisoner with his officers on board the *Raven* while Castlereagh, to whom the Lords of the Admiralty had passed the· papers, took counsels' opinion on what could be done with them. Senator Trichet lodged protests on Pétion's behalf that Britain was allowing Christophe to obtain men-o'-war and arms that she denied to his rival. Messrs Nicholl, Gibbs and Plumer of Lincoln's Inn advised that it would be possible to proceed against Goodall for having entered a foreign service "after a Proclamation which was as we understand duly issued and published whereby all His Majesty's Seamen were required to withdraw themselves from such engagements and return to the Service of their own Country." But, they added, "we do not recollect any instance of such a Prosecution and whether it be advisable under the Circumstances of the Present Case to proceed criminally against Captain Goodall must be left to the consideration and wisdom of His Majesty's Government."

The number of white mercenaries employed on both sides continued to increase, not in the land forces, where the Haitians were fully experienced, but at sea. While searching merchant vessels, Admiral Rowley's captains found documentary proof that during the previous summer the *Arrow* of Kingston, Jamaica, had shelled Christophe's troops outside Port-au-Prince; that recently the *Queen* of London and the *Ino* of Guernsey had been rearmed by Pétion and, voluntarily or not, used to convey reinforcements to Môle Saint-Nicolas; and that Christophe's envoy in Philadelphia – Toussaint's former treasurer, Bunel – was busy engaging seamen and supervising the fitting-out of a corvette for the northern fleet, which had also recently been augmented by the purchase of a 250-ton brig, the *Enterprise*, from Mr D'Arcy, one of the English merchants at Le Cap.

Christophe, writing to Bunel in March 1809, told him that "not having enough twelve-pounder cannon to arm the corvette . . . I beg you to arrange that its construction shall be such as to bear 20 twenty-four pounders instead of the 10 twenty-four pounders and 10 twelve-pounders. – You will oblige me by sending at the first opportunity 20lb of camphor, a quantity of sarsaparilla and some sassafras." These were evidently for domestic use, like the thousands of white and slate-grey marble slabs one foot square for which he asked Bunel a fortnight earlier, and which doubtless went to embellish the Palace which he was building in the place d'Armes. It was about this time that Christophe, having rapidly progressed through "Your Excellency" and "Monseigneur", began to have himself referred to in official communications as "His Highness the President" – probably more with the intention of staying ahead of Pétion than of catching up with the crowned heads of Europe. He was well aware of his countrymen's need of glitter and parade; his houses became palaces, his titles became more royal, his person was surrounded with more and more ceremony, his troops, whether in victory or defeat, remained smarter, better uniformed, better disciplined than those of Pétion. He was himself growing in stature and confidence. Where Pétion begged favours from the British Government, Christophe demanded that he should be accorded his rights. The dignity and dignities for which he strove were not for him alone but for every coloured soul in Haiti.

4

With Pétion's supporters still in control of a large part of the north peninsula, supplied and reinforced by sea through Môle Saint-Nicolas, Christophe had as great a need as ever to increase the size of his fleet. Goodall, released from the *Raven*, was seeking more vessels in London, where he had boldly resumed his Haitian rank and as 'Admiral Goodall' attended the Royal Humane Society dinner at the City of London Tavern on April 26, 1809, and promised an annual subscription of 20 guineas from Christophe. On Goodall's advice, Christophe bought the condemned 290-ton British sloop *Beaver* and rechristened her the *Haytienne,* but in December his navy was still inferior to Pétion's in ships and guns (7 ships, 1,570 tons, 1,029 men, 112 guns, against 10 ships, 2,010 tons, 1,028 men, 155 guns). Christophe daily awaited the arrival of the 730-ton corvette of 24 guns that Bunel had ordered in Baltimore; Pétion, on the other hand, had just bought a former East Indiaman, the *Duke of Montrose,* 970 tons, in New York, and was planning to arm her with 44 guns.

All these preparations prompted the British merchants at Le Cap and Port-au-Prince to renew their demands for the appointment of a consul or agent to protect their interests, but the government still refused to accord recognition to either side, or even to both, although trade with Haiti had been freed from restrictions by the order in council of December 14, 1808. Warships from the Jamaica station made frequent calls at Haitian ports for their commanders to keep watch on the treatment of British traders and were regularly assured that all was going well.

In March 1810 Christophe broached the ticklish subject of imposing a blockade of his own to Captain Charlton, formerly of the *Sappho,* and now of the *Garland,* who was making a routine call at the Cape after escorting the *Windsor Castle* packet through the Windward Passage on her return voyage from Kingston, Jamaica, to Falmouth. Christophe opened the conversation by complaining that the British were helping Pétion by fitting out vessels of war for him in Jamaica. He then pointed out that his forces controlled the approaches to Môle Saint-Nicolas by both land and sea and that he therefore considered himself entitled under international law to declare the port in a state of actual blockade. He protested that British vessels were still bringing in supplies for his "rebellious enemies and subjects" – and remarked that if his own ships prevented their doing so, there might well be loss of life and damage to property.

"And I wonder whether I should not feel perfectly justified in taking such action," he continued, as if thinking aloud. He spoke always in French, though his English was good, perhaps to allow himself time to think during the translation. He had appointed as his official interpreter his former secretary of state, Dupuy, an intelligent, mild-mannered mulatto, who returned to Haiti after making a good deal of money in America during Toussaint's governorship and had saved Christophe's life by warning him to stay away from Dessalines on a plea of ill health. Before Dupuy could begin his translation, Charlton who was sufficiently acquainted with French not to need his services, warned Christophe that any interference with a British subject "in either his person or his property" would result in the most unpleasant consequences. He added that if Christophe were claiming the right to blockade, he should discuss it with Admiral Rowley.

Christophe did not pursue the subject immediately, for within a few days he received news which posed urgent problems for both himself and Rowley. From Philadelphia, Bunel reported that Rigaud, still the most influential of the mulatto leaders, had arrived from Bordeaux in the American merchantman *Lovely Matilda* on March 7 and was preparing to leave for Port-au-Prince, where it was intended that he should take over command of the army while Pétion confined himself to the civil government. Rouanez, who had succeeded Dupuy as Christophe's secretary of state, informed Peltier in London, and Peltier passed the news on to Lord Liverpool. At the same time Rowley, having received similar information from Bond, the British Consul in Philadelphia, ordered his commanders to search all ships and seize Rigaud, who was understood to be travelling under the name of Dublin or Fillette. But the warnings had come too late. On April 23 Commander Evans of the sloop *Satellite* called at Les Cayes and learned that Rigaud had landed there a few days before and had gone straight to Port-au-Prince to meet Pétion, who at once appointed him governor of the South Province.

Christophe now set up a great clamour that Rigaud had been sent by Bonaparte for two purposes: to help Pétion win back the North Province and then establish the whole of the former colony as the base for an attack on Jamaica, using the battle-seasoned troops who now totalled between thirty and forty thousand; and to give aid to the French garrisons of the former Spanish part of the island where, since Bonaparte had foisted his brother Joseph on to the throne of Spain, the colonists led by the governor, Juan Sanchez, were struggling to eject them. Pétion argued that Rigaud, having been banished from Saint-Domingue by Leclerc and held in prison by Bonaparte, was a convinced enemy of the French. To this Christophe replied that Bonaparte would never have released him had not Rigaud agreed to serve France in the West Indies. He added that while the North was actively aiding Sanchez against the French with supplies of arms and ammunition, Pétion had significantly done nothing to embarrass the French.

Christophe realised that the British would be unwilling to quarrel with him at this moment. He chose it to make the first move in his proposed blockade of the ports held by Pétion. In May 1810 his fleet captured the *Crown*, of London, as it was attempting to enter Môle Saint-Nicolas. It was taken under escort to Port-de-Paix where its cargo was confiscated and sold and the ship held for several weeks before being allowed to sail for Port-au-Prince. Immediately upon its arrival there, Robert H. Windsor, the merchant who had chartered it, took the first available boat to Jamaica to complain to Admiral Rowley of the loss suffered by his partner, Archibald Kane, and himself. Their bill was large and detailed.

The *Crown*'s cargo, when it was despatched from London by Messrs Greaves, Sharp and Fisher, was valued at £26,431 18s 8d. The vessel sailed directly to Port-au-Prince, where Kane unloaded part of the cargo, put some flour and other provisions aboard, and then sent it to Môle Saint-Nicolas. The remaining cargo, when it was seized by Christophe, was cloth in the form of bales of Checks, Osnaburgs and Sheetings, valued at £4,857 3s 5d – 21,471 dollars and 45 cents, with the dollar reckoned at a little over 4s 6d. Kane and Windsor's anticipated profit of fifty per cent on this brought the value to 32,126 dollars and 17½ cents. To this was added the value of the stores shipped at Port-au-Prince: 1,345 barrels of flour at 14 dollars; 71 barrels of beef at 16 dollars; 89 barrels of pork at 20 dollars; and two months' charter fee of the vessel at £800 a month. The total came to more than sixty thousand dollars; and the indignation of Messrs Kane and Windsor was enhanced by the fact that they had learned that HMS *Hyperion* had stopped and boarded the *Crown* after her capture, but had allowed Christophe's fleet to proceed with her in custody.

Admiral Rowley, who had received a report from Captain Thomas Brodie of the *Hyperion*, promised to send an officer to demand the restitution of the cargo – or of its value, since it had already been sold – but added that "as I understand General Christophe has said that documents were found on board the *Crown* which proved that the Provisions were shipped by order, and for the account of, the chief to whom he is opposed, I am not sanguine that my application in your favour will be attended with success, and I therefore recommend that you should transmit authentic proofs of property to England and solicit the interference of His Majesty's Government." This they did, backed by a memorial drawn up by the egregious Robert Sutherland and signed by himself and twenty other British merchants, protesting at the extent to which Christophe had been permitted to build up his fleet. "The naval force of Pétion is commanded and manned by natives of his part of the island and has hitherto respected the British flag, and the flags of all other nations," they claimed. On the other hand, "the armed vessels of Christophe are commanded and manned by white men, renegades of all countries, and capture and condemn British, American and Spanish vessels and property."

Christophe had called the British navy's bluff. His fleet was for the moment in control of the territorial waters in the northern part of the island. In July he demonstrated his confidence in his command of the sea and also one of the more pleasing sides of his character. André-Juste-Borno Lamarre, the most distinguished of Pétion's generals and the man who had successfully defied Christophe's determined efforts to drive the Republicans out of the northern peninsula, was killed by a cannonball during one of the frequent attacks on Môle Saint-Nicolas from the landward side. ·When the news reached Christophe he ordered the whole of his fleet to sail to the entrance of the harbour. There, with colours at halfmast, they fired a ceremonial salute to his brave enemy. This grand gesture was followed by another. "Considering that the name of the town of Le Cap has not been changed since the Expulsion of the French and the Independence of Haiti," he announced on July 30, 1810, "and that the denomination of Cap-François was given it by foreigners", the capital of the State of Haiti was henceforth to be called Cap-Henry. This was scarcely dictated by the desire to bolster the morale of his fellow citizens; it began to appear that His Highness the President might be suffering from delusions of grandeur.

Pétion, apprehensive about the success of Christophe's naval forces, was also beginning to suspect that Rigaud intended to push him out of the presidency. He accordingly asked one of the British merchants at Port-au-Prince, William Doran, to renew the entreaties for recognition by the British government. Doran was very ready to comply with this request, since he and his fellow merchants in the South now faced two threats to their commerce – if Christophe's progress were not halted he might soon blockade all the ports through which they traded, and if the British government did not soon come to an agreement with Pétion he might decide to grant the Americans preferential terms instead. For the embargo that Congress had placed on trade with Saint-Domingue in 1806 and renewed in 1807 and 1808 had been allowed to lapse in 1809. Some Americans had continued to trade with the island under various covers (Robert Windsor, for instance, was American, though his partner, Kane, was British) and they might all now be expected to extend the contacts that they had made before the embargo.

Doran, who arrived in London late in July and put up at the St James's Hotel in Jermyn Street, pointed out in a letter to Lord Liverpool that formerly:

> The trade . . . was monopolized by the Americans, whose neutrality enabled them to dispose of [the island's] produce of 40 or 50 million pounds of coffee per annum in the European continental markets, at prices which prevented all competition on the part of British merchants and planters. The restrictions imposed by their Government at the desire of the French ruler, their embargo and non-intercourse laws, together with His Majesty's most gracious Order in Council of the 14th December 1808, at length put us in possession of this branch of commerce. . .
>
> We have had . . . till the late removal of the American commercial restrictions, the exclusive trade of the country. It has employed a considerable amount of British Tonnage and Capital; and, since the capitulation of Guadeloupe, has given us the monopoly of nearly all the coffee produced in the world.

Doran claimed that Pétion could "terminate the war whenever he pleases" but shrank from spilling more blood. He asked the British Government to restore and guarantee peace in the island in return for exclusive trade with the Republic and reduced tariffs.

The offer was too generous to have come from the strength that Pétion claimed. His anxiety to ensure some of his power before either Christophe or Rigaud succeeded in depriving him of all of it was made abundantly clear with the arrival of another of his emissaries, André Langlade, at the Globe Tavern in Fleet Street on September 21.

Pétion has charged me to inform you [Langlade wrote to Doran] that in the event of your not succeeding in obtaining the mediation of His Majesty's ministers for the re-establishment of peace between him and General Christophe, you should strive at least to obtain a decision from the British Government on the plan which he confided to you and which you strongly approved: viz. to subject the sovereignty of Haiti to His Britannic Majesty under his guarantee of the liberty and property of its inhabitants. . . . Except for the introduction of white troops, which should not take place without the consent of the representatives of the people, the President leaves to your judgement everything concerning the minor arrangements, in the certainty that your local and general knowledge puts you in a position to arrange everything for the best. . . .

This was an extraordinary proposal and a clear indication of the extent of Pétion's panic. He was prepared to surrender his country's sovereignty in order to keep himself in authority. It had been unlikely that Christophe would agree to mediation; it was impossible that he would agree to this.

He was indeed full of confidence, as Commander Lillicrap of HM sloop *Dispatch* discovered when he called at the rechristened Cap-Henry on August 24 to deliver Rowley's letter demanding the return of the *Crown*'s cargo, or the payment of its value. Christophe was away at the palace of Sans-Souci that he was building at Millot and Lillicrap had to wait until the next day for his return. When the audience was finally granted it was stormy from the outset. This may have been because Lillicrap was in a bad humour at having been kept waiting (he reported incorrectly to Rowley that the delay was for "several days") or it may have been because Christophe rightly suspected that Lillicrap was one of the British officers whom Robert Sutherland had won over by lavish wining and dining at Port-au-Prince and who were used, though they did not realise it, to provide Pétion with information on what was going on in Christophe's territory.

Whatever the reason, when Lillicrap informed Christophe that he had come to demand restitution of the cargo and had documents which he believed would prove the illegality of the seizure, Christophe bristled and answered roughly: "I am convinced it was a legal seizure, from the letters found on board of her, and I will not look at any other papers you have to produce."

Lillicrap, his face mantling at this rebuff, asked Christophe if he considered the Môle in a state of blockade.

"I do," Christophe snapped, "and I will thank you to tell the admiral from me that it is blockaded by land and sea by my forces, and no vessel whatever shall enter." Lowering his voice, but speaking sufficiently distinctly and slowly for Lillicrap to catch every word in French, Christophe said to the interpreter, Dupuy: "For two pins I would send his dispatch back to him." He swung round to Lillicrap and continued: "I have nothing more to say to you – I shall correspond directly with the British Government on the subject."

Lillicrap stood his ground, flushed pink face glowering at gleaming brown face. "Sir," he said, "the British Government will not notice any dispatch from you upon the point in question unless it goes through the proper channel, and that must be by the Commander-in-Chief."

Christophe glared at him for a moment and then strode out of the room; but the next morning, before he was ready to sail, Lillicrap received a message from Dupuy asking him to call again at the palace, where he was handed a letter that Christophe had written to Admiral Rowley.

I recall having already remarked to you in reply to one of your previous letters [Christophe wrote to Rowley] that you had been deceived in regard to the assertion that I had enticed subjects of His Britannic Majesty in order to detain them by force in my services on the ships of my squadron. You have now been strangely misled in the affair of the ship *Crown*, the value of whose cargo you ask to be returned. . . . I have unequivocal proof that the whole of this cargo, culled from several American cargoes, has been negotiated directly by the rebels for their accomplices at the Môle, and loaded into an English vessel to gain its protection. . . .

Neither is it inappropriate to tell you, Sir, that the captain, Robert Howland, who delivered to me all the . . . documents which were given him by the rebels . . . declared to me that on arrival off the Môle for the first time he was unable to enter because my Squadron was blockading that rebel town; and that on returning to Port-aux-Crimes, he was forced to go back again by the said Kane. . . . Thus this alleged claim is illusory and chimerical. The cargo of the ship *Crown*, clearly admitted to belong to the rebels, has been confiscated and condemned as a fair prize. The ship, admitted to be British, has been released; the personal property of the captain and his crew has been respected as belonging to a nation whom I pride myself on considering a friend.

The tone of the letter, firm and even aggressive, indicated Christophe's confidence. There had been a time when the white men had addressed him as 'Monsieur' refusing him the title of 'General'; now he had progressed beyond military titles and would make it clear to this mere admiral that he was president of a sovereign state. To emphasise the disparity in their stations he did not sign the letter himself, leaving that duty to his private secretary, Brigadier Prévost. There was one other point of interest for Rowley in the letter – Christophe had changed not only the name of his own capital but that of Pétion's as well: Port-au-Prince, rechristened Port-Républicain by the revolutionaries, was henceforth Port-aux-Crimes in all Christophe's letters and announcements, a name that had first been given it fifteen years before by the mulattos because of the maltreatment that they had received there from the whites.

Christophe had recently bought a former French frigate, the *Félicité*, which had been put up as a prize at Kingston, Jamaica, and named her *Améthyste* in honour of his elder daughter. Pétion had also obtained a ship of the line and a brig from America but, having lost four vessels in recent battles, he no longer had superiority at sea – and was now to lose his last foothold on the north peninsula. On October 10 Commander Lillicrap reported to Rowley from Port-au-Prince that Môle Saint-Nicolas had fallen and that "General Christophe caused every person in the place to be put to death". This lie, which Lillicrap too readily accepted from his congenial host, Robert Sutherland, was corrected at the end of the month by Captain Wooldridge of the *Rainbow*, who discovered that only one man had been executed at the Môle – a deserter from Christophe's army.

Having cleared the north peninsula, Christophe began preparations for an attack on the Republic; and as soon as this became apparent Rigaud launched his own attempt to overthrow Pétion. At the beginning of November he declared martial law at Les Cayes and proclaimed himself sovereign ruler of the South Province. He was joined by two generals from Port-au-Prince and, after raising funds by imposing a levy of 500 dollars on every foreign merchant in the province, he moved at the head of his troops to the town of Aquin, while Pétion sent 2,000 loyal troops to face him at Miragoane, twenty miles away on the other side of the peninsula.

It was now that Rigaud's earlier harsh treatment of the Negroes told against him. The Black troops whom the two mulatto generals had brought to support him from Port-au-Prince mutinied and, when Pétion arrived at Miragoane to take command on December 1, he found that his Black supporters had grown from 2,000 to 6,000. Rigaud was left with less than half this number and these, when summoned to surrender by one of Pétion's generals, promptly grounded their arms and began cheering. Rigaud very sensibly assured Pétion that the whole affair had been a foolish misunderstanding and was ordered to retire to his estates. Pétion returned to Port-au-Prince to prepare for the anticipated attack from Christophe. Christophe called upon the citizens of the Republic to have done with their disobedience and to accept the unification of Haiti – under his presidency – and, as he must have expected, received no reply; and Rigaud, after a short time in retreat, returned to his former post as Governor of the South Province.

In London, the waves set up by Christophe's blockade rippled up Whitehall. The Admiralty forwarded the documents that Admiral Rowley had sent them on the *Crown* affair to Lord Liverpool; a group of merchants trading to Port-au-Prince, headed by Staniforth and Blunt, submitted a memorial to the Privy Council, begging the government to take steps to prevent Christophe from blockading any other Haitian ports; and the Committee of the Privy Council for Trade and Foreign Plantations acquainted Robert Peel, for the information of the Earl of Liverpool, that in their opinion "the Order in Council of December 14, 1808, was an indirect and qualified recognition of the Independence of Haiti"; that "this order did not secure, nor could be construed as holding out any assurance of security to, vessels trading under the said order, or their cargoes, from the consequences attendant upon the intestine war, to which it was well known by all British merchants embarking in this trade, that they must necessarily be exposed; and that in the case of the *Crown*, not only did the merchants at Port-au-Prince know that the Môle was blockaded, but the cargo that they were attempting to deliver was provisions for the garrison and not part of the original cargo exported from Britain."

The committee arrived at its decision on December 27. Long

before news of it reached Cap-Henry, Christophe had arrived at his own. On December 30 he issued a proclamation:

> Having employed all the means of conciliation in my power, to put an end to the calamities of the Rebellion that has so long afflicted part of the West and South of this State,
>
> Desiring to curb the cupidity of certain foreigners who profit from the misfortunes of this land, by procuring for the Dissidents the means of continuing in their Rebellion,
>
> I declare in a State of Blockade all those Ports which are still in the Possession of the Rebels and which are now blockaded by my Squadrons, and against which I am directing my land forces.
>
> I consequently order my Admiral and other naval officers to take and capture, until the Revolt is crushed, all commercial vessels, of whatever nation they may be, which attempt to enter into any of the said Ports and to send them before the legal authority to be judged and condemned in accordance with the law of nations and the principles accepted in similar circumstances by civilised nations.

This outright defiance of the British government created as much alarm among the British merchants at Cap-Henry as among those at Port-au-Prince. They foresaw that if the Royal Navy broke Christophe's blockade, they were likely to be the first victims of his wrath.

> As we have a number of English merchants who trade to that part as well as to this, some misunderstanding will be unavoidable if an insult is offered to the British flag [they wrote to Admiral Rowley]. We . . . pray your Excellency, if such should be the case, that before the insult is revenged, you will have the goodness to send sufficient force to take us away, and all other British subjects that may be found here, otherwise our lives and property will be in the utmost danger. . . . We fully rely upon you for that assistance which every Englishman has a right to claim from his country. . . .

Trouble was not long in coming. At the end of January, Captain Brodie in the *Hyperion* called at Les Gonaïves, where a note was brought to him from Richard Simpson, a British merchant, asking for his protection and a passage in the *Hyperion* to Port-au-Prince. Simpson explained that he had sailed from Kingston, Jamaica, to

Jérémie, intending to collect money due to him at Port-au-Prince on a cargo with which he had come out from England. The vessel had been captured by one of Christophe's warships before arriving at Jérémie and he had been taken to Les Gonaïves, where he was placed in the custody of another British merchant, Matthew O'Brien. Letters and parcels that he had been carrying were taken from him and he had not been able to get them returned; neither had he been allowed to leave the town.

Brodie succeeded in smuggling Simpson on board, despite the close watch that was kept on him and the quayside guard which examined all boats going out to the *Hyperion*. The following day, February 1, the *Commandant de la Place* demanded Simpson's return, having heard of his escape from O'Brien. When Brodie went ashore to discuss the matter he was surrounded by the foreign merchants, led by O'Brien, who begged him to hand over the fugitive for fear of the reprisals that would fall on them. Simpson, on hearing of this, volunteered to return to O'Brien's custody.

All now seemed to have passed off harmoniously even though Simpson's personal problem had not been resolved, but on February 2 there was unexpected tragedy. Captain Brodie was in the town being entertained by the merchants when Mr Dillon, the officer in charge of the ship's launch, burst into the room. Dillon had been sent ashore earlier that day to procure fresh meat. He told Brodie that, after buying some bullocks, he had been returning with them to the *Hyperion* when the battery at Fort Castries had opened fire on the boat and three seamen had been killed.

Brodie at once went to protest to the district commander, General Raphaël, who made enquiries and then offered Brodie his apologies. He explained that, after Simpson's escape, orders had been given to stop all boats. The shot from Fort Castries had been intended to fall ahead of the *Hyperion*'s launch, not into it. Raphaël then placed the officer in charge of the battery and the *Commandant de la Place* in close arrest. Brodie, believing this explanation to be genuine, accepted it and even requested that the Town Major should be released from custody. The three seamen were buried with full military honours from the garrison and it was not until February 17, when he returned to Port Royal at the end of his ten-week cruise, that Brodie reported the incident to Admiral Rowley. The Admiral at once reprimanded him for not having taken a firmer attitude and for having been satisfied with anything less than a written apology.

Rowley was the more incensed because it was only a week before that he had received a copy of Christophe's proclamation of blockade. He had ordered Commander Henry Montresor of the sloop *Sapphire* to cruise in the Bight of Léogane and, if he found any British vessels detained by Christophe's cruisers, to demand their release; but – proof that the Admiral was himself unsure of his ground and of what support he might receive from Whitehall – "although in demanding the said vessels you are to use every means in your power to procure their liberation, without resorting to force, you are not to have recourse to that measure until you receive further directions, but to report your proceedings by the earliest opportunity to me." He intended to send the *Thalia* to join the *Sapphire* on her protective patrols, but by the time she was ready for sea Brodie had arrived and Rowley decided instead to send the *Thalia* with his senior captain, James G. Vashon, to demand an explanation from Christophe.

As soon as he heard of the tragedy at Les Gonaïves, Christophe ordered Simpson to be released from house arrest and sent back to Jamaica, where Rowley questioned him on board his new flagship, *Polyphemus*. Learning that he had been sailing in a ship falsely carrying Spanish colours, Rowley commented that "his imprudence is not to be justified". However, the merchants of Jamaica as well as Haiti, were in an uproar and the *Jamaica Courant* loosed a broadside against Whitehall and the navy, particularly complaining of "the growing piratical strength of our revolted neighbour. . . . "

Every man of common information in this Community, is sensible, we presume, of the injury, that by one dash, and in one night, in midst of all our naval force on this Station, the fleets of those rebels might do. . . . Every day we have in this harbour too many vessels with crews from the revolted part of St Domingue; and these persons are already disseminating corrupt principles among the sable inhabitants.

The letter which Vashon carried from Rowley to "General Christophe" was the more stern because of the pressure he was under. He expressed his "indignation and surprise" at the "outrageous Acts of Violence" committed on the three sailors and Simpson, complained that this was "not the first time that officers under your orders have shown a disposition to treat the British Flag with disrespect", and demanded that Christophe should "refrain hereafter from giving the least interruptuon whatever to British vessels employed in a Trade which His Majesty has been pleased to authorize."

Captain Vashon arrived off Cap-Henry ten days later, but a dead calm and poor light prevented him from getting into the harbour before the following afternoon, March 6. The audience that Christophe granted him was even more heated than the one with Lillicrap. When the translation of Rowley's letter was read to him, Christophe told Vashon that he was surprised to receive it.

"I lament the unfortunate affair of the British seamen as much as Admiral Rowley does," he said, "but it was an accident and has been most satisfactorily explained to the admiral by Captain Brodie." He told the interpreter to give Vashon a copy of a pamphlet that had been found among Simpson's belongings and continued: "The *Hyperion* cannot have arrived at Port-Royal before you left, otherwise Admiral Rowley would have been satisfied with the explanations already given to Captain Brodie. You have heard of the blockade?"

Vashon replied that, on the contrary, Brodie *had* arrived and it was just because the admiral was *not* satisfied with the explanations that he had sent the *Thalia* on her present mission. Knowing from gossip and from Christophe's reactions that he understood English perfectly well, Vashon read aloud a note which he had already written, and then handed it to the interpreter and took his leave. The note was even more aggressive than the admiral's letter.

Sir,

As Captain in His Brittanic Majesty's Navy, I do agreeably to my orders call upon you, for the *explanation* and *reparation* demanded in the letter I now deliver into your own hands from Admiral Rowley, Commander-in-Chief of His Majesty's Ships and Vessels of war etc., etc., for the acts of violence therein complained of.

His Majesty's frigate, under my command, will wait a reasonable time for your answer, which I hope, and am willing to believe, will be satisfactory to the Admiral.

The next morning, Dupuy brought Vashon a letter which, to his great annoyance, he discovered to be sealed – thus reducing him from the status of an envoy who read stern rebukes to that of a mere messenger. He told Dupuy that a sealed letter would not do and that he must have another interview with Christophe. After waiting for two days, during which no invitation came, he went to the Presidential Palace and demanded an audience. It was a foolish thing to do, inviting a snub which he duly received: a message was sent out informing him that the president was too busy to see him.

Christophe, however, realised that if he was going to be involved in a quarrel with the British he should not begin by cold-shouldering a mere captain. The following morning Vashon received a note saying that the president would see him at three o'clock that afternoon. He arrived promptly at the palace and was kept waiting long enough to indicate Christophe's displeasure and to rouse his own temper. When the president appeared Vashon ignored the interpreter and told Christophe in English that he had come to ask for a copy of the letter to Rowley, and to hear Christophe's own account of what he had done to satisfy the admiral's demands.

Without waiting for Dupuy to translate what Vashon said, and thus confirming Vashon's impression that he understood English perfectly well, Christophe replied disdainfully in French: "I have given Admiral Rowley my answer and that is enough." Then, with his eyes flashing:

"What do you want, Captain Vashon? Have you something to say against me or my country?"

"Nothing," said Vashon, "further than what the Admiral has mentioned in his letter to you – and it will be to your interest not to let me quit the Cape ignorant of the explanation and reparation I have received."

Christophe turned on his heel and, with a snort of contempt, made for the door.

"I desire you to hear that which I consider it my duty to tell you," Vashon continued, raising his voice.

Christophe swung round and began to reply, raising his own. It was almost an exact repetition of the scene with Commander Lillicrap, the two men scowling at each other, the white man's face growing redder with rage, the Black man's darker, only their overweening sense of their own importance prevented them from screaming at each other.

"I urge you to listen to me," Vashon protested. Christophe turned on his heel once more and strode out of the room. Vashon ordered the interpreter to go and bring his master back – an idea

that caused Dupuy to shake with fear. He would not even agree to
deliver a message from Vashon, who stormed back to his ship and
sent Christophe another letter, repeating his protests and con-
cluding:

I shall forward your sealed answer to Admiral Rowley with all
possible dispatch, acquainting him of my total ignorance as to the
contents, whether satisfactory or not, and at the same time
represent that your very disrespectful carriage to me was too
glaring to be submitted to with impunity by any British officer.

Vashon waited a day for a reply, but none came. He sailed westward to Cap Saint-Nicolas, and then down to join the *Sapphire* on
the anti-blockade patrol, sending his reports back from Port-au-
Prince, together with Christophe's reply and a letter from Harmer
Gaskell, on behalf of the Cap-Henry merchants, informing Admiral
Rowley that they assessed the value of the British property there
at a little over a million dollars, which "I look upon, as well as ourselves, to be in a state of security, so long as no very severe
measures are resorted to. I hope the answer to the dispatches
brought by Captain Vashon will prove satisfactory, in which case
our business here will go on as usual, but if anything disagreeable
should take place, we have only to repeat our wish to be enabled to
get away, although we should be obliged to abandon all our
property."

Christophe's reply was signed by Rouanez, the secretary of
state, on behalf of "Son Altesse Sérénissime, Monseigneur le
Président". It rejected all Rowley's arguments and accused
Simpson – apparently with justice – of having been caught while
taking to Port-au-Prince from Jamaica, where they had been
printed on Robert Sutherland's orders, bundles of libellous
pamphlets attacking Christophe. It protested that the death of the
three British seamen had been an accident which had been explained
to Captain Brodie's complete satisfaction. It finally complained that
"His Serene Highness could rightly be displeased with the parti-
ality and favour accorded to the rebels of the Southern group in
their illegal commerce with Jamaica. His Serene Highness has unequivocal proofs that this is increasing because of the licences that
are granted with an excessive indulgence." This dispatch was
followed a few days later by another, brought by Harmer Gaskell,
complaining of the second letter that Vashon had written to

Christophe. "Monseigneur le Président has charged me," Rouanez wrote, "to send you this offensive and insulting letter, in the hope that you will give him the satisfaction that he has a right to expect."

Christophe's annoyance at the magisterial way in which Vashon had tried to deal with him was increased by another factor, quite irrelevant to the squabble with the British. He had just learned that Pétion had been re-elected President of the Republic for a further four-year term, thus rejecting Christophe's offer to amalgamate the two states under his own presidency. Meanwhile, Pétion was still persevering with his attempts to get the British government to impose peace on both parties, allowing each to retain the territory it held; or alternatively to submit one or both parts to British rule. William Doran reminded Lord Liverpool about the proposal on March 13, 1811 and John Goff of Staniforth and Blunt was at that moment on his way to London from Haiti with a restatement of the offer from Pétion.

Whether the immediate impulse sprang from the rejection of his peace proposals and the re-election of Pétion, or because rumour had reached him of Pétion's plan to surrender sovereignty to the British, Christophe now took the final step on a path that he had, consciously or not, long been pursuing. At a council of state on March 28, 1811, he declared Haiti a kingdom, with himself as King Henry I.

V

King Henry I

1

He had many reasons for making Haiti a kingdom and himself a king. Vanity was not the least of them; but neither was it the greatest. A king was still a creature of power and splendour, not yet an antique oddity. The title would give him an advantage over Pétion in the eyes of both their peoples, brought up to honour kings. He could expect it to raise Haiti in the estimation of the white world, where Bonaparte was still setting up kingdoms for his relations. It was a valuable reinforcement of his authority in domestic affairs, now that he was about to turn to his long-contemplated but equally long-delayed reforms at home. As King of the Blacks he would have a greater chance to lead his people to equality with the whites.

Monarchy is an institution better bred by slow growth than by instant proclamation; but Christophe set to work with his customary briskness. On April 5 he created an hereditary nobility, with four princes, eight dukes, twenty-two counts, thirty-seven barons and fourteen knights, and two days later a spiritual hierarchy with Toussaint's favourite chaplain, Corneille Brelle, as Grand Almoner to the King and Archbishop of Haiti, with his seat at Cap-Henry, and suffragan bishops at Les Gonaïves, Port-au-Prince and Les Cayes – the last two still, of course, in Pétion's territory.

On April 12 he issued the regulations for the dress of the nobility. A white tunic reaching below the knee, white silk hose and red morocco shoes with square gold buckles, a gold-hilted sword and a round hat; a black cloak embroidered with gold and with red facings for the princes and dukes; simple coats of blue or red for barons or knights; and plumes of black, red, white and green in descending order of seniority. On April 20 he created his Order of Chivalry, the Haitian equivalent of the Garter or the Saint-Esprit

– the Royal and Military Order of Saint-Henry, whose members
wore a large cross set with brilliants, engraved on one side with
Christophe's head and the words *"Henry, fondateur,* 1811" and on
the other a crown of laurel, a star, and *"prix de valeur".* There
remained only the appointment of the officials of the royal household
and those of the households of the queen, the Prince Royal and the
two princesses. Having brought into being all these chamberlains
and pages, masters of ceremonies, governors of palaces and heralds
at arms, Christophe was ready for his coronation, which he set for
June 2.

The great church facing the place d'Armes was still shattered
and lacking a roof. In less than ten weeks Christophe had a new
church built in the Champ de Mars, 250 feet square with a cupola
80 feet high, beneath which stood the throne, 30 feet broad and
rising 70 feet to a crimson baldaquin, gold fringed, gold embroidered, and sprinkled with stars and phoenixes of gold. The
walls of the church were hung with sky-blue silk, again with
fringes and golden stars; the path to be taken by the king was laid
with carpets bearing his arms and more golden stars. To the right
of the altar stood the archbishop's purple-canopied chair, and
behind it a tribune for the choir who sang the motet; to the left of
the altar was the crimson-hung tribune of the queen and members
of her household.

The front of the church bore the royal arms, six feet high, the
national flag, and banners proclaiming Liberty! Independence!
Honour! Henry! To the right of the Champ de Mars the royal
pavilion, surmounted by two royal standards, was divided into
three rooms, carpeted in crimson and hung with green taffeta. The
roads leading to the royal palace (the former Presidential Palace in
the place d'Armes) were newly levelled, re-paved and gravelled;
along them Christophe drove in his state coach through the ranks
of his cheering and very impressed subjects to be crowned as
"Henry, by the Grace of God and the Constitutional Law of the
State, King of Haiti, Sovereign of Tortuga, Gonave and other
adjacent Islands, Destroyer of Tyranny, Regenerator and Bene-
factor of the Haitian Nation, Creator of her Moral, Political and
Martial Institutions, First Crowned Monarch of the New World,
Defender of the Faith, Founder of the Royal and Military Order of
Saint-Henry."

At the palace afterwards, King Henry presided at the first state
banquet of his reign. Among several foreign guests was Commander

Douglas of the sloop *Reindeer*, who proposed the health of the new monarch on behalf of himself and his crew. Christophe, thus given an opportunity of underlining his entry into the fraternity of kings, replied with a toast to "My dear brother, George the Third, whose life I hope the Supreme Arbiter may preserve to oppose an invincible obstacle to the ambition of Napoleon and to be always the constant friend of Haiti." The feasting over, he announced the members of his first royal administration – most of them the same men who had held the posts under the presidency, though now unfamiliar in their new noble names. In charge of Finance and the Interior was the Prince des Gonaïves who, as André Vernet, had held the office of Treasurer under Dessalines and had been raised to the dignity of princedom because of his old friendship with Christophe and because he was married to Toussaint's niece, Marie-Augustine Chancy; he was an old man now, past seventy, and full of honours, including the Grand Marshalcy of Haiti. The Minister of War and the Marine, Lieutenant-General Paul Romain, who as a colonel had commanded the 1st demi-brigade under Christophe's orders, was now Prince du Limbé, his birthplace. Joseph Rouanez, Minister of State, was the Duc de Morin; Councillor Juge, appropriately Minister of Justice, was the Comte de Terre-Neuve; Julien Prévost, the king's mulatto secretary, became Foreign Secretary, Comte de Limonade.

Despite Commander Douglas's friendly toast Britain was still far from recognising Christophe's kingship, or even his authority over the north of Haiti. Pétion's envoy to London, John Goff, had succeeded in interesting Wilberforce in his cause and during the week before Christophe's coronation Wilberforce wrote to Lord Liverpool setting out a little unquestioningly the case that Goff had outlined to him. This was that Pétion and Christophe "have both become fearful of a new power which has lately attempted to establish itself in the south-western part of the island, that of Rigaud, who was formerly in St Domingo a Jacobin *enragé*. There is . . . little or no doubt of his being in reality an emissary of Bonaparte." The great reformer, despite his gullibility in accepting Pétion's version of what was happening in the south, was a man of practicality, as he demonstrated in the conclusion of his letter. If Britain were to mediate successfully between the contending parties, he pointed out, "we should then secure to this country the exclusive commerce of that great island, which commerce, already great, is likely to become immense if the island should be restored once more to quiet." In fact, the estimated value of exports from Britain to Haiti in 1811 was £1,200,000.

For the moment, the British government had no hope of bringing Christophe and Pétion to accord and was interested principally in restricting the area of the quarrel. On July 16 Admiral Rowley sent a letter to "General Christophe" warning him of the "immediate interference of His Majesty's Naval Forces" if any British vessels from Britain carrying British cargoes were arrested by armed vessels belonging to Haiti. To this Christophe had his foreign secretary, the Comte de Limonade, reply that no such vessels had ever been arrested by one of his warships and that he would "always endeavour to preserve the amity and good harmony which exists between the two peoples". Pétion's answer to a similar letter from Rowley was longer, blander and perhaps more heartfelt in its assurances that he desired to maintain the existing good relations with Britain, for he had just blundered into serious trouble.

With the help of the brigand Goman – an unreliable partner at the best – he engineered a rising at Les Cayes against Rigaud and marched south "in answer to the appeals of the oppressed multitudes" in the South Province. He had, however, grossly overestimated Goman's support and underestimated Rigaud's hold over the province. Rigaud seized the excuse to strike back and was counter-attacking strongly in the direction of Port-au-Prince when he was unexpectedly struck down by yellow fever, to which his long absence in France may have rendered him insufficiently immune. He died on September 18, 1811, at the age of 50. His successor in opposition to Pétion was General Borgella, the mulatto son of the white president of Toussaint's *assemblée centrale*; a brave man but lacking in Rigaud's dash and popularity, he was content to remain on the defensive.

The year 1811 ended on a sour note for Christophe. As a genuine admirer of many things English, and because he could not do his royal shopping in republican America and would not do it in imperial France, he had bought almost all his regalia in London and was still having various expensive afterthoughts shipped out to him. He was consequently very annoyed to learn that the customs agents had, at the end of October, seized many of his new purchases from a vessel about to leave the Thames for Cap-Henry. Among the confiscated items were several enormous mirrors, a gold sceptre, a sword of state nearly eight feet long, several other

swords and a Herschelian telescope. It was possibly the last item
that Christophe regretted most of all. Springing, no doubt, from
the anxiety that every Black in Haiti shared – that he might not get
sight of the expected French invasion until it was too late –
Christophe's passion for telescopes went beyond their installation
in every one of the palaces that he was now constructing. Everywhere that he went, he was accompanied by a page carrying a spy-
glass wrapped in a napkin, and his subjects soon began to believe
the stories that he used the instrument to oversee them from afar,
that he would send soldiers to beat any man who was not working
hard enough, and that in one instance he had trained a gun on an
idler and blown off his head at a range of two miles.

The detention of his property did not last long. His agents
had failed to obtain the necessary clearance certificate from the
Ordnance Board; when they had completed this formality the ship
was allowed to proceed on its way. It arrived at Cap-Henry in the
New Year and, if the episode had raised doubts in Christophe's
mind about the friendly attitude of the British Government, these
were soon dispelled by the *Améthyste* incident.

In January 1812 Christophe ordered Rear-Admiral Bernadine
(Goodall and most of the British officers had now been replaced in
their commands) to cruise along the southern passage of the Bight
of Léogane in his flagship *Améthyste* (officially *Princesse Royale
Améthyste* since the previous March), accompanied by the corvette
Athénaïs (named after the younger of the princesses) and the brig
Jason. The admiral's mission was to intercept any vessels trading
with Pétion's part of the island. He was unaware that he was carrying some of Pétion's sympathisers among his crew.

The chief of these conspirators was the mulatto paymaster,
Eutrope Bellarmin, whose position gave him ample opportunities to
preach mutiny among the crew. By the time that the *Améthyste*
reached the Straits of Miragoane, Bellarmin had enlisted so many
dissidents – and Admiral Bernadine had foolishly got so far ahead
of the two other vessels – that the senior officers were overpowered
without difficulty and the ship was taken into Mirogoane harbour,
where the rich prize was greeted with great enthusiasm.

Miragoane was one of the towns that had been overrun by
Rigaud when he counter-attacked Pétion in the previous summer,
but Pétion's propaganda had led Bellarmin to believe that the
president had recaptured it. It was with some embarrassment that
he discovered that it was still in the hands of the southern rebels;

however, since General Borgella greeted him with great warmth, he offered the ship to the general as if that had always been his intention, and even broached to him a plan for capturing the other two. The new *coup* seemed even more brilliant than the first and Borgella sent Bellarmin off in the *Améthyste*, now renamed *L'Heureuse Réunion*, its crew strengthened with local volunteers, and commanded, since Bellarmin was no sailor, by a French ex-corsair captain, Augustin Gaspard.

Once out of the harbour again, the *Heureuse Réunion* soon came in sight of her slower sister ships, the *Athénaïs* and the *Jason*, and Gaspard, in accordance with Bellarmin's plan, signalled for their officers to come aboard the flagship for a conference. They were seized before they had time to realise that the ship had changed hands and, though some of the officers remained loyal to Christophe, Gaspard and Bellarmin were able to persuade the crews of the corvette and the brig to accept new officers pledged to support Borgella.

The whole operation passed off without bloodshed. There was only one small cause for regret: by the time that the three ships arrived within sight of Miragoane it was already late afternoon. The rapid fall of night would at any moment make it impossible for the citizens of Miragoane to see and acclaim Gaspard's triumphant entry. He accordingly decided to wait until dawn in the Gonave channel, between the island and Miragoane.

It was a moonlight night. At three o'clock in the morning, HM frigate *Southampton*, sailing southward along the coast from Port-au-Prince, sighted the three vessels. As the *Southampton* turned to approach them in a light SSE wind, the three ships began to run before her. At 5.45 the *Southampton* had closed the gap sufficiently to be within hailing distance and her captain, Sir James Lucas Yeo, asked the frigate who she was.

The captain of the *Heureuse Réunion* answered that they were a squadron from Les Cayes. Captain Yeo then sent Lieutenant Gordon, his second-in-command, on board the *Heureuse Réunion* to ask its captain to return with him to the *Southampton* and to let Sir James inspect his commissioning papers. Gaspard refused to do this, but instead sent his second-in-command, Captain L. A. Daunec, to show the orders that he had been given by General Borgella, "Commander-in-Chief of the Department of the South of Haiti."

I know of no authority [Yeo told him] that the said Monsieur Borgella has to employ a naval force at sea. I have no orders to respect such a force. I know of only two contending chiefs of Haiti: Generals Christophe and Pétion. It is therefore my duty to take your ships to my commander-in-chief in Jamaica for his superior decision respecting them. It is very far from my wish to use any violence and I hope that you will proceed to Jamaica for examination quietly, at the same time it is my fixed resolve that you shall go. You will please inform the commander of your squadron that I give him five minutes to decide how he will act.

Yeo sent Lieutenant Gordon back to the *Heureuse Réunion* with Daunec, to make sure that his message was understood. At 6.29 Gordon returned with Gaspard's answer – that he would rather sink than comply with Yeo's demands, and that if Yeo intended to enforce them would he please fire one gun ahead of him as a signal. "After such a message," Yeo reported to Admiral Stirling, who had taken over command at Port-Royal following Rowley's death from yellow fever, "there was only one way of supporting the dignity of the British Flag. The bow gun of the ship was immediately fired and almost at the same instant our broadsides were mutually exchanged."

The *Heureuse Réunion* had taken 300 soldiers on board at Miragoane and at 7 am they made an unsuccessful attempt to board the *Southampton*. Until now, the British ship of 38 guns, with a complement of 215 men (she was the oldest frigate in the navy, built in 1757) had been fighting all three of the Haitian ships, with a total of 75 guns and 1,000 men, but at 7.15 the corvette and the brig turned tail and ran for Miragoane, leaving the two frigates to fight it out. At ten minutes to nine the mizzen mast of the *Heureuse Réunion* fell, shortly afterwards followed by the main mast; her colours had been shot away early in the action and Yeo was convinced that another broadside would sink her. He ordered his gunners to cease fire and hailed the *Heureuse Réunion*, asking if she surrendered. Gaspard replied that she did and, after putting Lieutenant Gordon on board of her, Yeo set sail to pursue the vanishing corvette and brig.

The wind was light, the two fleeing ships were using their sweeps to get under the protection of the coastal batteries at Miragoane, and Yeo saw that the foremast and bowsprit of the *Heureuse Réunion* had gone over the side and that she was drifting fast on to the rocks. He gave up the chase and returned to take the *Heureuse Réunion* in tow. He landed her dead and wounded – more

than a hundred of each – at Miragoane, together with any other
members of the crew and soldiers who wished to support the
South, but did not allow them to take their arms with them. He
continued to Port-au-Prince, where he landed the remainder of the
Heureuse Réunion's crew (a few Americans and three other men)
and then turned back to Jamaica.

The majority of the dead and wounded soldiers on the *Heureuse
Réunion* had come from Les Cayes, on the opposite side of the
peninsula from Miragoane. Borgella ordered the military commander of Les Cayes, Bonnet, to arrest all the British merchants
there and put them in prison. Bonnet, however, realising that when
they were in prison they were in grave danger of having their
throats cut or being lynched, lodged them under guard in the house
next door to his own, where, during the following week, mobs
gathered and the merchants were in hourly danger of losing their
lives. On February 11 they obtained permission for one of them,
a man named Edgar, to board a ship leaving for Jamaica, carrying
a letter to Admiral Stirling which they all signed.

> We do not pretend to know the merits or demerits of Captain
> Yeo's conduct [they wrote] but we beg leave to mention as
> British subjects . . . that such hostile proceedings were very
> impolitic, he being from his frequent visits to this country per-
> fectly acquainted with the natural disposition of the natives
> towards foreigners, consequently he must have been well aware
> of the alarming consequences of such measures. . . .
>
> The result of this unfortunate affair has been succeeded by the
> arrestation of all His Majesty's subjects in this department, not
> adopted as a measure of retaliation alone, but also as a necessary
> precaution taken by this Government to preserve our lives from
> an outrageous mob, and to which we are still exposed, and will
> be until you will be pleased to interfere in the business, and we
> are fearful that unless a restitution is made of their frigate and
> people, that our properties in this country (which amount at this
> moment to about half a million dollars) will be confiscated to
> reimburse their loss.

Edgar arrived under a flag of truce in one of Borgella's ships,
bearing a letter from the general demanding the return of the
Heureuse Réunion. Stirling replied to Borgella telling him that the
question of whose property the ship might be – Christophe's,

Borgella's, Pétion's (for Pétion was claiming that the mutineers would have entered Port-au-Prince had they not been carried on to Miragoane by unfavourable winds) or a legitimate prize of Captain Yeo and his crew – would be referred to the Admiralty. Meanwhile he called on Borgella to release the British merchants if they wished to leave the island. He charged Commander Richard Plummer Davies of the sloop *Brazen* with the task of delivering this message. It was a good choice since Davies was well known and liked by the authorities at Les Cayes – in common with many of the leading mulattos, including Borgella himself, Davies was a freemason and a welcome guest in the Les Cayes lodge.

First news of the mutiny reached Christophe on February 13.

The King, my Master, [the Comte de Limonade wrote to Stirling] has ordered me to inform Your Excellency that, following the revolt and treachery of some scoundrels who raised their guilty hands against their admiral, His Haitian Majesty's Frigate *Princesse Royale Améthyste* was delivered into the hands of the southern rebels and eventually captured, after stubborn fight, by His Britannic Majesty's Frigate *Southampton*, Captain James Yeo, who conducted her to Jamaica, together with two other vessels of war.

His Haitian Majesty, confident of Your Excellency's respect for equity, the law of nations and the accepted customs of civilised powers, and particularly that of the English nation whose probity is well known, as is its rigorous attitude towards such crimes, has charged Mr Hardy, a merchant of Jamaica, to hand you this communication, whose intention it is to ask Y.E. for the return of his frigate, his two other vessels and the guilty authors of this treason together with those of his subjects who were victims of the crime and may have been left on board these vessels. . . .

Stirling was still without instructions to recognise new monarchies in the Caribbean. He addressed his reply to "General Christophe" and compounded this offence by referring to the "letter I have received from one of your officers" – a ludicrously inadequate description of Limonade's introduction of himself as *Comte de Limonade, Maréchal de Camp des Armées du Roi, Commandeur de l'Ordre Royal et Militaire de Saint-Henry, Secrétaire de sa Majesté, Membre de son Conseil Privé et Major Commandant les*

Chevaux-Légers du Prince Royal, Secrétaire d'Etat et Ministre des Affaires Etrangères.

I agree most fully with you [Stirling said] in reprobating every species of treason, but as your ship after arrival at Miragoane had her name changed to *L'Heureuse Réunion,* and was officered and manned by General Borgella, and fought most desperately the ship belonging to my sovereign, I do not think myself authorized to give her up to any power, and therefore, I shall send a Ship of War immediately to England with a copy of the letter containing your claim, as also the demand of General Borgella and General Pétion on the occasion, and I will write to you as soon as I get an answer.

In the meantime, as it is probable the Captors may libel their Prize in the Court of Vice-Admiralty at Kingston, I presume you will employ Counsel to argue your cause if you think proper . . . but whatever judgement may be awarded I shall not suffer the captured Ship to depart until I hear from my Government. . . .

Christophe took the seizure of the *Princesse Royale Améthyste* as a declaration of war by Pétion. On March 8, in a proclamation to the people and the army of Haiti, he accused the 'rebels' of "making use, on this occasion as on all others, of their natural weapon, treachery! Sailing thereafter without a commission from any legitimate power, these vessels were captured as pirates; for no sovereign is immune from becoming the victim of treason, but all have an interest in punishing traitors. Now I rise. I rested like the lion. I am determined to march against Port-aux-Crimes, to crush the rebels. For too long have I restrained the ardour of my brave soldiers. . . ."

His attack was not attended by good fortune. The day before he issued his proclamation, Pétion engineered a successful revolt in the South Province against Borgella, who had lost a great deal of respect because of his failure to get back *L'Heureuse Réunion* from the British. Colonel Henri, the commander of the 18th Regiment of the Line stationed at La Grande-Anse, declared for Pétion, who marched south from Port-au-Prince and within a fortnight had taken Les Cayes and received Borgella's submission. He thus not only increased his prestige and supply of men and material, but he also regained control of several of his former ships, including a corvette and a brig at Les Cayes as well as the *Athénaïs* and the

Jason, which Christophe mistakenly thought had been taken to Jamaica.

It was the rainy season of what was to be a notably rainy year. Through violent storms, the main body of Christophe's army marched south-east along the Artibonite river to Le Mirebalais, and then swung south-west through the gorges of the Pensez-y-Bien range down into the Plaine du Cul-de-Sac, while the king and his household troops took the more direct coastal route through L'Arcahaye. The whole of his fleet was used to bring stores and provisions down by sea.

When Pétion went south to take advantage of Colonel Henri's rising against Borgella, he left his secretary, General Boyer, in command at Port-au-Prince, and it was Boyer who offered the first resistance to Christophe's troops, setting up his headquarters at the Santo plantation, between Fort Cibert and the town of La Croix-des-Bouquets. Christophe had marched slowly along the coast to give the main body of the army time to catch up with him in the Cul-de-Sac plain, and it was they who made the first contact with Boyer's forces at Santo, inflicting a heavy defeat on them. Boyer fell back on Port-au-Prince with most of the survivors, but some managed to get across into Fort Cibert before Christophe – now marching at full speed – came down the coast road.

His first attempt to take the fort by storm was unsuccessful. Unwilling to leave this strong position in his rear, he ordered the main body of the army forward to Port-au-Prince while he personally supervised the siege of Fort Cibert. The defence was stubborn; the construction of counter-works and approach trenches threatened to consume much time and many lives. Christophe determined to appeal to the defenders in person. Accompanied by his aides-de-camp, wearing his uniform as commander-in-chief and his considerable array of medals and decorations, he entered the trench, ordered his men to hold their fire, and then climbed onto the parapet. The defenders also ceased fire and the Comte de Limonade – it having been decided that it would be lacking in dignity for the king to bawl his offer across no-man's-land – shouted Christophe's message:

"Generals, officers, subalterns and soldiers! I address you in the name of the King, our beloved Sovereign, who is here present." It was an opening that might well have brought a hail of bullets, but the silence remained undisturbed.

"Surrender!" Limonade continued. "You shall be maintained in your present ranks and offices; you are in error, you have been deceived; refrain from pursuing this unjust and barbarous war! You are reduced to the last extremity; you can no longer defend your-selves! Surrender, then! No harm shall be done you. We urge you, for your own sakes and in the name of our country, to surrender!"

There was a confused noise of argument among the garrison, but the men finally obeyed their commander's orders to resume firing. The artillery officer standing beside Christophe fell dead at his feet; guns on both sides began to batter at walls and trenches. At nightfall the defenders made a sortie but were driven back. Before dawn they again left the fort, this time noiselessly. Passing them-selves off in the darkness as members of Christophe's army, they infiltrated his lines and made for their homes.

Christophe had secured his line of retreat; but in doing so he had compromised his advance. Before he could get the remainder of his troops in position around Port-au-Prince, Pétion had swung round and, by forced marches, got most of his army back into his capital. The odds at once shifted round in Pétion's favour, for Christophe now had only 15,000 men to attack a fortified town defended by 13,000. The steadfastness that had endeared him to his superiors in early days was developing into a royal stubbornness that was the despair of his subordinates. Instead of recognising the impossibility of bringing the campaign to a successful conclusion and cutting his losses, he doggedly sat down before the walls of the city and began a siege.

Everything was against him. The weather continued bad. The warships that Pétion had found in the South were refitted and by May had seriously disrupted Christophe's seaborne supplies. The roads over the mountains were too rough and damaged to bear the necessary amount of transport. Provisions ran low and his troops found themselves being bombarded with bread instead of cannon-balls. Across the trenches that were in some places almost touching each other the besieged yelled to the besiegers that this was the sort of reward the Republic gave them, not the beatings that they got from their officers under a king.

Admiral Stirling kept three warships patrolling the coast to watch over the welfare of the British merchants. Their commanders had orders to observe the strictest neutrality but were also told to try to persuade Christophe to agree to an armistice and to accept mediation by the Prince Regent. British policy remained what it had always been: non-interference so long as the civil war merely weakened the participants and rendered them less able to attack Jamaica, but attempted reconciliation if one seemed likely to gain an outright victory over the other, or, as with Rigaud, a third party seemed more dangerous. As soon as it became apparent that sickness, lack of supplies and growing discontent among his troops would make it impossible for Christophe to take Port-au-Prince by storm, and that he had so exhausted his strength that he might be cut to pieces on the long retreat back to the North, Stirling made his offer of mediation. Christophe's terms, however, were indistinguishable from those he would have demanded as a victor, and Stirling did not even trouble to communicate them to Pétion. In June, when he returned for a short visit to Saint-Marc, where he had left his family and the civil administration, Christophe still maintained, and possibly believed, that he would eventually capture Port-au-Prince.

This was the moment that Pétion had been waiting for. Christophe was now neither in his capital nor at the head of his army. He was unarmed against the expansive plot that Pétion, a master at promoting treachery, had long ago prepared to bring him down.

The plan hinged on Christophe's punctilious performance of his religious duties. Like Toussaint, he was regular at mass and always took communion before embarking on a campaign. (He was also as firm with the clergy as with his officers – attending church one morning and finding that the priest was not yet there, he sent a squad of soldiers to arrest him and take him straight to gaol.) Pétion had arranged to have Christophe killed as he knelt at the altar. The murder would be carried out by officers from Christophe's staff and from the garrison of Saint-Marc. He now set the date as the second Sunday in June.

Christophe arrived outside the church and rode along the ranks of the troops drawn up for his inspection. Then, instead of dismounting, he unexpectedly wheeled his horse and shouted to the soldiers: "I take charge of this parade! You will receive your orders from me!" In the ensuing silence he drew a paper from his pocket and handed it to one of his aides to read aloud.

Christophe's intelligence had proved superior to Pétion's. One by one the conspirators were lined up in front of the troops. It was the drama of Toussaint and the mutineers at Le Cap being repeated. When the reading of the list was complete, Christophe gave the order to load, aim and fire. Then he entered the church.

But assassination was only one part of Pétion's plan. The flank of Christophe's besieging army, stretching from the coast to Fort-National, was commanded by one of his oldest and most trusted officers, the quiet General Magny, who had led Toussaint's body-guard in the battle of Crête-à-Pierrot and was now Grand Chamberlain and Duc de Plaisance. The three regiments under his control were less reliable. One had been commanded by Pétion in the war of independence and still had some of his former officers serving with it; the second had mutinied when stationed at Le Gros-Morne; the third was tainted with disaffection spread from the other two.

On June 12 an officer crossed to the southern lines under a flag of truce and reported to Pétion that the three regiments were ready to join him. The following afternoon Pétion rode out to the porte Saint-Joseph at the entrance to Port-au-Prince and took the salute as they marched in, shouting *Vive la République!* and *Vive le Président d'Haiti!* With them came the Duc de Plaisance. It was said that he was the prisoner of his own men, but he did not return and Christophe never discovered to what extent his old friend willingly betrayed him.

Christophe was still at Saint-Marc when this crushing news arrived. He returned at once to his headquarters on the Drouillard plantation and found an officer from HMS *Brazen* waiting there with a letter from the captain, Richard Davies, who had already consulted with Pétion on Stirling's proposal of mediation:

> Impressed with the necessity of concluding an armistice between you and General Pétion to afford time for the discussion of your respective claims, and knowing at the same time the anxiety of Admiral Stirling to use every persuasion in his power to effect so desirable an object, I have to request you will be pleased to acquaint me if you are still averse to the pacific measures I had the honour to propose? And if not, at what time and in what place you will meet deputies from General Pétion to acquaint you with his propositions. Should you have any immediate com-munication to make to General Pétion I beg leave to offer myself as the channel through which it may be made. . . .

Even with his army disintegrating around him, Christophe did not hesitate for a second. With a ferocious glare he thrust the letter aside and summoned a conference of those generals who remained

loyal to him. He agreed with them that it was no longer possible to
hold the remaining positions before Port-au-Prince and ordered
evacuation to take place under the cover of darkness. The British
officer was sent back to the *Brazen* at sunset and the following
morning Commander Davies could see through his telescope that
Christophe's lines were no longer manned, though his guns
remained in the positions where he had been forced to abandon
them. Davies went ashore to tell Pétion that he meant to follow
Christophe up the coast and renew his offer of mediation and to ask
Pétion's assurance that he would still consent to negotiate, even
though the tide had swung so dramatically in his favour.

Pétion agreed. He also pointed out that he was making no
immediate efforts to harry Christophe's forces as they filed northwards. He had good reasons for staying his hand: the final phase of
his plot had now been reached and he believed that the remainder
of Christophe's army would desert him as soon as they learned of
the new revolts that were about to break out against the king.

At Mirebalais the garrison mutinied and killed its commanding
officer. All along the Cahos mountains and in the hills south of
Saint-Marc the field hands flocked from the plantations and formed
themselves into guerilla bands, fighting against Christophe and the
hard work that he forced upon them. Christophe set his half-
mutinous army in position before Saint-Marc and waited for
Pétion's attack. Instead, on June 17, he received another note from
Commander Davies, who had sailed up from Port-au-Prince.
Christophe listened impatiently while it was translated to him.

"Hand it back," he said to Dupuy; and to Davies's messenger:
"You may tell your captain that I will never answer any letter that
proposes reconciliation between myself and the rebel Pétion."

"Any comment of mine upon the General's conduct on this
occasion," Davies wrote to Admiral Stirling, "would I am sure be
quite superfluous." And the admiral, passing on Davies's report to
Mr Croker at the Admiralty, remarked, "I had hoped that when
Christophe saw that there was no possibility of success he would
have been disposed to agree to amicable terms. . . . But his disposition seems so violent that he must be left to his fate."

It was his violence and obstinacy – together with Pétion's lack of
perseverance – that enabled him to ride out the storm. He ordered
his local commanders to suppress the slightest indiscipline with the
utmost severity. He rode daylong, as Toussaint had ridden, to
make sure that his orders were obeyed. With fierceness and energy

he re-established his control over the army and throughout the countryside. When Pétion realised that Christophe's remaining troops were not deserting as he had expected, a characteristic listlessness took hold of him. Although a man of courage as well as of intelligence, he was incapable of following up the plots that he contrived so ingeniously. He led his army to Saint-Marc and then lost interest, leaving the command to Boyer while he went down to the tip of the south peninsula where Goman had changed sides once more and raised a revolt against him – but Goman and his petty rebellion were of no importance and could well have been left to burn themselves out while Pétion obliterated Christophe.

The war dragged bloodily and inconclusively on into 1813. Christophe gradually built up his strength again and edged southward until, with the recapture of Fort-Boucassin, beyond L'Arcahaye, he was back on approximately the line he had started from when he lost his temper over the capture of the *Améthyste*. The frontier, unconfirmed by any formal peace treaty but respected by both sides, ran from Le Boucassin on the coast eastwards between the Pensez-y-Bien range and the mountains of La Selle, then along the valley of the Tombe to the Artibonite river and on to the former Spanish frontier at Lascaobas. Holding the whole of the North Province and almost half of the West, Christophe at last resigned himself to leaving the 'rebels' unvanquished, though he continued to list the districts of the remainder of the West and the South in his *Almanach Royal*, with spaces left blank for the names of the governors whom he one day intended to appoint to them.

2

The pervading, continuing, inexpungeable nightmare of another French invasion had been expressed in the fifth article of the constitution of May 1805, "At the first shot from the warning gun, the towns shall be destroyed and the nation shall rise in arms", in the embargo on ownership of land by whites, and in the local regulations – much more strictly enforced in the North than in the easygoing South – forbidding white merchants to stray out of the towns towards the mountains which concealed the strong points and stores of food and ammunition against the attack that might always come. The greatest and most fantastic of these defence works was the fortress which Christophe built on the Pic de la Ferrière.

The bricks for the inner walls were made on the site, but the enormous blocks of stone of which the face of the stronghold was constructed were dragged up precipitous paths where often even mules could not tread. The road rose like a staircase, with platforms cut as resting places for the animals. On the final stage of the climb, after the track emerged from the forests and reached the last village, where each of the huts was a concealed watchpost or block-house and wisps of cloud began to obscure the view of the summit, it was impossible for anybody, workman or king, to proceed except on foot, so treacherous was the smooth surface of the rocks over which scores of guns had been hauled. From below, the fortress, shaped like the prow of a ship, seemed to ride almost lightly on the crests of the clouds, and only from the top of the path could its true size be appreciated, its walls, varying from eighty to one hundred and thirty feet high, lined with cannon and dominating the approaches. This was the ultimate impregnable stronghold to which the king would retreat with his personal guard and con-tinue the fight against the worst that the white man could send against him. The German military engineers who designed the citadel and supervised its construction lived on inside its walls, forbidden to leave for fear that they would betray its secrets. Throughout the whole of Christophe's reign the work on building and fortifying continued, never finishing, never so secure that more might not be added to make it stronger.

It was not only military architecture that occupied his attention. He was a king of many castles and many palaces. His châteaux, built for relaxation, had fanciful or evocative names: Victory, the Cloak, the Sceptre, the Necklace, Embuscade, Belle-vue-le-Roi; the palaces were set in or close to the principal towns of the kingdom, Cap-Henry, Fort-Royal, Le Limbé, Port-de-Paix, Môle Saint-Nicolas, Les Gonaïves, Dessalines, Saint-Marc and La Petite-Riviere (to which the *Almanach Royal* added the national palaces of Port-au-Prince, Léogane, Jérémie, Les Cayes and Jacmel in the un-submitted West and South). The last, the largest, and the favourite of his palaces was completed during the course of 1813, at Millot, his former headquarters, where he had long had a flourishing sugar plantation. Here, at the foot of the Pic de la Ferrière, guarded by the fortress that he called Citadel-Henry, he built Sans-Souci, naming it out of admiration for Frederick the Great and despite the fact that it was also the name of the bitter enemy whom he had murdered.

In his other palaces Christophe was soldier, administrator, law giver. At Sans-Souci he was monarch, King Henry I, the sun round whom all splendour and regal panoply revolved, Here he held his Thursday levées, circles, receptions and the public audiences at which any subject might submit a petition to the king, in writing or by word of mouth, with the assurance that an answer would be given him on the next Thursday at the same hour of 10 am to11 am. At 5 pm their majesties held a *cercle* which all the nobility and senior military officers who could not plead urgent business elsewhere were required to attend, in uniform or the appropriate court dress. Christophe was as great a stickler for etiquette as his fellow parvenu, Bonaparte. Princes and princesses, ducs and duchesses were privileged to seat themselves on the traditional *tabourets*; comtes and comtesses, barons and baronnes, chevaliers and chevalières made do with the lesser *pliants*. They were placed in order of precedence by a Master of Ceremonies and sat bolt upright in stiff silence, knowing that "one may not address the King or the Queen without having obtained permission through the Grand Master of Ceremonies for the King, or the Lady-in-Waiting for the Queen. . . ."

But though Christophe could coerce them into the mute immobility of courtly poses there was nothing he could do to still the joyful clamour of their dress. "Their coats were so bedecked with gold lace," wrote one observer, "that it was difficult to determine of what material they were made; their shoulders were burdened with epaulets of an enormous size; their caps were adorned, among other ornaments, with feathers nearly equalling their own height; and these articles, together with their beautiful white small-clothes and elegant silk hose, rendered their appearance supremely fantastical."

Newly-appointed officers of state kissed hands at the king's levée, but on all other occasions were presented to both the king and the queen and then to the remainder of the royal family. François-Ferdinand, whom Christophe sent with General Boudet to be educated in France, died in exile, a sad little hostage at the Orphans Hospital in Paris, in October 1805; a second son, whose name has not been recorded, died before Christophe came to the throne; and the sole surviving boy was His Royal Highness, Monseigneur Jacques-Victor-Henry, born in 1804. His other children were the two girls, six and four years older than their brother, Améthyste-Henry and Anne-Athénaïre-Henry who, in addition to having been given the suffix Henry, had her second name changed from Athénaïs to Athénaïre for some unexplained reason.

In December 1813 Christophe and his people mourned the death of the venerable André Vernet, Prince des Gonaïves. The body of the seventy-two-year-old Grand Marshal of Haiti was taken to Cap-Henry to be embalmed and was then exhibited to the people, not recumbent in a coffin but sitting nobly upright in an armchair, with his clothes changed on each of the three days that he received the homage of his fellow citizens. On the fourth day, at 6 am, he was carried to his princely coach and, still upright, set off to his funeral. Accompanied by six thousand mourners, each carrying a lighted taper, the cortège passed out of the town gate, along the road to Le Haut-du-Cap, across the river and on to Sans-Souci, where it halted at the church just outside the palace gates. There the Grand Marshal was carried to the crypt and, to the sound of solemn music and the discharge of cannon, committed to the newly-constructed Haitian Pantheon.

These displays of pomp, rivalling the ceremonies that the whites set such store by, delighted Christophe's subjects and in an equal measure annoyed the lackadaisical southerners, whose state occasions were in comparison shabbily-dressed, inadequately rehearsed and slovenly. But there was no such enthusiasm for his measures to strengthen the country's economy and restore prosperity to the ravaged land. His *code rural*, incorporating the system of *fermage* that he had worked out with Colonel Vincent and directly descended from the earlier *codes* of Polverel, Toussaint and Dessalines, was sternly framed and rigorously enforced.

Saturday was a holiday, when the workers cultivated their own small fields and took their produce to market. Sunday was a day for relaxation and religious observance. On each of the other five days the foreman summoned the field hands with a bell at 3 am to rise, take breakfast and say prayers. At 4.30 they went to the fields where they trimmed hedges, burned refuse and did other tidying jobs until it was light enough to begin the serious work of the day. After a short break for food between 8 am and 9 am they worked until midday, when they were allowed two hours of rest. From 2 pm they laboured uninterruptedly until sundown when they gathered for prayers again before going home. The sick or crippled were employed in looking after the children and taking water to the workers.

In return for all this toil the plantation owner was obliged to distribute one quarter of his gross earnings to the workers, to feed and lodge them, to provide a nurse and midwife and a weekly visit from a doctor. Overseeing them all – owner, foreman and field hands – were the military police, who might descend on the plantation at any time from 3 am to dusk and mete out instant punishment to any whom they suspected of idleness.

These severe regulations brought a much higher standard of production in the Kingdom of Haiti than in the Southern Republic and some of his contemporaries argued that Christophe, a Black, could impose such measures on his fellow-Negroes without resistance, whereas Pétion, trying to rule 250,000 Blacks in the interest of only 12,000 mulattos, had to govern with a light hand. There is clearly some truth in this, but even had Pétion been set in authority over a nation totally composed of mulattos it is unlikely that his conduct would have been more energetic. A brilliant, brave but dissolute man, he brought scarcely more order to matters of state than to his own affairs. Liberty, in the Republic of Haiti, verged always on licence; corruption in public office was matched by a laxity of moral standards; marriage, as in the old slave days, was the exception and concubinage the rule.

In the Kingdom of Haiti, where Roman Catholicism was the state religion and others were tolerated although not recognised, Christophe insisted on every union being regularised by marriage and every marriage enforced by a civil contract. His habit of roving the countryside and marrying extempore any couples whom he suspected of living in sin gave rise to some of the island's merriest anecdotes; but any of his ministers or officials who contracted irregular unions soon discovered that their offence was no laughing matter. To Christophe, none of his subjects was above punishment.

His own marriage had been entirely happy, though he was a stern father and an undemonstrative husband. He expected his wife and children to approach life with an earnestness equal to his own. His only surviving son he brought up strictly. In those of his letters to the boy that have survived he is often chiding and seldom affectionate. "When I looked at the latest example of your writing," (he was, of course, dependent on his literate secretaries for criticisms of the weekly exercises that the Prince Royal had to submit to him), "I noticed three erasures, as well as other mistakes. . . . In future, pay more attention if you desire to please me," he wrote when the boy was nine; and, when he was twelve, "Your studies should have all your attention – I do not consider that you are devoting yourself to them with all the application that they deserve." This letter was the only one that he subscribed *votre bon papa* instead of his usual *votre père, Henry*, and in none of them did he use the normal *tutoiement* of family life.

His attitude to his wife was often magisterial, even by nineteenth-century standards. "The King to his Spouse, the Queen," was the only superscription of a letter that he wrote to her from his palace of Cap-Henry in March 1815.

I have just seen the doctors, my dear; they tell me that my daughter, Madame Première, has a badly coated tongue, which is a sign that she is very much out of sorts. You will therefore have her take senna tomorrow, Sunday, and again on Monday, copiously. The physicians will be with you at Sans-Souci on Monday afternoon, to give her another purge on Tuesday, which she greatly needs. I told you eighteen months ago, my dear wife, that Madame Première needed to be purged and you should reproach yourself for not having done it long ago. I reproach you for it and I shall always reproach you for having left it so long.

Henry.

Yet he was undoubtedly fond of the plump, kind-hearted Marie-Louise and demonstrated it by including among the national holidays of the kingdom – in addition to Independence Day, the King's Birthday and Coronation Day – their Majesties' Wedding Day (July 15, 1793, when he had been 25 and she 15). Before their marriage he had had an illegitimate son, Armand-Eugène, whom he recognised and created prince and Duc du Môle. Otherwise, unlike Toussaint, Dessalines, Pétion and all the others to whom power had brought the opportunity for promiscuousness, there was no suggestion of marital infidelity until very late in his life. It was then the occasion for one of his rare bursts of humour. Discussing what title he should give to the bastard child just born to a casual mistress he said: "I know – prince des Variétés. He's here only because I wanted a change from my wife."

Proud by nature, resolved to win respect for his people and conscious of the white man's habit of equating 'field hand' and 'thief', he made death the penalty for stealing and used the 4,000 gendarmes of his Royal-Dahomets to enforce the law. These were recruited direct from Africa as a surety of loyalty (the idea was Toussaint's in origin); a hundred and fifty of the youngest were formed into a cadet *corps d'élite* under the name of the Royal Bon-

Bons and the remainder were distributed through the Kingdom, seventy to each of the fifty-six arrondissements. They visited the plantations to ensure that the *code rural* was being observed; they checked the passes of any workers whom they found absent from the fields, and made sure that they were decently dressed if they intended to enter the towns. But their most feared activity was the setting of traps for thieves. They had been known to leave money or jewellery in the streets and to arrest anybody who picked it up and did not report it immediately. The device became legendary and a peasant spending the day in town would, if he saw some object of value lying on the ground, stand stock still in terror and then, like as not, take to his heels in panic. Or, fearing that even this might expose him to punishment, he would stoop and pick it up and then race breathlessly in search of somebody in authority to surrender it to.

Each arrondissement had an army officer acting as justice of the peace and empowered to deal with minor crime; above him was one of the ten district *sénéchaussées* and courts of admiralty, and above these the *cour souveraine* from which there was a final appeal to the king's great council of state. This was less military than Dessalines's grand council, on which every general had the right to sit, but even more despotic – for Christophe alone appointed its nine members: six generals and three ministers of state. In a land where illiteracy was the rule, the qualifications of the judges were seldom high: one had been the cook on an American merchantman – but then the king his master had been no more than a headwaiter in civil life. And all were encouraged by Christophe to exercise their powers with intelligence and incorruptibility. If not, they too were sent off to the Citadel for a spell of hard labour on the fortifications that were always being built and never reached completion.

For ordinary misdemeanours prompt punishment was the usual rule. The cart-whip, symbol of slavery, had been abolished through-out the Kingdom and the Republic and it would have gone hard with anybody, whatever his colour, who tried to make use of one. But sticks and canes and the thick stems of lianas were commonly used to enforce discipline in the army and, since most field hands were in the reserve of the army and all policemen were soldiers, the labourer who broke the regulations was usually flogged.

Christophe himself carried a stout silver-knobbed cane with which he dealt out summary guidance to the anti-social and the idle as he stalked about the streets, dressed in imitation of his model monarch, George III, in a severely plain jacket with no decoration other than the gold star of the Order of Saint-Henry. His justice, though rough, was impartial, taking no more notice of nationality than of social status. It often fell harshly on the American merchants who never won from him the respect and even affection that he felt for some of the Britons – perhaps because of a natural preference for monarchies over republics, perhaps because of the United States's flirtations with Napoleon and the consequent reflection that it was only the Royal Navy that he could completely trust to keep the dreaded French invasion ships away, perhaps because the Americans were now lagging behind the British in the march towards the liberation of slaves. He was conscious of them as oppressors and hypersensitive in their company.

Once, when he was giving the skipper of an American merchant-man a dressing-down for a breach of Haitian regulations, the American muttered under his breath, "I wish I had you at Charleston now." Christophe's sharp ear caught it and, breaking his firm rule never to reveal that he spoke the language, he snapped back in English, "And how much do you think I should fetch?" The Black king had reverted twenty years to the insecure Negro. He traded with Americans because it suited him to buy flour and other perishable goods from them, but even in his commercial dealing with them he was not happy.

In 1810 he became convinced that the Baltimore firm of Von Kapff and Brune had swindled him out of a cargo of coffee and bills of exchange to the value of 124,000 dollars. He demanded the money that was due to him, or the goods that should have been bought in Baltimore with it. When neither arrived, he ordered five Britons and Americans to inspect the books of all the American merchants. They reported that the total assets exceeded 130,000 dollars, which Christophe then compelled the Americans to pay into the privy purse in settlement of the debt, telling them that they had his permission to collect the money back from Von Kapff and Brune in Baltimore.

The king was himself a smart trader. He had a large storehouse built at the docks and this, filled with the produce of his own plantations, had to be cleared each season before any other producers were allowed to offer their goods. Since the demand for coffee, sugar, cotton and the other principal crops always exceeded supply, this did no great harm to the other merchants, but it certainly ensured that the king sold his own at good prices. It also resulted in Christophe paying frequent visits to the docks, riding down on horseback from the palace, and then stomping about on foot dealing out admonitory thwacks in all directions.

To protect the home-produced and government-controlled *tafia*, the king banned the importation of brandy and rum. This led to a considerable amount of smuggling, since there were many who desired, and could afford, to drink something smoother than the fiery *tafia*. Determined to stamp this out, Christophe issued orders that he should be personally notified of the next breach of his regulations. A few days later he received a message that among the cargo of wine in a newly-arrived schooner had been found some casks of brandy.

He galloped down to the docks in a tearing rage and had two customs officers hanged on the spot. He then sent for the merchant to whom the cargo was consigned – an American named Hall – and slipped a noose round his neck and threw the end of the rope over a beam in the customs-shed. He informed the startled merchant that he had the choice of paying a fine of 20,000 dollars or of being hanged in twenty-five minutes' time. Hall's fellow-merchants managed to raise the money with five minutes to spare. He was more fortunate than another American, Harris, who uttered remarks that Christophe held to be seditious, and was not even given the option of a fine. He was straightway tied by his hands to the tail of a dragoon's horse and dragged off into the mountains for a fortnight's *travaux-forcés* on Citadel-Henry.

The unfortunate Americans complained to their government, but neither redress nor even negotiation was possible for several years. Increasing British interference with American shipping on the pretext of searching for contraband or for naval deserters culminated in war between the two countries in 1812. Until the summer of 1815, Christophe saw very few American vessels and received only occasional visits from British men-o'-war, come to Haitian ports to collect the homeward-bound merchantmen and shepherd them to Jamaica to join the convoys for the eastward crossing of the Atlantic.

There was one moment, in May 1813, when it seemed to Admiral Stirling at Port Royal that trouble was about to break out again. "I understand," he reported to Mr Croker, "the President intends to march shortly against General Christophe, whose army is much reduced, and sanguine expectations are entertained of success, altho' I shall regret to see the present balance in Haiti destroyed as, however moderate General Pétion has hitherto been, there are those who believe he is not so partial to us as he professed to be when under apprehension from the attack of his enemy." But Pétion, as so often happened, failed to summon up the energy to persevere with his plan. The border remained inviolate. In the twenty miles of no-man's-land that was left uninhabited and un-cultivated along the whole length of the dividing line, the jungle grew taller and denser under heavy rains and burning sun in the rich wasted earth.

It was true that Christophe had reduced his army – to between 20,000 and 25,000 men. Driving his people on towards his dream of a European way of life and standard of living he had brought his sailors as well as his soldiers back to the land. Almost all of his foreign mercenaries had gone and, in this summer of 1813, the Court of King's Bench in London heard the distressing epilogue to the career of one of them.

On July 19 Thomas Goodall, admiral of Haiti, brought an action against his former partner, William Fletcher, attorney-at-law, "for criminal conversation with the plaintiff's wife". Sally Edwards, chambermaid at the White Horse Inn at Uxbridge, gave evidence that Fletcher, a married man with three children, and Mrs Goodall, still the mother of only eight, had spent the night in the same bed in Room 27 towards the end of July 1812. Goodall was awarded the verdict. But the forty-year-old ex-admiral had not long in which to enjoy his victory. He had been as forgetful of marriage vows in Cap-Henry as his wife had in Uxbridge and was now a broken man, so riddled with syphilis that no surgeon in London would risk his reputation by treating him: a fact which the judge no doubt took into sympathetic consideration when awarding him damages of £5,000.

3

Since Christophe could neither read nor write more than his signature – always 'Henry' with the English 'y' – his thirst for information on what was happening in the world outside Haiti had to be satisfied by relays of readers, with whose aid he followed, in newspapers, magazines and the fortnightly newsletter that Peltier sent him from London, the progress of Napoleon's decline from Moscow to the abdication at Fontainebleau. His fear of the emperor turned to contempt when he learned that he had neither died in battle nor killed himself in defeat. "If he had to fall, then he should have buried himself in the ruins," he said. "I never would have thought he would end his career in a manner so unworthy of a soldier."

He had the Comte de Limonade write to Peltier in June 1814 telling him that he was maintaining all his defences, since "the repose of the world will never be secure while Napoleon lives." On the other hand, "His Majesty has never confused the French people with the government which oppressed them. To peaceable traders he has always offered security, protection and commerce. . . . You may declare . . . that His Majesty will with pleasure receive the vessels of French merchants. . . . They shall be protected and treated like the subjects of other friendly powers who trade peaceably with Haiti. . . ."

It was a shrewd move, not only to benefit trade but also to match Pétion in any approaches that he might make to the French. It was expressed in terms calculated to impress the new royalist government, which, Christophe trusted, "would not forget, among our claims, that of having combatted its most implacable enemy from the commencement of his reign to his fall. . . . His Majesty flatters himself that he will find humane sentiments in a sovereign instructed by misfortune."

The great objective, as always, was to persuade Louis XVIII – who was to prove himself even less susceptible to instruction by misfortune than most sovereigns – to grant recognition to Haiti; and Christophe optimistically directed Peltier "to prepare the channels by which the two powers may come to an understanding for their mutual interest". His hopes did not last long. He soon learned to his dismay that the Treaty of Paris, signed at the end of May, granted France the right to continue the slave trade for a further five years; and the list of members of the chamber of peers revealed many ex-colons and others with claims to land in Haiti from whom came a swelling clamour for an expedition to reconquer the island.

When the reactionary character of Louis XVIII's government became evident, common danger drove Christophe and Pétion to agree to common resistance. An English merchant writing home from Haiti discussed "with a feeling of horror, the scenes of bloodshed and massacre that must take place in the island in the event of the French attacking it. . . . It is indeed a sight that makes humanity shudder, to see the preparations making for the destruction of the cities and everything in them, not portable to the mountains. . . . The arsenals are full of torches ready to be lighted. . . . The two parties, those of Pétion and Christophe, can bring into the field upwards of sixty thousand fighting men, in the event of a French invasion; and the soldiers are inured to fatigue and danger. . . . A few months will decide whether the finest country in the western world is to be a dreary desert or a flourishing state."

In July the alien agent at Falmouth was visited at his office in the Customs House by three Frenchmen who told him that they were leaving the next day in the Jamaica packet. When the agent informed them that they could not go to Jamaica without permission from the Colonial Office, they expressed surprise and said they understood that the French Ambassador in London had completed all the formalities. Since the agent still hesitated, the leader of the party, Colonel Dauxion Lavaysse, asked for a word in private and produced secret instructions from Monsieur Malouet, Minister of Marine and Colonies in the new French administration, together with a letter from the French Ambassador to the Duke of Manchester, Governor of Jamaica, introducing Lavaysse and his companions, Lieutenant-Colonel de Medina and Monsieur Dravermann. The agent reluctantly allowed them to go aboard the packet and by late August they were in Jamaica.

Lavaysse decided to conduct negotiations with Pétion himself, leaving to Medina the unenviable task of dealing with Christophe. The third member of the party, Dravermann, had been included because he was married to General Borgella's white half-sister and was to try to win over the general if Pétion proved difficult. Only when they arrived in Jamaica did the conspirators, who were imperfectly informed on many essential matters, learn that Borgella had lost all standing as a political figure since the *Heureuse Réunion* fiasco – a discovery which allowed the septuagenarian Dravermann, who had a slight stroke the day after they landed, to return gratefully to his home in Bordeaux, leaving his two colleagues prostrate with yellow fever.

Lavaysse sent a letter to Pétion by HMS *Moselle* on September 6, asking for an opportunity to set Louis XVIII's proposals before him, and Pétion replied on September 24, agreeing to receive him. It was not until October 24 that Lavaysse arrived in Port-au-Prince, still suffering from the effects of the fever, and was lodged in the luxurious apartments of General Boyer, Pétion's secretary. After a month's discussions, Lavaysse brought Pétion to the point of agreeing to pay compensation to the French government for the benefit of the dispossessed planters. Heartened by this progress, he was trying to persuade Pétion to renounce independence in return for the assurance of being retained as lieutenant-governor, when developments in the North brought all his hopes crashing to the ground.

Christophe learned early in September of Lavaysse's mission, from Peltier, who had returned to Paris with the other *émigré* royalists. On September 18 he published a royal manifesto in which he once more recounted the events of the Haitian revolution and called on the good offices of all the sovereigns of the earth, all philanthropists and all mankind to preserve the liberty and independence which his compatriots had won at such a cost.

We believe that His Majesty Louis XVIII, in accordance with the philanthropic views for which his family is noted, and imitating the attitude of his unhappy brother, Louis XVI, towards the United States of America, will follow in the steps of that monarch and recognise the independence of Haiti. This would be only an act of justice, a feeble recompense for the ills that the French Government brought upon us. Free by right and independent in fact, we will never renounce these privileges. . . . We solemnly declare that we will never accept any treaty, nor any condition, capable of compromising the honour, liberty and independence of the people of Haiti. Loyal to our oath, we will bury ourselves beneath the ruins of our country, rather than permit the slightest impairment of our political rights.

On October 1 Lavaysse informed Christophe that Colonel Medina would present Louis's proposals to him. Since Christophe was known to be more determined to resist than Pétion – and perhaps because Lavaysse himself was not to have the ordeal of facing him – the letter was more sternly worded than the one he had sent to Port-au-Prince three weeks earlier. It made the open threat that the Bourbons had asked the victorious allies to permit France to continue the slave trade for a further five years so that she should be in a position to 'replace' the Black population of Haiti if they resisted Louis's demands. Christophe's reply was to send Lavaysse a copy of his manifesto of September 18.

While Lavaysse journeyed to Port-au-Prince, Colonel Medina went further afield – to Santo-Domingo, capital of the former Spanish part of the island which, ceded to France under the Treaty of Bâle and captured by British troops in 1809, had recently been returned to Spain under the Treaty of Paris. Agostino Franco de Medina was in a peculiar position. Spanish by birth, he held a colonelcy in the French army. His family owned property at Vega, in the Spanish part of the island, where he had been appointed mayor by Toussaint and had later commanded the department of Cibao under the French general Ferrand. Although the primary purpose of his mission was to present the French proposals to Christophe, it seems likely that he was also sounding the possibility of an eventual French return to the Spanish part of the island. From the city of Santo-Domingo he went north-west to inspect the Medina estates and then crossed the border into the Kingdom of Haiti – where he was arrested on November 11 and taken as a prisoner to Le Cap.

Christophe's object in arresting Medina was undoubtedly to give a public demonstration of his refusal ever to discuss any matter touching on the independence of Haiti. But what was to have been a simple propaganda gesture turned into something far more serious when Medina's baggage was examined. The imprudent colonel was carrying with him papers which proved beyond doubt that he and Lavaysse were the outriders of the return of slavery. "As for the class that is numerically the most important – that of the Blacks employed in agriculture and the manufacture of sugar, indigo etc.," said one memorandum, "it is essential that they should remain in, or return to, the condition in which they were before 1789."

Medina was brought before the military court of Cap-Henry, charged with spying. The trial produced further revelations from the frightened Medina, including the allegation that Pétion had made approaches to Bonaparte in 1813, and that Lavaysse intended to use the Republic as a base for the invasion of the Kingdom. The royal printing presses poured out hundreds of copies of the court-martial proceedings, for distribution in Europe and across the border in Pétion's Republic. For Medina there was the expected sentence of death. But Christophe ordered the execution to be postponed. Not because of any disposition to leniency or doubt about the legitimacy of the verdict – he had made it clear, in sending his manifesto to Lavaysse, that he refused to accept an envoy and Medina had therefore entered the country at his own risk – but because he saw an opportunity to squeeze still more publicity out of the incident and to dramatise his own steadfastness of purpose. He conceived the macabre plan of giving Medina a state funeral – with the condemned man attending in person. The church of Notre Dame was hung with funeral draperies. Medina was perched on a platform high enough for all the congregation to see him, with the empty coffin beside him. The archbishop, the aged Corneille Brelle, conducted a requiem mass in the presence of the entire royal family, members of the nobility, ministers of state, and a packed throng of soldiers and civilians. He read, and commented on, the instructions that had been found in Medina's possession, and was then followed in the pulpit by the Baron de Vastey, a brilliant, acid-tongued mulatto who was the Prince Royal's tutor as well as Christophe's most spirited and skilful propagandist. Vastey's address was so passionate that the congation burst into shouts of rage against France and many of its military members drew their sabres and seemed likely to execute Medina on the spot. The poor man fainted and was escorted back to gaol where Christophe, his purpose amply fulfilled, ordered that his life should be spared.

It was no longer possible for Pétion to continue his negotiations with Lavaysse, who left Port-au-Prince on December 2 and arrived back in France in January 1815 to be met with a rebuke for "exceeding his instructions", though it would seem that his only offence was to have been unsuccessful. For Christophe, Lavaysse's mission had been timely, since it gave him the opportunity to confront Pétion with a new proposal of union between the two halves of Haiti at a moment when the president was at his most vulnerable: his second four-year term of office was about to expire.

Christophe chose as his representatives four men who all had links with the West and the South: the Comte du Trou had served with Pétion as Colonel Dupont; the Baron de Dessalines was a nephew of the emperor; the Baron de Ferrier had lived at Jacmel and had been a senator in the Port-au-Prince assembly; the chevalier Edouard Michel had formerly traded in the South. They made a stately and overdressed arrival at Port-au-Prince on February 18, each wearing a costume of a different colour, enormous military hats, a wealth of gold braid and decorations, their hair and long queues heavily powdered. (Rigaud, acutely conscious of his crinkly Negroid hair, always wore a very straight-haired wig; Christophe ordered any of his courtiers who suffered from the same disability to roll lead weights in the ends of their curls.)

The commander of Fort Cibert detained them on the road while

he sent to Port-au-Prince for instructions and Pétion thus had time
to place some of his paid supporters among the crowd that watched
the envoys enter by the porte Saint-Joseph. The northerners rode
with their escort down the principal street, the rue Républicaine, to
the accompaniment of laughter and jeers from Pétion's men, who
shouted to each other, *"Cé Pagnols! Cé mascarade! Gardé yo donc!
Ça yo vini chaché?"* ["*They're Spaniards! It's a carnival! Just look at
them! What are they after?*"] Amid mounting ribaldry the four men
were taken to the Palais National where Pétion had called a number
of generals and magistrates to listen to Christophe's proposals.

The Comte du Trou presented a long letter signed by His
Majesty's Secretary of State for Foreign Affairs, the Comte de
Limonade, addressed to 'Général de Division' Pétion. It adjured
him to consider that:

> The plans of Haiti's implacable enemies having been laid bare,
> the people of Haiti can no longer hesitate to reunite and offer a
> massive resistance [to] the imminent attacks with which our
> oppressors threaten us. Knowing the wishes of the Haitians in the
> sector under your command, and in the profound conviction that
> their reunion with the great Haitian family depends on you
> alone, General, the King, head and father of us all, would be
> justified . . . in waiting for you to take the first step towards
> reunion; but so that it may not for one moment be said that it is
> His Majesty's fault if such a reunion does not take place, His
> Majesty is once more pleased to give the people of Haiti proof
> of his benevolent disposition and to demonstrate before God
> and man that he has never ceased to cherish the public weal and
> common interest. The King has consequently ordered me,
> General, to make this approach to you and to propose:
>
> 1. The total obliteration of all memory of the past.
> 2. Open and genuine reconciliation.
> 3. Retention of Your Excellency's rank and command.
> 4. Retention of their rank and employment by all general
>   officers, magistrates, military commanders, officers and
>   non-commissioned officers, with the titles appointed in his
>   Majesty's Regulations, examples of which are attached.
> 5. Admission to the Hereditary Order of Nobility of the
>   Kingdom in accordance with the scale of ranks laid down
>   for senior civil and military officers.

6. Guarantee of their possessions to all Haitian property-
owners.

There was little in this to compensate Pétion for loss of the
presidency, but he was obliged to pretend to consider the proposal.
Ever since the arrest of Medina, Christophe's agents in the South
had been spreading word that Pétion was prepared to hand over
power to the French rather than submit to Christophe (a story that
would have gained a great deal more credence if his approaches to
the British government four years before had been known)and that
the result of this would be the return to slavery of most of the population. These rumours had been supported by the pamphlets containing the account of Medina's trial. In less than three weeks' time – on
March 9 – Pétion would be offering himself for re-election. If
there were the slightest hint that he might bring back slavery, the
whole Black population would reject him.

He faced the challenge boldly. He invited the Comte du Trou to
read Christophe's letter aloud, before the throng that had followed
the northerners into the Palais National, and himself led the
laughter at its terms while his retainers among the crowd continued
to shout, *"Cé Pagnols! Cé mascarade!"* He even turned to the attack
and accused the Baron de Ferrier of having absconded from Jacmel,
when he was plain Senator Félix Ferrier, with 50,000 piastres
belonging to his business associates. Robert Sutherland, who was
prominent among the foreign observers, seized this cue to shout to
the president that he requested permission to arrest Ferrier on
behalf of the creditors. Pétion retorted amid roars of laughter, that
"a King's envoy" could not be held for debt. He sent for the
members of the deputation two days later and handed them his
reply, mockingly expressing the hope that they would have a good
journey home and keep their heads at the end of it.

His letter to the Comte de Limonade was full of recriminations
against Christophe:

You speak to me, General, of amnesties, pardons, expunging
the past, paternal authority, monarchs, ranks, distinctions, titles
of hereditary nobility! We were very far from such bizarre ideas
when I begged General Christophe to leave Le Cap to escape the
gallows, and when I awakened his distrust of the French, whom
he understood so little that shortly before he had entrusted his
son to General Boudet to be taken to France. . . . Yet it is he who

is so gracious as to pardon us, to raise us to hereditary nobility and to decorate us with his orders!

Christophe's epistolary style inclined to the florid – when one of his secretaries wrote that an enemy had "died", the king ordered him to substitute "bit the dust", an expression that he picked up from Toussaint – and was not as well suited to public debate as Pétion's sharper wit. The president published the exchange of correspondence and was duly re-elected. The great majority of his fellow citizens had, in any case, little property to be guaranteed and no hope of earning hereditary titles. The Republic might have a smaller revenue despite its larger population but the disadvantages attendant on this were trifling compared with the unremitting toil to which they knew they would be forcibly exposed if they came under Christophe's firm hand.

The Hundred Days of Napoléon's return from Elba flared up and flickered away almost unnoticed in Haiti, except that Christophe's contempt for Bonaparte increased when he learned that, for a second time, the emperor had allowed himself to be captured alive. But one of Bonaparte's actions during this period – the hypocritical abolition of the slave trade – though it did nothing to help his own cause, served to make the Bourbon retention of the trade even more difficult to defend, and when the gross Louis was once more dumped into the throne of France Christophe gave vent to his rage and fear in a declaration that he would convert his kingdom to Protestantism and introduce English as the national language. The task would have been formidable and there is no indication that he really meant to attempt it, but the outburst revealed the extent to which he was now emotionally wedded to his 'native country' and the admiration that he felt for the English philanthropists: Wilberforce, Clarkson, Archdeacon Wrangham, James Stephen, Zachary Macaulay.

He began corresponding with Wilberforce in 1814 and in the following year first wrote to Thomas Clarkson, the originator of the abolition movement and the man who persuaded Wilberforce to become its spokesman in parliament. Their letters brought him reliable news and informed views on events in Europe and his own gave him the opportunity to express the very real gratitude that he felt towards these men who had impelled their country, against its own selfish interests, to abolish the slave trade. More than this, the correspondence allowed him to hope that with their help he would some day gain the one thing that he desired above all others:

British recognition of Haiti's independence, for without the protection of the Royal Navy his people could have no assurance that their freedom would endure. There had been no mention of Haiti in the Treaty of Paris. In the eyes of all its signatories the country was still a disaffected colony of France. In one of his earliest letters to Clarkson, Christophe told him frankly, "we hope, if the French Cabinet is ever again led to venture on inhuman measures against us, that our virtuous champions will enlighten the public opinion of Europe and attempt to prevent the execution of such a plan. . . . We count on them at least to warn us of any such moves aimed at our destruction."

It was partly to impress his people, partly to satisfy his own vanity, partly even as a reply to Pétion who, in June 1816, had put through a new constitution for the Republic under which he was to remain president for life, and partly also to show the European powers that his kingdom lacked nothing in display and military might, that he organised the protracted celebrations of the queen's patronal festival on August 15, the Feast of the Assumption, in 1816. On the 14th the court made a ceremonial progress from the palace of Sans-Souci to the palace of Cap-Henry. Detachments of the artillery, royal bodyguard, Haitian Guard, *chasseurs de la garde*, and the King's, Queen's and Prince Royal's Light Horse were followed by the king's aides-de-camp bearing the royal standard and preceding the king's eight-horse state carriage, recently made for him in London and admiringly described in the British journals. Constructed "peculiarly for the country, . . . the front projecting for the purpose of shade," its lower panels were painted the royal colour, celestial blue, and the interior lined with "the richest velvet, embroidered with the star of the Order of St Henry". The cornice, with a phoenix in each corner, was "supported by the emblematical figures of Liberty, Justice and Fortitude, and surmounted with the royal crown"; and everywhere was a profusion of gilt lions, trophies and arms.

Following the king, each in an eight-horse carriage, were the queen; the Prince Royal; Madame Première, the elder daughter; Her Royal Highness Princess Athénaïre, the younger; all attended by the officers of their households. Then came the six-horse carriages of HRH Madame la Princesse Jean, wife of the king's nephew; HRH Madame la Princesse Noël, wife of the queen's brother; the four-horse carriages of the two princesses' governesses, a long string of countesses and "an infinity of persons of all ranks

and both sexes, in carriages and on horseback". Just before the
bridge at Le Haut-du-Cap, where the side road from Sans-Souci
met the main road from the south, Prince Jean, Grand Admiral of
Haiti, and son of Christophe's sister, Marie, joined the procession
with high naval officers.

At the other side of the bridge the foreign merchants, on
catching sight of the king, dismounted from their horses, lined both
sides of the road, and greeted His Majesty *"par des cris de huzza, en
agitant en l'air leurs chapeaux."* * The procession passed under a
triumphal arch inscribed with encomiums and loyal salutations, and
at La Barrière-Bouteille, on the outskirts of the town, the king
descended from his carriage and mounted his horse, to be welcomed
and conducted into his capital by the governor of Cap-Henry,
General Richard, now Duc de la Marmelade. (The duke's name,
like that of the Comte de Limonade, provoked much merriment in
Europe although both were simple territorial titles, taken from
towns that had been named by Frenchmen long before the revolution – and, as Christophe pointed out on one occasion, no more
comical than such honoured French titles as the Duc de Bouillon
or the Prince de Poix. Or, he might have added, the Prince of
Orange.)

From this point onwards the route was lined by the Régiment du
Roi and the Régiment de la Reine. From the forts and town
batteries there came the slow, solemn thunder of a hundred-gun
salute, and from the warships and merchant ships in the harbour
another hundred guns echoed back. The citizens were now thick
along the sides of the road, waving and shouting. The king, in the
uniform of a colonel of his own Light Horse, saluted or removed his
hat, revealing a mass of pure white hair, crisply curled, for he did
not himself observe the rule of wearing lead weights.

His Grace, Monseigneur Corneille Brelle, Duc de l'Anse, Archbishop of Haiti, stood with his attendant clergy beneath a canopy
beside another triumphal arch, flanked by the senior magistrates
and native merchants of the town and their wives. After receiving
their greetings the king continued along the rue Espagnole, where
once he had worked as maitre d'hôtel at the long-since destroyed
Auberge de la Couronne and so to the palace, at which point the
crowd dispersed to watch the fireworks or to join in the dancing
that struck up all over the town.

The next morning, the day of the festival itself, guns began

* *"With shouts of hurrah, waving their hats in the air."*

firing at dawn. At 8 am the queen received the congratulations of the town worthies and their wives, who warmly applauded her as she entered the throne room on her husband's arm, dressed in a gown of white satin, richly embroidered with gold sunflowers and with a broad gold fringe at the hem. The white satin train, embroidered to match the gown, was looped on each side with gold tassels. A gold net fell from her left shoulder, finished at the corners and along the edges with more gold tassels and fringe. Combs, studded with precious stones, held her tall nodding headdress of white feathers in place. Her broad black face beaming with good nature and gratitude, she thanked them charmingly for their good wishes and assured them that "to do all that I can do to be agreeable to my august Spouse and to contribute to the happiness of the Haitian people, will always be my sole aim and the object of my liveliest solicitude".

At the conclusion of this audience the king and queen went on foot across the place d'Armes lined by troops of the royal household to the cathedral, preceded by heralds at arms and pages and flanked by the king's barons, counts, dukes and princes.

After Mass and the Archbishop's address, the *Te Deum* was sung to the ringing of all the bells of the city and the firing of guns from every battery; 400 guests assembled at the palace to feast amid the glitter of candelabra and the glare of torches reflected from the mirror-hung walls of the banqueting hall. The richly-decorated ceiling rang with applause and musical echoes as toasts were drunk to the Royal Family, individually and collectively, to Liberty, Union and the memory of those who had died in the fight for independence.

The official programme completed and the musicians and artillerymen stood at ease, the afternoon continued with a profusion of additional toasts, proposed and drunk with increasing enthusiasm and incoherence, and would have endured far into the night but for the need of the celebrants to move on to the theatre where the amateur company of court players performed Grétry's *Zémire et Azor*. The opera was followed by a firework display on the square in front of the palace, and a ball that went on until dawn.

The next afternoon the Duc de la Marmelade gave a banquet to the foreign merchants at which the diners drank the health of the King and the Royal Family, of George III, the Prince Regent and William Wilberforce, the President of the United States, the King of the Low Countries and the King of Prussia.

As the toasts indicated, there were merchants from several countries present, including Messrs French, Beesley and Myers from the United States and Herr Strickmann from Bremen, but they were outnumbered by the British contingent, and it was one of these, John White, wearing his old army uniform in honour of the occasion, who rose to say:

Gentlemen, I am an Englishman and accustomed to express my feelings freely. I have seen all the sovereigns of Europe and the troops of all nations. I have observed the laws and customs of the people of all the countries I have visited. Well, gentlemen, I can honestly say this: I have seen the King of Haiti at the head of his troops; I have examined the richness of the uniforms, the bearing and discipline of the Haitian army; I have observed the morals and studied the laws of this country. And I have not seen anywhere in Europe any Sovereign of better presence, any troops better dressed or better disciplined, nor any better order, regularity and justice than in this Kingdom. In your present situation, gentlemen, you need fear no enemy – you are invincible!

To a roar of cheering, Mr White resumed his seat, only to be lifted out of it again and embraced by a large part of the company.

On Saturday, the court moved to the château of Plaisance de Tivoli, returning to Le Cap for Mass in the cathedral on Sunday, followed by a march past of the garrison with their majesties taking the salute on the palace balcony.

Heavy clouds and the threat of rain sent the ladies to their carriages and the infantry back to their barracks to protect their uniforms, but Christophe took personal command of the cavalry, leading them in extended manoeuvres and charges from the place d'Armes along the former rue d'Anjou, now renamed the cours de la Reine, and then along the quays and back up the rue Notre-Dame to the place d'Armes once more, riding his favourite charger, Bois-Rouge, and wearing the full-dress uniform of Colonel of the Haitian Guards. The twelve-year-old Prince Royal, in a green tunic with pink facings and green satin breeches trimmed with yellow, took command of a detachment of his own Light Horse, while his illegitimate brother, Prince Eugène, marched at the head of the Chasseurs de la Garde, in red and green tunic and white breeches.

Each company carried its colour, embroidered by the ladies of the court with one of the royal emblems, the regimental designation and device, and an appropriate motto: *I triumph over my enemies* and *I disperse my enemies* for the first and second companies of the Royal Artillery; *God, my cause and my sword* and *I am reborn from my ashes*, for the Garde du Corps; *He shines for all* for the King's Light Horse; an olive branch entwined with the delicate and unforeseen legend, *May the arts and agriculture flourish in her fashion*, for the Queen's Light Horse; for the Prince Royal, his arms and *The Sports of Childhood foretell great men* on one side, and on the other the genius of the country setting a trumpet to her lips and *I will inspire him and he shall prosper*; the ten standards of the Garde Haitienne all bore the same motto, *Valour crowned by Victory*; while the Chasseurs de la Garde shared three legends on six banners, each as brisk as their own marching step: *I disperse the darkness*, *Quick as lightning* and *I sound terror*.

At nine o'clock on Monday morning the king received the foreign merchants, recovered from their banquet. On Tuesday the whole court rode out to spend the day at Port-Dahomet, the former Port-Français, the queen and the ladies on horseback, dressed *en amazone* and wearing small hats with very large ostrich feathers. On Wednesday, their majesties were occupied with good works during the day, the queen dispensing money to the aged or incapacitated poor and discussing arrangements for the banquet which she intended to offer to the ladies of Le Cap on the following Sunday, the city's patronal festival, as a repayment for the kindness that she had received from them; the king granting pardons to prisoners. The ball at the palace that evening continued until four o'clock in the morning, when the royal family and their retinue drove back to Sans-Souci. The king had been in the best of humours all night, smiling and chatting with the crowds of people who thronged the doors and craned in at the windows, and promising them that after the feast that the queen was giving on Sunday they too should dance in the royal ballroom.

On Saturday, the foreign merchants returned the governor's hospitality at a magnificent banquet at the *Café des Etrangers*. On Sunday they joined Prince Jean and other notables in waiting on the 800 prominent ladies of the capital who had been invited to the queen's banquet. After many loyal toasts, and more gunfire there was a performance of the *Barber of Seville* and, in accordance with the king's promise, dancing in the palace ballroom.

4

Christophe was a convinced believer in the value of publicity: he
had John White's speech at the Duc de la Marmelade's banquet
reprinted on the royal presses and distributed at home and abroad.
But though he hoped to impress others with bravado and the noisy
vulgarities of royal pomp, he did not deceive himself. He remained
level headed, determined and worried, a man in his late forties
with so much to do and so little time to do it in.

The project closest to his heart was the education of his people.
He saw clearly that learning was the only sure safeguard of their
continuing freedom. And it was with the setting up of schools and
the provision of teachers for them that his early correspondence
with Wilberforce and Clarkson was principally concerned. Wilberforce recommended the British and Foreign School Society in the
Borough Road, London, and at the same time – towards the middle
of 1815 – sent out to Haiti an educated American Negro named
Prince Sanders who had been working with the abolitionists
in England. Christophe asked Sanders to go back to England to
bring out the first of the teachers from London – he had sent
Wilberforce £6,000 to be used in advances for salaries and travel
expenses – and gave him a letter to deliver to Clarkson.

For a long while [he wrote to Clarkson] my intention and
dearest ambition has been to obtain for the nation which has
entrusted to me its destiny the benefits of public instruction. . . .
I am completely dedicated to this project. The buildings required
for the institutions of public instruction in the cities and in rural
areas are under construction. I await the teachers and craftsmen
for whom I asked, who will undertake the training of our youth.
. . . If God blesses my labours, and grants me time enough,
I hope that the people of Haiti, overcoming the odious prejudice
that has so long oppressed them, will astonish the world with
their knowledge.

The first of the British and Foreign School Society's teachers,
T. B. Gulliver, arrived at Cap-Henry in mid-September 1816 and
in the absence of the king, who was "engaged in an excursion to
make observations on the state of agriculture", he was welcomed
by Baron Dupuy and became his guest until his own lodgings and
the schoolroom were completed. Gulliver, like all the teachers

from the British and Foreign School Society, had been trained in the system introduced by Joseph Lancaster in 1798, whereby "one master may conduct a school of 1,000 children with perfect ease". The Society's *Manual of the System of Teaching Reading, Writing, Arithmetic and Needlework*, published in that year, laid down in great detail the physical requirements of the school. The ground on which it was built should be high and open to the south; the school yard should be of sand to the depth of one foot, enclosed by a wall, part covered, and one side furnished with stone seats. In the single schoolroom, the master's desk stood in the centre of a platform, flanked by the smaller desks of the two principal monitors. In front of these stood three sand-desks, the surface painted a dark colour with white sand sprinkled in a thin layer on it. On these the children of the first class copied the letters from the alphabet wheel fixed to the master's desk.

The pupils of the second to seventh classes, whose benches rose in front of the master on a floor that sloped at a degree of 1 in 20, learned to write on slates, while the most senior boys, in the eighth class, were allowed to use pen and ink. Suspended on the walls were more alphabet boards and other lesson boards with the aid of which the monitor of each class and the assistants he had chosen examined their classmates' work, corrected and dictated. The master was armed with a bell, a whistle and "a collection of amusing instructive books, to be chosen by the committee, which may be lent to the best pupils as a reward for good conduct".

Joseph Lancaster disapproved of corporal punishment and devoted much time to the invention of ingenious forms of non-violent public humiliation which must have left far deeper scars on his pupils' characters. He had now severed all connection with the Society, but some of his aids to discipline lived on in the "Badges of Merit and Disgrace-marks . . . made of little pieces of wood 6 inches long and 3 inches broad and 1 inch thick. They have two holes in them to admit a piece of pack thread by which they are suspended round the neck of the children. On one side of the badge are written the words First boy, Playing mark, Idle mark, Talking mark, Dirty mark etc." These methods did not appeal to Christophe's less philosophical nature. In the ordinance that he was having drawn up for the Haitian National Schools, he prescribed six to twelve strokes of the cane for lateness, idleness, noisiness, quarrelling, lying or damaging school property, and one to two weeks' imprisonment on bread and water for absence, not attending

Sunday devotions, disobedience or blasphemy. These punishments could be doubled for a second offence, or if the offender was a monitor.

The pupils, aged from six to fifteen, were to bring with them a doctor's certificate that they had no contagious disease and, if their parents lived in the country, were to be put in the care of somebody living near the school who would provide board and lodging. In addition to the national and principal religious holidays, Thursday and Sunday were rest days, though on these days they had to attend at the usual time in the morning for "prayers and a lecture within the comprehension of the pupils". They were to be taught English as well as French, reading, writing, simple arithmetic and grammar. During the summer their hours were from 6 am to 11 am, and 2 pm to 6 pm; in the winter they began work an hour later and ended an hour earlier. To cure a problem common to all day school masters, Christophe also inserted a clause that "the monitors shall ensure that pupils leave classes properly and in the strictest order; pupils may not loiter in the streets, but shall go straight home".

The pleasant and exciting work of drawing up this system of education and discussing its details with the young and sternly enthusiastic Tom Gulliver was interrupted by the arrival early in October of a new French mission. As before, the softer landing at Port-au-Prince was chosen by its members, all of whom were former *colons*, headed by the elderly Vicomte de Fontanges, who had distinguished himself twenty years earlier in the campaigns against Jean-François and Biassou.

Fontanges, while still at sea in the frigate *Flora*, sent a message to Pétion that the royalist flag "which you defended so long and so courageously" already floated over the other territories that France had lost during the war and that Louis XVIII "wishes to re-unite all the members of his family in bonds of friendship, and his children in Saint-Domingue are no less dear to him than those in Europe". Fontanges added that he had been commanded by the king "to repair to Saint-Domingue for the purpose of consulting with those in authority there on the measures to be employed to give that country the security which it cannot enjoy in its present precarious situation; to legalise in his name all the necessary institutions; to reward the care and services of those who have restored and maintained order in the colony; to confirm by his royal will all such institutions and changes in the status of persons and things in this island which the course of events may have rendered necessary and which are not incompatible with the dignity of the crown or the interests of the colony and the mother country."

There was very little gilt on the pill. The island was referred to as Saint-Domingue, not Haiti; Pétion was addressed as General, not President. This, from a Bourbon, might have been anticipated; but the message clearly postulated the end of independence and the right of Louis XVIII to ratify or rescind at his pleasure any of the colony's new laws – including the abolition of slavery. Pétion, however, replied to the commissioners that he was prepared to discuss the proposals with them and they conferred with him for two days following their arrival at Port-au-Prince. It was then agreed that they should go to Cap-Henry for talks with Christophe before entering into any final settlement with Pétion.

Their journey northward was beset by calms. They left Port-au-Prince on October 9 but it was not until October 17 that the lookout at Fort Picolet spotted the *Flora* with her attendant brig, *Le Railleur*, and identified them as French ships of war. The governor, Marmelade, rode out to the fort to confirm the news, leaving behind him a city in which tension was mounting rapidly. By nightfall rumours were circulating that these two ships were the precursers of a great armada; it was the invasion of 1802 all over again. There had been considerable discussion of such an expedition in the French newspapers since the Bourbon restoration and much of it had been reproduced in the pamphlets that Christophe printed on the three presses that he now had working at Cap-Henry, Citadel-Henry and Sans-Souci to cope with the flow of royal proclamations, official publications, news sheets and tracts, many of them written by his ministers.

Yellow fever, the advocates of invasion had suggested, could be warded off by sending the troops to be acclimatised on the small islands around the coast where the air was purer; and they could be reinforced by other seasoned troops brought from the Windward Islands. Tortuga in the north, Gonave and the Cayemettes in the west and the Ile à Vaches in the south were proposed as suitable islands to be captured and held for this purpose. It might be, thought the agitated citizens of Cap-Henry, that while the frigate and the brig cruised offshore to prevent countermeasures, French soldiers were already landing from transports at Tortuga.

Dawn showed the frigate and the brig still offshore, hove to about ten miles distant. Throughout the morning they remained without sign of purposeful movement, the brig drifting a little from the frigate; but at two in the afternoon the watchers who now lined the shore and all the points of vantage from Fort Picolet along the Morne du Cap saw the brig approach the frigate in answer to a signal and a boat cross from one to the other. Half an hour later both ships hoisted the red and blue Haitian Republican flag at the mizzen and, with the royalist white flag at the main and foremasts, headed towards Fort Picolet.

With all the batteries in the town and its protecting forts prepared for action, the governor sent the pilot boat to wait within the range of Fort Picolet, ready to escort the vessels into harbour; but at a distance of five miles the French ships again hove to and the brig fired a gun. The next likely move seemed to be the lowering of a boat under a flag of truce and the arrival of a French officer to speak with the commander of Fort Picolet or to ask for a pilot. Instead, there was a long pause, then another gun was fired from the brig. As the two vessels lay offshore throughout the afternoon, one of them lugubriously firing a gun at long intervals, it became apparent that they dared not risk coming closer for fear of the coastal batteries, but had a message to communicate. The Duc de la Marmelade, on the other hand, was unwilling to send out the pilot boat in response to what might be interpreted as a summons by the French.

As dusk approached, the French vessels hoisted more sail and made off to the west, but before they were out of sight they fell in with a brigantine, also heading west, stopped and spoke to her for half an hour and then continued. The brigantine, the *Sidney Crispin* of New York, came about and made for Cap-Henry; but she, too, continued beyond the harbour entrance, then put about and so continued until the following morning. Like the French men-o'-war, the American merchantman then approached the harbour but, as soon as the pilot boat put out, turned away again. She finally entered the harbour and took up moorings in the Royal Dock, whereupon an interpreter was sent aboard and was told by Captain Elisha Kent and his supercargo, Jacob M. King, that the French brig had entrusted them with two letters for King Henry.

The interpreter sent word to the governor who, on his arrival on board ship, at once realised the reason for the American captain's hesitancy in entering port. It seemed, indeed, almost incomprehensible that the two men should have accepted the missive for, as the Duc de la Marmelade pointed out to them in a great rage, they were in the habit of trading with Haiti and must

have known that it was both impossible and insulting to attempt
to deliver letters addressed to "Monsieur le Général Christophe"
at "Cap-François" – an affront both to the king and to national
independence. He returned the letters unopened and told the
Americans to leave port, bellowing the order with such ferocity
that Captain Kent at once hired all the longboats in the harbour
to tow him out.

Meanwhile, the French frigate carrying the commissioners came
upon a Haitian ship off Cap Saint-Nicolas, bound from Cap-Henry
to Les Gonaïves. Knowing that the letters they had given to the
Americans were likely to be rejected, they put further documents
in a cover addressed to the Governor of Les Gonaïves and
persuaded the Haitian captain to carry them with him. One was a
copy of their commission from Louis XVIII; the other was a letter
informing Christophe that "the King is desirous of extending to
Saint-Domingue the blessings he has bestowed on France"; and
that they awaited the general's reply and did not doubt for an
instant "that you will seize with eagerness the opportunity of
proving to your countrymen that in such important circumstances
you are desirous of promoting their welfare."

The French commissioners continued to Port-au-Prince, arriving
there on October 23 and exchanging letters with Pétion until
November 10, when they decided there was no hope of persuading
him to accept their proposals and they sailed for France. On
November 12 Pétion published the correspondence that had passed
between them, together with a declaration to the people of the
Republic of Haiti, who had been demonstrating against the continued stay of the Frenchmen. He assured them that they had done
their duty in restraining themselves and that "your confidence
shall never be abused". How far he himself had been tempted to
negotiate with the French remained obscure.

Christophe, on the other hand, made his position clear with his
usual vehemence and volubility. On November 20 he issued a
declaration of more than 5,000 words in which he reviewed Haiti's
grievances against Louis and made known to the world "our
unshakable resolution either to live free and independent or to
die . . ."

He accused France of retaining the slave trade as a means of
"replacing the population of Haiti, in case of its destruction in the
contemplated war of extermination." He recounted the missions
of Lavaysse and Fontanges and accused the French cabinet of

inciting the South to attack the North. "They are unaware . . . that the cause of Haitians of both colours is one and inseparable . . . that all are embarked in the vessel of independence, and must save her from shipwreck, or perish with her. . . . . The Haitians will be unanimous on this point at least, *to fight to extinction rather than submit again to the yoke of France and slavery. . . ."*

The sovereign of France has declared that in negotiating with us nothing should be done which could detract from *what he owes to the dignity of his crown, to justice and the interest of his people!* And we – we also declare that we shall not be found wanting in what we owe to the interest of our people and the dignity of our crown.

We do solemnly declare that we will not negotiate with the French Government on any other footing than that of power with power, sovereign with sovereign. . . . And that no definitive treaty shall be concluded with that Government without having previously obtained the good offices and mediation of a great maritime power which will guarantee the integrity of the treaty against its ever being broken by the French:

In the event of our negotiating we will withhold our consent from any treaty which does not admit the liberty and independence of all the Haitians who inhabit the three Provinces of the Kingdom, known by the names of the North, the West and the South; the cause of the Haitian people being one and indivisible . . .

Neither the French flag nor individuals of that nation shall be admitted within any of the ports of the Kingdom, until the independence of Haiti has been definitely recognised by the French government. . . .

We declare and affirm that, whatever be the menaces employed by the French to intimidate us, whatever their attempts to subjugate us, the nature of their attack, or the magnitude of the crimes and barbarity they count upon employing for the attainment of their end, nothing shall for an instant shake our determination. Should the whole universe conspire for our destruction, the last Haitian will resign his last breath rather than cease to live free and independent.

We leave the justice of our cause in the hands of that God who always punishes the unjust and the aggressors. We will maintain the dignity of our crown, with the rights and interests of the Haitian people; and we rely with confidence on their bravery, their zeal, and their patriotism, to second all our efforts in defence of their rights, their liberties, and their independence.

5

The great maritime nation which Christophe hoped to persuade to be the arbiter in any dealings he might have with France was, of course, Britain. But at this moment he was not in good odour at Whitehall, where the friends of Mr James Davison, of the firm of Davison and Hill, had complained to the government of an "act of barbarity" that he suffered at Christophe's hands earlier in the year.

According to Davison's story, he had gone from Cap-Henry, where he had his headquarters, to Puerto Plata on the northern coast of the Spanish part of the island and there met James Reid, the master of the Belfast merchantman, *Lady Gambler*, who delivered some letters and papers to him and told him that he had come for a cargo of mahogany and dye-woods but was finding difficulty in obtaining them. Davison recommended him to sell all the cargo he had brought to Puerto Plata, take on board a hundred logs of mahogany that Davison's firm had in the port and, if he could not complete his cargo locally, to sail for Port-au-Prince where he would find plenty of log-wood and fustic.

Captain Reid did, in fact, fail to complete his cargo at Puerto Plata and was on the point of sailing for Port-au-Prince when he received news from the city of Santo-Domingo that a revolution in favour of Christophe had broken out in the South. There had been two attempts to unseat Pétion in the second half of 1815, and Davison had heard that a secret expedition to support the rebels had sailed from Cap-Henry just before he did. He told Reid that he would return to Cap-Henry at once and try to discover what was going on. A few days later he wrote Reid a letter saying that "King Henry's expedition against the South side of the island has been completely unsuccessful. His vessels have returned here, having been frequently chased by those of Pétion, and the troops upon landing at Jérémie immediately went over to the opposite party. You may now therefore go round to Port-au-Prince without any danger. I understand the price of logwood there is seventeen dollars."

Davison hired a small sloop to take this message to Puerto

Plata, but it returned ten days later with its mission uncompleted
– the easterly headwinds had been too strong. The master of the
sloop refused to make a second attempt. Davison, having received
urgent enquiries from Captain Reid – which had come overland by
horseman – was forced to send his letter by the same route. To do
this he had first to submit it to the censorship instituted on all
letters passing between the kingdom and the Spanish part of the
island.

Baron Dupuy, the court interpreter, was in charge of the
censorship office and many of the merchants, to guard their trade
secrets, were in the habit of getting him to countersign their letters
personally – which he usually did without reading them – instead
of passing them through one of the junior interpreters. When
Davison brought his letters to the office, Dupuy told him to leave
them with the messenger who was to carry them across the frontier
and that he would sign them when he had a moment to spare.
Davison, displeased at being kept waiting, came back into the
room shortly afterwards and said that his messenger had to leave
at once.

Dupuy took the letters and had signed three of them – all open
– without reading them, when he noticed that the fourth was sealed.
His suspicions aroused, he broke the seal, unfolded the paper, and
read Davison's account of the alleged defeat in the South. This
made him more suspicious than ever, for he had himself received
no news of the expedition that had sailed three weeks before. He
asked Davison where he had obtained his information, to which
Davison replied that he had overheard it in a café.

Dupuy pointed out that in that case Davison would have been
more likely to write "I have heard that" instead of making the
firm statements in the letter. He again asked Davison for the
source of his information and, when Davison answered curtly that
it was a business matter and no concern of the government, Dupuy
ordered him to accompany him to the Governor's Palace. The
Duc de la Marmelade was ill and received the two men in his
bedroom. Dupuy repeated his questions, Davison refused to reply,
whereupon the governor, who had already heard reports of seditious rumours circulating in the town, had him taken to the prison
of La Barrière-Neuve.

The truth of what happened next was never agreed between the
parties concerned. Davison said that after being cast into a cell he
was fettered and had thumbscrews applied. Dupuy said that Davison

never complained of this to him, while the Duc de la Marmelade said that, as far as he knew, there were no thumbscrews in the prison. It is quite possible, however, that Davison's story was true – the thumbscrew was a common form of torture at the time. Bonaparte ordered its use on political prisoners after one of the royalist plots in Paris.

On Christophe's orders, Dupuy assembled the fifty or sixty foreign merchants, read them Davison's letter, and told them that he had been imprisoned and would be accused of espionage. There was no protest from the merchants; a fact which Dupuy attributed to their acknowledgement that there was a prima facie case for Davison to answer, and also to Davison's being heavily in debt and not in good standing in the community. Davison's fetters and thumbscrews were, according to his own story, not removed until after four days of torture, and it was more than a week before one of the British merchants, Strafford, asked Dupuy for permission to see the king, to obtain Davison's release pending trial. This Christophe agreed to and Davison emerged from prison on February 2. He was allowed to leave Cap-Henry, neither Dupuy nor the governor having managed to find any further evidence against him, but it was not until almost a year later that he reached London and lodged protests with the ministry about his treatment.

All this happened before the celebrations of the queen's fête in August 1816, at which the foreign merchants – and the British in particular – were so fulsome in their praise of Christophe and his government. Some of the panegyrics could be attributed to sycophancy, but not all, though this did not deter Davison's friends from representing the British traders at Cap-Henry as feeling the greatest anxiety that "while prosecuting their mercantile speculations with that spirit of adventure peculiar to Englishmen, they can be deserted by the powerful protection of their own government." And on March 4, 1817 Mr Sharp presented a petition to the House of Commons on Davison's behalf.

Rumours were circulating in Britain at this time that the United States government was about to take firm steps to recover from Christophe the money that he had confiscated from the American merchants after the Von Kapff and Brune swindle. President Madison had in fact decided to send Septimus Tyler to Cap-Henry as a commercial agent, and there were suggestions that he should travel in a frigate to give more force to his arguments. But this proposal was dropped and Tyler's stay in Haiti proved to be very short. To avoid any suggestion that the United States was recognising Haitian independence, his letters of introduction referred to "Cap-François in the island of Saint-Domingue". They were rejected by Christophe as "improper and insulting", and Tyler was sent away with a copy of the king's declaration of November 20, 1816, to study.

Although Christophe was at loggerheads with Anglo-Saxon officialdom, his relations with the philanthropists remained excellent. Tom Gulliver, while waiting for the completion of the school that was being built in the rue Royale, formed a small Bible class, with Christophe's full approval, for although Roman Catholicism was the authorised religion, he had decreed complete religious toleration within the Christian faith. "Every one is free to serve the Almighty according to his own opinion," the Comte de Limonade wrote to the secretary of the British and Foreign School Society on September 18, 1816; "the wish of my august sovereign is to extend light and civilization, and to promote the knowledge of the English language among his people, being persuaded that he will thereby secure their prosperity and happiness".

In a letter to Wilberforce a few weeks later, Christophe went much further, reverting to his former plan of establishing Protestantism and the English language. After assuring Wilberforce that "Sanders was correct in telling you that I understand English perfectly, and I wish you always to correspond with me in that language," he continued:

> I have tried as far as possible to inculcate the principles of religion and morals in my fellow-citizens; but you must consider, my friend, the extent to which a people newly emerged from the twilight of ignorance and slavery, after 25 years of agitation and revolution, still has need of time and care and effort if religion and moral principles are to be disseminated through all classes of society. My object is therefore to spread them more widely; but not the principles of that religion which is marred by fanaticism and superstition, but the religion which you profess, full of the essence and humanity of its divine author. . . . The teaching of English literature in our schools will eventually, I hope, cause the English language to predominate over French; the only means of preserving our independence is to have absolutely nothing in common with a nation against which we have so many grievances and whose conduct tends only to our destruction.

Sanders, who had returned to Haiti from England with letters from Wilberforce and Clarkson, was in disgrace. During his stay in London he had published a translation of several of Christophe's manifestos and Vastey's pamphlets under the title of *Haitian Papers*, without Christophe's permission yet claiming to do so "by Authority". He had also engaged teachers without reference to Wilberforce and in general acted in a bumptious way that Christophe felt compelled to apologise for. "You must think me quite devoid of sense, my friend," he wrote to Wilberforce, "to send a man like Sanders. . . . You can be assured that he will not return to England. I have employed him here with Mr Gulliver."

The interest aroused by Christophe's educational project began to embarrass Pétion and in May 1817 he gave two Methodist missionaries permission to found a school on the Lancastrian plan at Port-au-Prince. The British and Foreign School Society once more supplied the teacher, Thomas Bosworth, and in its annual report expressed the hope "shortly to receive accounts that the blessings of instruction have been diffused by means of this Society throughout the whole of that interesting island; and that the foundation of moral improvement and happiness in a degree never before known, will be deeply laid in regions which, though richly blessed by the hand of the Creator, have been too long blasted by the ignorance and vices of man". A similar unfavourable view of the moral state of the Republic had already been expressed by the two missionaries, John Brown and James Catt, who described it on their arrival as "a land . . . where Christianity is unknown, save through the disguise of Popery, and where no cheering sound of Salvation breaks through the horrid silence". Not unexpectedly, these stern, uncompromising men had a hard and eventually unavailing battle against the entrenched champions of Rome. Tolerated but not financially supported by the government, the school never developed beyond a sort of Bible class with a maximum of thirty members. Brown and Catt, denounced by the Catholic priesthood as infidels, were ordered out of the country in 1818 and, though other Methodists were later admitted, they too were harassed and in 1820 imprisoned on the false rumour that Christophe had been converted to Protestantism and they were therefore liable to overturn the Republic in his favour.

Even had the missionaries been less dedicated and more tactful it is unlikely that they would have made much headway against Pétion's inertia and Francophil preferences. Conversely, no obstacles could have withstood Christophe's drive and enthusiasm. To National Schools he added Royal Academies for secondary education from which the outstanding students were to continue to Royal Colleges. He set up a Royal Chamber of Public Instruction to supervise all these and, in his address to his subjects on New Year's Day, 1817, told them:

> To form good citizens we must educate our children. From our national institutions will proceed a race of men capable of defending by their knowledge and talents those rights so long denied by tyrants. It is from these sources that light will be diffused among the whole mass of the population, teaching them how to appreciate their duties and love their country. The moral virtues which distinguish man in a civilised state will replace the ignorance and depraved manners which are the unhappy result of barbarity and slavery.

The first of the National Schools was now fully functioning – "a fine and commodious room capable of containing nearly three hundred children," Tom Gulliver reported. "Through the zeal of His Majesty . . . to promote education, nothing has been left deficient respecting this establishment." By April 1817 he was convinced that "my scholars possess great abilities, they make rapid progress in the English language. It is now six months since I commenced to qualify some monitors and at present they are capable of teaching a class of thirty or forty boys. . . . They have advanced in six months to the *sixth and seventh classes, and go through the four first rules of arithmetic in English* with facility."

At the end of April John Daniell, a former instructor at the Borough Road Training College, arrived at Cap-Henry after "a pleasant six-week passage from Portsmouth". He was given an order on the Treasury for 300 dollars to furnish the house that was being built for his use at Sans-Souci, where he was escorted by Dupuy three weeks later and formally presented to the king. Daniell, as senior of the British teachers, was given partial responsibility for the education of the Prince Royal and was also to take charge of a Grand Central School intended to cater for 400 boys. Another teacher, Mr Sweet, came out on the boat with him, but he remained at Cap-Henry with Gulliver, who found him not at all sympathetic.

"I am afraid he will do us little credit," he wrote to James Millar, the secretary of the society. "He has never been master of a school, and the good he will do . . . will never make atonement for the badness of his character, which is of the most immoral cast. Of this perhaps you have heard from others who know him better than I, and especially from his fellow passengers." The truth was that Sweet was too fond of the bottle. Fortunately, he was sent off to take charge of a new school at Les Gonaïves early in July, just before Christophe made his first official inspection of the school at Cap-Henry, overawing the pupils with his briskness and the splendour of his attendant staff, barking shrewd questions at them and, on leaving, expressing his great satisfaction with Gulliver's work by presenting him with a sheep and some coffee and sugar.

Schools were now in full operation at Cap-Henry, Port-de-Paix (where Prince Sanders had been sent to take charge of 100 pupils), Sans-Souci and Les Gonaïves, and another school for 200 boys was opened at Saint-Marc before the end of the year. In his speech on November 29, the national holiday celebrating the anniversary of the expulsion of the French, Christophe praised those heroes who had given their lives for the independence of Haiti and the liberty of its people and declared:

> We will confound the calumniators of our race by proving ourselves in no respect inferior in moral and physical powers to the other inhabitants of the Globe, and by showing that we are capable of acquiring and practising the sciences and the arts and attaining to an equal degree of improvement and civilisation with Europeans.

During 1818 the increase in the number of National Schools was complemented by the setting up of the first Royal Academy, to provide secondary education in grammar, history, geography, arithmetic and the Latin, English and French languages. The Reverend William Morton, a recently ordained Protestant clergyman who had formerly been an usher at a school in Plymouth, came out to take charge of the academy, and was shortly presented with forty of Gulliver's best scholars from Cap-Henry, and ten from Sans-Souci, where John Daniell had to attend at the palace twice a day to teach the Prince Royal and Prince Eugène and was therefore not yet able to expand his school beyond thirty-five boys.

Daniell, like Gulliver, was delighted with the enthusiasm of his pupils and the farsightedness of his patron. "Were all monarchs animated with a zeal for the present and future welfare of their subjects, equal to that which animates the enlightened mind of Henry the First of Haiti," he wrote to James Millar, "your labours [towards universal education] would soon be crowned with complete success. . . . Ours is an undertaking which was, I believe, never before tried – to teach a foreign language to those who can neither read nor speak a written language – for Créole is as different from French as French is from Latin."

The Prince Royal was not an easy pupil to handle, His education had until now been supervised by the brilliant, bitter Vastey, who had instilled in him an exaggerated sense of his importance as heir-apparent and a deep distrust of white men. He had been brought up in the shadow of a great and domineering and often nagging father and much of his arrogance was a cloak for his sense of insufficiency, for he was an unprepossessing lad, squat and corpulent, looking ten years older than his true age of fourteen. Yet Daniell gradually discovered under the sulkiness and bluster a depth of frankness and good nature.

Both Daniell and Gulliver suffered severe attacks of fever, Daniell's almost proving fatal, despite the ministrations of the king's personal physician. Less fortunate were the unreliable and regrettable George Sweet, who died at Les Gonaïves in June 1818, and Tom Bosworth, the society's only representative in the South, who died in February of the same year. Prince Sanders, not fully restored to Christophe's good books, lost interest and went back to the United States. He was replaced by Mr Meyer, sent out by the society together with William Simmonds, a Negro trained at the Borough Road Training College but unfitted for teaching in England because of the climate. After a few weeks with Gulliver at Cap-Henry, where he learned a smattering of French, he was sent to open a school at Port-Royal and later transferred from there to Les Gonaïves on the death of Sweet. With the school at Saint-Marc opened by Thomas Oxley, another society man, in November 1817, there were now more than 700 children being taught in the National Schools. The Reverend Mr Morton was joined at the Academy by the painter Richard Evans, who had earlier set up a private drawing school at Sans-Souci. Duncan Stewart, a Scottish surgeon, was appointed professor of Anatomy.

Two years later, a visiting Methodist inspected the Cap-Henry school, describing it as:

. . . a large building, situated in a retired and elevated part of the town, and as properly arranged and perfectly furnished with all the necessary apparatus as the best schools conducted on this system in England. [I found] one hundred and fifty to two hundred boys from eight to sixteen years of age. . . . At this period, all the boys of the school could read and write; many of them were acquainted with the introductory rules of arithmetic; and some spoke the English language with considerable ease and propriety. At the request of the master I called several of his pupils indiscriminately, and proposed to them questions, according to the classes in which they stood; and the result of this examination was a conviction that, whatever may be affirmed of the stupidity of the Negro, he is no further inferior in intellect to others than the system of slavery renders him. . . . I directed a certain number of these lads to commit to memory selected pieces in English and French, some in poetry and others in prose; and promised to encourage them by bestowing appropriate rewards on those who should repeat these pieces most readily and correctly. At the expiration of the time appointed them for learning, they each recited their respective portions with so much ease and propriety that it was difficult to determine to whom the prizes should be adjudged; and the only satisfactory mode of arrangement appeared to be that of increasing the number, so as to give each boy a trifling reward. A short time afterwards, I heard them repeat the same pieces; and they rehearsed them with nearly the same readiness and correctness as they had previously done.

6

At the end of March 1818, a few days before his forty-eighth birthday, Pétion died, seeming to fade from life almost inadvertently, his strange listlessness having increased to the point where he could no longer be bothered to take food. Under the revised constitution of 1816, he had the right to nominate his successor, and it was without surprise that the country learned that his choice had fallen on his secretary, General Jean-Pierre Boyer, a friend so intimate that the two men shared the same mistress, the beautiful Joutte Lachenais. Boyer, six years younger than Pétion, was the son of a white man and a Negress. He had been apprenticed to a tailor before the revolution, had fought with Rigaud against

Toussaint and escaped to France, and, like Pétion, had returned as an officer in Leclerc's army.

For a few days after Pétion's death there was fear in the Republic that Christophe might seize the opportunity to invade; and from Jamaica the new naval commander-in-chief, Rear-Admiral Sir Home Popham, sent warships to Port-au-Prince and Les Cayes to provide protection for British merchants. Their captains reported that the new president was well disposed to the British and that there was no sign of any aggression from Christophe. It was not until June that he made any move, progressing in great state to Saint-Marc, where he established his court and sent envoys to Port-au-Prince to repeat the offers of union that he had made three years before. He cannot have been greatly surprised to see them return empty-handed, for he realised by now that, despite some reforms and relaxations in his system of government, the thought of coming under his driving hand attracted very few of the citizens of the Republic.

The most important of his reforms was the breaking up of the large estates that had been created under the original system of *fermage* and the sale of land to small farmers. This produced a momentary ray of hope among the ordinary field hands that their lives would be a little less hard, but they soon found that the king had no intention of relaxing his supervision, the troopers of the Royal-Dahomets remained always at their elbows, the hours and the labour as long and arduous as ever. There were many who gazed enviously southward where, as one British observer reported, "under Pétion's government there was a great affectation of promoting every sort of industry, especially that of agriculture, but the desire of propitiating all classes, by giving way to their favourite passion, idleness, was all-powerful."

Christophe had long been conscious of the waste of man-power involved in maintaining a large army and wrote to Thomas Clarkson of "my favourite project, to send the soldiers back to agricultural pursuits". But he was still fearful of a possible French invasion. "I have made a beginning, but only peace and security will allow me to carry it through to a satisfactory conclusion. . . . I must have positive assurance that England will recognise our independence, or will take some equivalent step such as guaranteeing that the French will not undertake an expedition to blockade our ports and attack our territory, and also that Spain will not be permitted to cede her part of this island to our enemies, thus permitting them to establish themselves in our rear." This thought that the Bourbons might arrive at an agreement with the King of Spain to buy or exchange other territory for that part of the island and use it as the base for an attack against Haiti was a continuing nightmare to him and accounted for the strict frontier surveillance which had led to Davison's imprisonment.

Although he dreaded the French, he appreciated his country's need for white men and their skills and knowledge. He hesitated to flout public opinion by directly contravening the law that Dessalines had originated and Pétion had promulgated in the South – that "no white man whatever his nationality may set foot on this territory in the capacity of master or proprietor" – but he issued an edict in the spring of 1818 under which a white man who married a Haitian woman would qualify for full citizenship after one year, and a white man of any nationality who married a Negress anywhere in the world might settle in Haiti and even have his fare paid.

Later that year a convention of American abolitionists meeting in Philadelphia discussed the possibility of sending to Haiti the many 'people of colour' who found themselves free but socially outcast in the Northern States; Christophe showed interest in the scheme and Clarkson, whose enthusiasm sometimes outstripped his commonsense, suggested that it might be possible to persuade the United States to buy the Spanish part of the island, people it with freed slaves from the American plantations, and then cede it to Christophe. In the same letter he proposed that Christophe, who was infuriated by the knowledge that the Spaniards were still importing slaves, should fit out "a small ship of war to prevent the landing of slaves in the Spanish part of the island. . . . Suppose [it] were to capture an English slave ship. . . . Would you by so doing involve yourself in a quarrel with the English Government? What damages could any English merchant or captain whose ship you had taken, obtain against you by making a complaint at home? None at all. . . ."

It is proof of Christophe's level-headedness that he placed less faith in Clarkson's knowledge of the law than in his own experience of practical politics. He was aware of British sensitiveness to the presence of armed vessels in those waters and knew that any excursion by one of his men-of-war against a ship of any other nation (except perhaps the Haitian Republic) would bring the whole Jamaican squadron down on him. He bided his time, since he knew that Spain was already committed to abolish the slave trade – for which she had been promised compensation of £400,000 from Britain, a gesture which, Christophe wrote, "redoubles our affection for your incomparable nation".

His fear of a sudden attack kept him continually strengthening and improving the fortifications of Citadel-Henry. Under the supervision of the German military engineers the rock had been tunnelled and casemated to provide stores and shelters and battery positions. Above ground the Citadel's massive walls enclosed barracks for the garrison, great cisterns of water, and private apartments for the royal family, as ornately furnished as they were stoutly protected. He would not allow himself to be tricked as Toussaint had been, despised and left to cough out his life in the icy dampness of some distant French prison. He would defy them from his fortress and fight on through the years; and if food and ammunition ran low, he would finish in one last sortie, his sword in his hand and his brazen cannon blazing. For this he kept the Citadel always fully garrisoned with detachments from his household troops, and the governor – his brother-in-law, Prince Noël, Duc du Port-de-Paix – always in residence.

On August 25, 1818, Cap-Henry sweltered in the summer heat. Even at Sans-Souci the air was uncomfortable with the weight and breathlessness of the storm that hung over the mountains. Lightning flickered and cracked across the sky. Suddenly there was a sharp report and then a tremendous detonation from Citadel-Henry. From far off, flames could be seen raging up from the top of the mountain, where the fortress now sailed across the sky like a ship on fire. Christophe leaped to his horse, sending officers to fetch troops and round up plantation hands while he rode up the six miles of serpentine mountain paths, perilous with loose stones, with nothing around him to be seen but the deep green trellis of trees and lianas – until suddenly he was out and above the tree line and there above him was the Citadel, half hidden in flames and smoke. He raced up the last long flight of steps, shouting at his staff to follow him; some of the garrison were already trying to fight the fire and others were conscripting helpers from villages lower down the slopes of the mountain.

The lightning had struck a powder magazine above ground, exploding it and scattering burning fragments around the whole of the area within the walls. Before the last of the flames had been beaten out, the fire had destroyed all the troops' quarters and the royal apartments. The thirty-four-year-old Prince Noël was dead, with 159 men of the garrison. But the underground stores and powder magazines were untouched and Christophe began feverishly rebuilding.

President Boyer seized this moment to renew the campaign against Goman, who still ruled his own bandit state in the mountains of the south peninsula and whom Christophe had created Comte de Jérémie – partly for the malicious pleasure of annoying Pétion and partly to re-affirm his claim to that part of the island. The title had no effect on Goman's actions; he remained unattached, owing allegiance neither to the kingdom nor to the Republic. But he was useful as an irritant and, as soon as Christophe heard that Boyer had begun to move troops towards Jérémie, he mounted a naval expedition against Port-au-Prince. The threat was enough to force Boyer to withdraw.

A British naval officer, visiting Cap-Henry after an absence of four years, sent this description of Christophe to a friend in September 1818.

The King is in his person what in England you would call a fine portly-looking man about 5 feet 10 inches. He is now growing stout, and on horseback, where he certainly looks his best, has much the appearance of old George. His dress, except on state days, is very like the Windsor uniform, without lace or star. He is quite black, with a manner and countenance, when in good humour (and I have never seen him in any other) very intelligent, pleasant and expressive – his features are much that of his countrymen – his nose rather long but flat at the nostrils – his lips are not thick – his eyes, except when in a rage, rather small, but quick – his forehead, which gives so much character to his countenance, high – when I saw him last his hair was gray, and until he remarked it to me himself (for I thought he wore powder) I did not observe that it is now grown quite white.

I am told by those who have seen him in one of his gusts of passion, that it can only be compared to a hurricane for its fury; but fortunately the fit now comes very seldom, and does not last long. A friend, who has seen a great deal of him, told me he one day saw him in one – his form absolutely dilated, his countenance changed, and his eyes became enlarged and rolled in his head. He looked like a demon – it was over in five minutes, expending itself in words, and he was then as quiet as a child. None but the queen dare go near him in these paroxysms.

It is his mind, and his alone, that governs all; he has the ablest men of his kingdom employed about his person, but they are mere executors of his will. One proof of his being neither a very changeable or cruel man, is that almost all the great officers of the palace, who were there four years ago, are there now. . . .

There is one striking part of his character – he never forgives a fault. He even sent his own son, the Prince Royal, a prisoner to the Citadel, to show he paid no regard to high rank. But before you judge too severely of him for this, think who he has to govern – a set of slaves brought up without any principle of either religion or morality, and who have, in the sanguinary and dreadful contest for liberty, been accustomed, by the example of their enemies, to all sort of butcherous and dreadful crimes. . . .

Sweet, the teacher at the school of Les Gonaïves, was already dead, and it seemed likely that he would soon be followed by Meyer, who had replaced Sanders at Port-de-Paix. The king, arriving unannounced one day, found Meyer incapably drunk at noon and only the shortage of teachers saved him from an awful visitation of the royal wrath. But the standard of teaching and the progress made by the boys in the other schools was remarkable.

"When I mentioned to him the talent which I thought I saw in the boys", the naval visitor reported, "he said with a smile 'I think we shall be able to prove that we are capable of thinking and acting for ourselves.' He certainly is bringing that great question to a fair trial, whether the Negroes possess sufficient reasoning powers to govern themselves or, in short, whether they have the same capacities as white men. And he is the only man, I think, in the world who could have given it so bold a trial. . . ."

Even though Christophe was growing stout, his energy and command of detail were as surprising as ever.

The King went round the hospital while I was there. I saw Dr Stewart just after it; he was perfectly astonished. He said there was not an individual that he did not know by name, his character, his regiment, disease, and everything about him; and whenever he came to a blackguard (and the Doctor said every one he singled out had been a troublesome patient) he gave him a confounded crack on the head with his cane saying,——. There were above 300 in – the soldiers were all delighted to see him and cut jokes – not so the officers, they looked frightened – the wards for the officers are really elegantly fitted up, and he sends them of all ranks there, from a Duke downwards. . . .

In September 1818 the representatives of the great powers met at Aix-la-Chapelle to discuss the re-admission of France into the councils of Europe. Thomas Clarkson attended as a private individual in the hope of persuading them to bring pressure to bear on Portugal to abolish the slave trade in 1820, the date to which Spain had already agreed. He was welcomed by the liberal-minded Alexander I of Russia and took the opportunity of speaking to him of Christophe. The Czar, who obtained his information on Haiti from French and German sources, believed its inhabitants to be unredeemed savages, and was amazed at the style and content of one of Christophe's letters, which Clarkson showed him.

He exclaimed that it "contained wise, virtuous and liberal sentiments. It would have done honour to the most enlightened Cabinets of Europe," Clarkson reported to Christophe. "A person rising up in the midst of slavery and founding a free Empire was of itself a surprising thing," the Czar remarked, "but to see him, in the midst of ignorance and darkness, founding it on the pillars of education under Christian auspices was more surprising and truly delightful." The Czar "hoped he should see a new Empire rivalling the whites in all that was great and good."

Clarkson assured Alexander that Christophe planned great things for Haiti but that all his projects were impeded by fear of a French invasion. He begged him, if ever the French seemed inclined to send another expedition against the island, "to use his high influence with the King of France to prevent it". But he also warned Christophe that Boyer had been making approaches to the French government. He urged Christophe to try once more to effect a union with the Republic, or at least to arrive at some treaty of mutual aid.

What I most fear is that if you should keep [Boyer] in a state of fear or alarm respecting your own intentions, you will oblige him to have recourse to France for protection, though probably much against his will. In this case he will offer France his trade, but he will call upon her in return not only to acknowledge but to *guarantee* his independence; and if France should guarantee his independence and Your Majesty should afterwards see occasion to quarrel with him, he will call in the French to his assistance, and you will then see French armies finding a safe and easy passage through his territories into yours.

Shortly afterwards Limonade, now elevated from comte to duc, received a private letter from Colonel Vincent from which, as Christophe said when he sent a copy to Clarkson, "you will see that the French Government is looking for means of sounding us out; but before I undertake any negotiations, I am anxious to have your advice and to profit by your wisdom. I shall be profoundly grateful if you will write to me in your usual forthright way, telling me what course I should pursue in the event of the French Government proposing the signing of a treaty with me."

Before Clarkson's reply could reach him – the mail between Britain and Haiti took six weeks at the best of times – Christophe changed his mind. Vincent, the old comrade of whom Christophe had once said, "You are the only Frenchman with a love for the inhabitants of Saint-Domingue", had been living in France for twenty years. Christophe now thought of him more as a Frenchman than as a friend and, finding his next letter to Limonade "more aggressive", let the correspondence drop. But Clarkson's report on his conversation with the Czar had raised other hopes. Christophe wrote a letter to Alexander which he sent unsealed to Clarkson with the request that he could "please read it, my friend, and if you consider that it may be sent on to him, I beg you to forward it to its destination."

It was, like so many of Christophe's letters, rather long.

I have always believed [he wrote] that a Sovereign so enlightened, just and humane, who in the midst of his conquests and victories gave the strongest proofs of justice and moderation, must take a lively interest in the situation of the Haitians, those unfortunate people who have risen from the midst of ignorance and barbarous slavery to the rank of a free and independent nation, after having experienced the greatest misery and misfortune, and I am happy to see my hopes realized.

He outlined the history of the past twenty years; the granting of liberty by the French during the Revolution; the army sent by Bonaparte "with the criminal intention of destroying a peaceable and defenceless population, or to plunge it again into the horrors of slavery"; the proclamation of independence in 1804. Since then the nation "has advanced rapidly towards civilisation and is continually improving its social situation. . . . Too long has the African race been unjustly calumniated. Too long has it been represented as deprived of intellectual faculties, as scarcely susceptible of civilisation or government by regular and established laws; these false assertions spring from the avarice and injustice of men who have had the impiety to degrade the finest work of the Creator, as if mankind had not one common origin. These persons attribute to difference of colour that which is only the result of civilisation and knowledge."

He complained that the attitude of France had not altered with the return of the Bourbons and hoped for the Czar's "powerful and generous protection and benevolence to the cause of the unfortunate, oppressed Africans, and of the good and interesting people of Haiti".

Clarkson wrote to Christophe in June that he had read the letter "with interest and satisfaction. . . . Nothing could have been more proper. I sent it without delay to Count Lieven, His Imperial Majesty's Ambassador in London."

Christophe was not indulging in flattery when he told Clarkson how much he valued his advice. He paid great attention to all of Clarkson's proposals and acted on many of them. His sharp intelligence must by now have discerned the contrast between Wilberforce's attitude towards him and Clarkson's. Wilberforce was the missionary, eager to bring the light of the true Protestant religion and the high moral principles of Kensington Gore to the interesting but inferior Negroes of Haiti. Clarkson, on the other hand, filled the role of colleague and collaborator, showing from the earliest days a genuine excitement and sincerity in setting about obtaining a public recognition of complete equality for the Haitians – as human beings and as a nation.

While Clarkson lobbied Alexander of Russia, Wilberforce was typically urging Christophe to suppress the frivolous Roman Catholic Sundays in favour of the Protestant sabbath of pious inactivity. He sent him "a great variety of excellent little works [which] have been published in this country of late years for the purpose of inculcating useful knowledge and good morals. Many of these, though professing to be intended for the use of young people, may be read with advantage by persons of any age." And in sending him volumes of the British Encyclopaedia, "you will also do me the honour, I hope, of accepting and placing by their side the

History of the Inquisition, and that of the Jesuits." Christophe, not usually addicted to little jokes, passed most of this literature on to his new archbishop, successor to the recently defunct Corneille Brelle, a white Cuban named Juan Gonzalez. "Christophe is not himself, I fear, governed by religious principles," Wilberforce wrote to Zachary Macaulay in July 1819.

Two of Clarkson's projects which were occupying Christophe's attention at this time were the suggestion that he should accept some of the 200,000 Negroes who wished to leave the United States (and who ultimately went to Liberia), and the possibility of returning many of his soldiers to agriculture by reorganising the army on a militia basis. Observers were never able to gauge the exact size of his army, for he had the habit of inflating two regiments into three on paper in order to confuse Boyer and the French. A lieutenant of the *Iphigenia*, who accompanied Sir Home Popham on a courtesy visit to Cap-Henry in May 1819, assessed Christophe's forces as two regiments of cavalry, (masquerading as three), two of artillery (similarly described as three), one of engineers and nineteen of infantry, a total strength of about 35,000 men, not counting the Royal Amazons, a company of fifty handsomely-uniformed young women who, despite being armed with bows and arrows and sabres, were a non-combatant force with the queen as their commander.

In July 1819 Christophe made a free distribution of land to all serving soldiers. The land, situated close to their barracks and divided into units of a little more than 100 square yards, was allotted at the rate of one unit to a private, two to a corporal and proportionately up to twenty for a full colonel. The recipients might sell the land if they wished, but those who kept it would be expected to grow foodstuffs and would be given time off for that purpose.

I shall begin little by little to accustom the troops to the transition from the soldier's life to that of the farmer by giving them leave, a group at a time, to go and tend their land for short spells [he wrote to Clarkson]; then when I can do so with complete safety, I shall go further and carry out the whole of your proposal of maintaining only a militia. You see, my friend, how much value I attach to your kind advice. . . . However, my position is very difficult, since I am forced to guarantee the security of my compatriots and calm their fears for the future.

Mr Morton, the clergyman from Plymouth, had recently upset the king by insisting on leaving the country on grounds of ill-health, which the hard-driving monarch described as "the most frivolous of excuses". He appointed John Daniell to take charge of the Royal Academy in Morton's place while a monitor took over from Daniell in the Ecole Nationale at Sans-Souci, thus demonstrating the efficacy of the Lancastrian system. A Scotsman named Moore arrived to take up the chair of mathematics in the Royal College; and to extend the scope of the work at the Academy, Christophe asked Clarkson to find him two more teachers, to take French, English and general subjects. He offered seven-year contracts, free passages for the teachers and their families, and the attractive salary of 250 gourdes (about £57) a month.

He had more important tasks for Clarkson to perform. In the hope of finally laying the ghost of French aggression, and in accordance with Clarkson's own recommendations he wrote in November 1819 to ask the Englishman to "make an overture toward opening negotiations for the signing of a treaty between Haiti and France". To cover Clarkson's expenses he sent him a letter of credit for six thousand pounds, drawn on Reid, Irving and Company of London. A formal letter from the Duc de Limonade invested Clarkson with authority to open negotiations "through whatever channels he may deem advisable". Another instructed Clarkson that King Henry made one "indispensable condition": that Louis XVIII should, on behalf of himself and his successors, recognise Haiti as a free, sovereign and independent state and renounce all claims on it. Clarkson was empowered to offer in return a commercial treaty under which France would receive most-favoured-nation treatment, and the promise of Haitian neutrality in the event of a European war (although this would in fact have been more to the advantage of Britain than France).

Clarkson, on receipt of these instructions, wrote to his friend the Baron Turckheim, at the French Ministry of Marine and Colonies, praising Christophe ("we who live in England, having better opportunities of knowing his character than you who live in France, have good reason to esteem his talents and his virtues, and to be assured that he will be ranked by posterity, not only among the best of kings, but among the benefactors of mankind"), and setting out his hopes and his former grievances against France. Clarkson spoke of Christophe's desire for peace and willingness to disband his army and concluded that "I think it my duty to offer my services to the French Government through the medium of you." He also added, with unexpected sophistry, "King Henry is entirely ignorant of my writing this letter."

There could be no doubt about Christophe's sincerity in seeking peace that would give him the time and the resources to continue and expand his work. "I assure you that I have no intention of committing any hostile act against Boyer," he had told Clarkson, and in the second half of 1819 he proved it when Boyer once more took the field against Goman. Christophe allowed his Comte de Jérémie to be defeated without raising a finger to help him. And when Boyer brought this campaign to a successful conclusion in February 1820 and showed indications of wishing to try another adventure – northwards against the kingdom – Christophe again held his hand and accepted Sir Home Popham's offer of mediation. It was the first time that he had ever refused a challenge.

He was busy with the nation's health now. Duncan Stewart, promoted to *maréchal de camp* as director of the army's medical service, had also been placed in charge of the civilian hospital. "The King has given me complete power to order what I think necessary for the dieting, clothing and accommodation of the sick in his hospitals," Stewart wrote to Clarkson. "I can safely say there is not an hospital in England where the sick are better supplied with all conveniences and necessaries than the hospitals of Haiti." But he failed to mention one of the most interesting of these conveniences – "a pair of stocks fitted to every bed-place, in which the legs of the occupier are immediately put on the least symptom of insubordination". It was the lieutenant of the *Iphigenia* who remarked on these, and Dr Stewart assured him "that coercive measures were absolutely necessary: as from the great ignorance of some of the negroes, it was impossible to induce them to take their medicines by mild ones." From more than one point of view, Christophe's kingdom was a doctor's dream come true.

The plough was an unknown instrument in Haiti. On the plantations, shovels and mattocks were used to make holes for sugar-canes and cotton-plants and coffee-bushes; and on the field hands' small holdings, mattock and hoe were supplemented by pointed sticks. Christophe had written to Sir John Sinclair, first president of the Board of Agriculture, for advice on modernising agricultural methods and was delighted when Arthur Young found two ploughmen willing to make the journey to Haiti to demonstrate their art. "The honest rustics and their apparatus are about to embark," Wilberforce told him in November 1819, "one of them . . . encumbered with a wife and children." Unfortunately, they met with little success. One was sent to a district where the terrain was so rugged and stony that his plough had no advantage over the existing primitive tools; the other became discouraged in the face of the native farmers' conservatism; both shortly went home again.

The enthusiastic Dr Stewart made a tour of some of the royal estates and remarked that the workers "are well used and are as comfortable and happy as any peasantry I ever saw in any part of Europe", but even he was compelled to admit that the kingdom still lagged behind in the areas of "true religion, with its many beneficial effects on life and manners, and the education of the female sex, which would lead to their obtaining that rank in society to which they are entitled, and without which civilisation can advance but very slowly. I am sorry to say that females are used very ill in Haiti, being often forced to submit to the hardest labour and the greatest iniquities at the capricious will of their rulers."

It was true that religion was more professed and publicly practised than believed. The court was conscientious in performing its duties, the army had no lack of church parades, but there were increasing signs that the old dark cults were creeping back, that balancing the growth of education there was a proliferation of the blind profanities, a return to the sinister mysteries of vaudou. It had never been quite stamped out on the plantations and was now beginning to get a hold again in the barracks.

The education of women was a project that Christophe had in mind. His ordinance of December 1818, setting up a Royal Chamber of Public Instruction, implied this in the stipulation that "children of opposite sexes shall never be brought together in the same school to receive instruction". There were two private schools for girls at Cap-Henry and he had already persuaded two American women teachers to come out to start a public one. They were greeted a little alarmingly by the sardonic Baron de Vastey but accompanied on their journey out to pay their respects to the queen – the court was then at Sans-Souci – by the "polite and gentlemanly" Dupuy. After a short pause at the house of Prince Jean, to be entertained by his wife, "a stout, fat, well-looking mulatto", they were taken up to the palace and shown into the library, where the Duc de Limonade was waiting for them.

In about a quarter of an hour we heard a bustle in the adjoining passage – the door opened – and Christophe, preceded by six young Negroes, as pages, and accompanied by some of his nobles, made his appearance. We rose and made a profound *salut*; he desired us to be seated; we knew better, and stood while he remained; not in the least intimidated by the appearance or manner of his sable majesty. He said little to us, but turning to baron de Dupuy, he inquired if our house at the Cape was in readiness – finding it was not so, he said, 'Oh, these ladies can come here and instruct my daughters,' and immediately left us to prepare them for our reception.

We were now conducted to another part of the palace, and shown into a spacious saloon, furnished with great magnificence and taste. We had scarcely seated when the large folding doors by which we had entered again opened, and Christophe, with the Queen, the Prince Royal and the Princesses appeared, dressed most handsomely, and with a degree of elegance that we had not expected. The Queen was exceedingly obliging and affable; she made kind inquiries respecting our passage and health; she expressed her hope that we should be perfectly happy as long as we should remain with them; and she assured us that she would be always ready to assist us – and her evident sincerity convinced us that she had a kind and affectionate heart. Her daughters were equally polite; and appeared quite pleased at the idea of our coming to reside at the palace. On the whole we were much pleased and satisfied with the interview. . . .

When arrangements had been completed to provide them with lodgings and a schoolroom at the palace, they drew up a syllabus of English, French, Composition and Drawing and a time-table whose hours did not tax their royal pupils unduly — from "between seven and eight till ten, in the morning and three to five in the afternoon". They found that "the princesses differed much in their abilities and dispositions. The elder sometimes appeared to think the difficulty of acquiring knowledge greater than it was worth. She was disposed to learn, but often yielded to that listlessness so common among natives of tropical climates. The youngest was lively and amiable; she had great quickness of apprehension; but was rather averse to application and careless of improvement. Yet the progress of both was considerable; and the queen, and we believe the king also, felt perfectly satisfied with our endeavours."

The teachers themselves, however, were not so happy.

A few months only had passed away, ere we felt our situation disagreeable in the extreme. We occasionally dined with the queen; our pupils also sometimes stopped after the hours of instruction for conversation, or we accompanied them to the gardens; but we felt, in a great measure, excluded from society; for there was none with whom we could hold a free and friendly intercourse. If we used the carriage which was at our service, we could only ride to a prescribed distance; and we were perpetually annoyed by the guard, if we ventured on a ramble, inquiring who we were and whither we were going. The etiquette of the court was intolerably irksome; and the inquisitiveness of the officers whom we occasionally met, not to be endured. We had come from America; and the confinement, restraint, and cere-mony, we had been quite unaccustomed to, and could not suffer. The queen's kindness and attentions, indeed, made up for many inconveniences; nor was there any thing in her power which she would not have gladly done to render our situation agreeable. Circumstances, however, continually recurring to render it unpleasant, we determined at length to resign our charge. . . .

Clarkson had by now engaged two teachers to take up the professorships at the Royal College: William Wilson, who was working as tutor with a wealthy family in Ipswich, five miles away from Clarkson's own home at Playford Hall, and George Clarke, who had been born in Ipswich but was teaching at a London school.

They arrived at Cap-Henry in the brig *Aimé* on March 21, 1820, but did not increase the number of British pedagogues in the kingdom, because Gulliver and Daniell, after nearly four years' service in the treacherous climate, had prevailed on Christophe to give them a few months' leave. This necessitated a change of plan, Clarke taking over Daniell's duties in the Royal Academy while Wilson took over the tuition of the Prince Royal as a full-time task. The Prince found Wilson a congenial teacher, and Wilson in return spoke of him as an "amiable and interesting boy". He was still as fat as ever. Christophe, talking to British naval officers in the palace at Cap-Henry, spoke of the malicious lies published about him in the French press, including a recent one that he had "in a paroxysm of rage, thrown the Prince Royal from a window of the palace, for having disturbed his sleep. Pointing to his son, he laughingly observed, 'These Frenchmen highly compliment my strength; I fear it would require more than I am master of even to lift so stout a fellow'."

Admiral Popham, continuing his attempt at reconciling Christophe and Boyer, spent a great deal more time cruising about his station than his predecessors had done. He had visited Christophe on several occasions since taking over command early in 1818 and had developed a great respect and admiration for him, a liking that Christophe returned, taking great pains over the entertainment that he provided for the admiral and paying marked attention to his advice. Having persuaded Christophe to accept mediation – the hardest part of the task as he thought – he arrived at Port-au-Prince on April 27, 1820, and was lodged in the elegant mansion that had been Boyer's before he succeeded to the presidency. But, to Sir Home's dismay, Boyer proved to be much too pleased with his recent victory over Goman to be interested in the proposal of a treaty with Christophe, whom he described as a rebel against the Republic.

"In less than a year his reign of terror will be ended," he told the admiral, "and the Haitians of the Artibonite and the North will be once more united with their brothers in the West and South. Christophe is reduced to complete impotence. When he came as far as Saint-Marc last year he did not dare to cross our frontier – his troops would have deserted him and joined ranks with ours."

With this uncompromising reply Sir Home sailed up to Cap-Henry, accompanied this time by Robert Sutherland, junior, who had been serving with his regiment in Canada when his father recently died and had come down to Port-au-Prince to settle his affairs. Young Mr Sutherland was given a very frigid welcome by Christophe, who knew all about his father's efforts on behalf of Pétion in Jamaica and London, but he was, nevertheless, impressed by the great progress that had been made in the North. "Pétion's policy," he later stated to a Royal Commission, "was this: by giving the people as much liberty as possible, in fact a liberty amounting to licentiousness, to undermine the absolute monarchy of Christophe." That policy, continued by Boyer, was still lowering the standard of living in the South but it was also beginning to bear fruit in the North, though it is doubtful if Sutherland was aware of this during his brief stay.

Sir Home determined to make one last effort and, after his new talks with Christophe, he wrote to Boyer on May 14 repeating that, as a defensive measure against the possibility of a French attack, "the King is sincerely disposed to enter into an agreement in the most perfect friendship with his friends of the West and South. . . . You can be assured that he will scrupulously fulfil all his undertakings. . . . Consider this proposal very seriously; it is the cause of humanity and it rests with you alone to give me all your help in accomplishing it. . . . Do not ever contemplate going to war; do not attempt to advance beyond your frontiers, for, if you do so, I shall consider you to be an aggressor, and you will be responsible in the eyes of the whole world for the consequences of such a civil war, and the more so because I can testify to having witnessed the King's good intentions in this matter."

7

Sir Home's persistence merely confirmed Boyer's opinion that Christophe was enfeebled and even frightened; and there were now some among Christophe's generals who began to think that he had grown too old. Certainly his character was changing. Even in the few years since the British teachers had been coming to Haiti the alteration was marked. To Gulliver and Daniell he had been a paragon; to his naval visitor of 1818 he was a man whose rages were a thing of the past; yet to Wilson in 1820 he seemed "a most tyrannical and cruel man".

He was approaching fifty-three. At times he had the old man's habit of reminiscing about his youth and the battles he had fought. He liked to sit on his mahogany throne under the star-apple tree in the *cour d'honneur* at Sans-Souci, the terrace on his right, the queen's garden, the military hospital and the printing works on his left; below him the stables and, west of them, the Treasury and the Prince Royal's apartments, the Petit Palais; behind him the barracks of the household troops, the arsenal and its three protective forts; far out ahead the sea with Monte Christi and the Spanish border and leftwards his city of Cap-Henry; and high above him the great last stronghold, Citadel-Henry. Here he would gather his family and favourite officials around him, to listen while he talked. But he was far from being in his dotage. A rage for more time to live had overtaken him. He was obsessed with his dreams of greatness for Haiti, with the consciousness of how much remained to be accomplished if he were to leave his people strong and fit to control their own fate; and he continued to squeeze every drop of effort and sacrifice from them apparently without reckoning that there might be a point at which their docility would crack.

With this great greediness for time went all the lesser lusts. There was talk of mistresses and, though envy and hatred exaggerated the stories of his lechery, as they did of his impatience and quick temper, there is no doubt that latent vices now found an outlet. His eyes roved among the women of his court, and few among his officers and ministers had the courage that Philippe Guerrier showed in thwarting the royal will. Guerrier, colonel of the 7th demi-brigade in the war of independence, now commanded the first arrondissement of Christophe's western province and had been ennobled first as Comte du Mirebalais and then Duc de L'Avancé. Suspecting that Christophe had designs on his wife and learning that she had been invited to a function at the palace without him, he went to Sans-Souci and, entering the room unannounced, said to Christophe: "Sire, you are known as the father of all the children of Haiti – but I have no desire to be the father of your son." He then offered his arm to the duchess and led her out of the room.

Guerrier's temerity was all the more remarkable since Christophe did not exempt from punishment even the highest in the land or the closest to his household. The Duc de la Marmelade, governor of Cap-Henry, having been ordered to carry out a commission for the king, performed what he had been told to do, but in a different manner. Christophe promptly ordered him off to Citadel-Henry for several months' hard labour on the fortifications before reinstating him in his rank and office. The Prince Royal had received similar treatment in his early teens, and when the Comtesse de Rosier, wife of Juste Chanlatte, one of his secretaries, was caught in adultery, Christophe revived the old French punishment for prostitutes and had her paraded through the streets astride an ass, naked and facing its tail. Not unexpectedly, the king was beginning to show signs of suspiciousness; he carried his pistols with him everywhere, and rumour said that he was making more and more use of the telescope with which he was believed to be able to pry into everybody's lives.

Chief among his interests during the spring and summer of 1820 was the rebuilding of Cap-Henry. So many houses had been rendered uninhabitable by the two devastating fires that whole streets were choked with rubble, overgrown with weeds and overrun with vermin. Stately buildings had crumbled, looters had stolen what the fire had not consumed, trees grew through the great gaps where once roofs had been. Among a people whose belief in *zombies* was still unshaken, there were many who also believed that the ghosts of former inhabitants haunted the blackened and tumbled blocks of masonry and only the boldest or most wicked ventured along the more desolate streets at night. As trade returned, some of the less grievously damaged houses were patched up and for the sake of appearance Christophe rebuilt the entire range of buildings along the quay. He had completed the handsome palace on the west side of the place d'Armes during his presidency, the main hall decorated with prints of famous statesmen, soldiers and sailors – all British – and the audience chamber glittering with one million francs' worth of furniture panelling, gilt and crystal – all French, but installed by a German because Christophe would not allow even one Frenchman to set foot in the kingdom. The church of Notre Dame on the south side of the place d'Armes was still without an adequate roof, though it had been a cathedral for nearly ten years; but he had now begun the systematic rebuilding of his capital city. For those who claimed that he was growing feeble there was clear disproof in the energy he displayed as he galloped about the streets or strode around the building sites, vigorously applying his silver-mounted cane to idle shoulders and dealing out summary prison sentences to those who gave more serious offence.

He was a tyrant and no matter how benevolent his intentions his hand was heavy and often resented. The field hands and labourers had always had grave doubts about the benefits that their driving, domineering king bestowed upon them. Now he was also beginning to lose the support of the army, which had brought him to power and sustained him there. At first it was the familiar grievance of arrears of pay. Christophe could argue that, since he distributed land to all his soldiers, they had the means of supporting themselves and their families. But now that there was no fighting to do they often found themselves employed on heavy fatigues – and regarded this as an indignity as well as a hardship.

The men of the 8th Regiment of Foot considered themselves more hard done by than the rest. From their station at Saint-Marc they were charged with bringing loads of timber the whole length of the Kingdom to Cap-Henry for the work of reconstruction, officers and men being forced to carry the planks and logs on their heads and shoulders whenever the roads were too bad for carts to pass. No sooner were they back at Saint-Marc than they were set to repairing and reinforcing the frontier defences because of Boyer's continuing aggressive talk. Their discontent became so noisy that the military governor of the district, General Jean Claude, sent for their commander, Colonel Paulin, to administer an official rebuke. Paulin, however, refused to accept the general's reprimand and defended his men in such insubordinate language that Claude reported him to Christophe, who summoned both officers to Cap-Henry.

Paulin was well acquainted with the king – his sister was said to have become Christophe's mistress during his last visit to Saint-Marc. Presuming on this relationship, Paulin offered no apologies for the words he had used to the general and even tried to defend his insubordination. This disregard for the military proprieties, and perhaps a guilty resentment that Paulin should be able to take advantage of him in this way, sent Christophe into a sudden gust of rage. He ordered Paulin to be stripped of his insignia on the spot.

As one of his aides stepped forward to carry out the king's command, Paulin raised his hands to his epaulets and answered: "These badges of rank I won by my own effort – they are not your property!" And then, growing enraged in his turn, he tore the cross of Saint-Henry from his tunic and dashed it on the floor.

"I got this from you," he shouted, "but Negroes and men of colour have no use for crosses!" Christophe remained silent for a moment, suspended between surprise and shock, then he ordered Paulin to be taken off to Citadel-Henry.

The king kept watch over the masons and carpenters sweltering under the summer sun in Cap-Henry until the second week in August, when he left for the château of Belle-vue-le-Roi, fifteen miles up in the hills, for the celebration of the queen's fête. The queen and the rest of the royal family, who had gone to Sans-Souci a week earlier, joined him at the château and at eight o'clock on the morning of August 15 the whole court set out for mass at the parish church of Limonade – a smaller copy of the church of Notre Dame at Le Cap – with rather more splendour than was usual even with Christophe's royal progresses, as if he were trying to abash the mounting criticism with a show of magnificence. The long cortège of carriages bearing the duchesses, countesses and baronesses who had come to offer their compliments to the queen was preceded by the King's Light Horse and the Queen's Corps of Amazons.

He seemed in perfect health and was as sharp-eyed and critical as ever during most of the service, but at the moment when the Archbishop raised the Host a whisper swept through the circle of attendants: "Water! The King is unwell!" The Grand Master of Ceremonies hurried forward with a glass of water; Christophe drank from it and then began sweating profusely. As he handed the glass back, he said: "Have my carriage brought up. I am not well!"

The procession was being re-formed for the return journey and the other vehicles were so numerous that it was ten minutes before the carriage could be brought to the church door. Christophe, meanwhile, leaned forward in his seat, resting his weight on his silver-topped cane. The queen and his children, who occupied chairs facing the throne, came over and tried to help him out of the stiflingly-crowded church into the open air, but he would not admit his weakness. Instead he made an effort to raise himself from the throne. His arms refused to support him and he crumpled to the floor, kneeling, his head slumped on to his chest and his shoulder resting against the seat of the throne.

There was a gasp, then complete, terrified silence, then a hubbub of voices. Some of his attendants ran forward to carry him out, while others struggled to clear a path. He was lifted and borne out to the church porch in an eddy of jostling, and raised voices. "It is difficult to describe the frightful disorder which took place on this occasion," said William Wilson. "The people and the soldiers of the guard, leaving the church in great haste to ascertain the extent of the malady, occasioned so great a press that several were killed and their terrible shrieks portended a still greater calamity!"

The royal carriage having now been brought to the church door, the king was laid on one of the seats and Duncan Stewart, crowded in with the queen and the princesses, cut away the sleeves of his uniform and at once began to cup him. As the carriage trundled carefully back to Belle-Vue the surgeon took two pints of blood from him and piece by piece cut away nearly all his sweat-soaked clothing. The queen and Stewart spoke to him several times, but he was unable to reply. They carried him into the château and Stewart, reduced to heroic measures in this crisis, again bled him. It was not until four in the afternoon that he recovered sufficiently to ask for his wife and children, and he then uttered the words so painfully and indistinctly that only those close to the bed could understand what he was trying to say.

Three days passed before Stewart was able to announce that the king was out of danger. He made no mention of the paralysis that had succeeded the stroke and had deprived Christophe of the use of the whole of the right side of his body: but this was a secret that could not be kept. When Christophe went back to Sans-Souci it was on a stretcher, in a carriage that had been converted into an ambulance. He was carried to his bed and remained there, while the rumour that he was sick and powerless rippled from the court to the towns and then through the countryside.

This was the moment of opportunity for those who had long feared or hated him.

Many of them possessed courage to undertake any enterprise [Wilson wrote to Clarkson] and fortitude to execute it; although they had long trembled before Christophe, because none could resist singly and none could confide the thought of resistance to another. But now that their dreaded superior was impotent to punish them, these men became daring; and it was not long before some of them began to consult privately on the safest means of destroying the King and changing the government. The most moderate proposed to effect this by instituting a milder and more liberal institution, without, however, using violence against their present ruler and his partisans, who, they rightly judged, would not now be numerous; others, found mostly among the military, thought it now advisable to take up arms and finish the tyranny by the death of Henry and all his adherents.

There were many in the king's council of state who suspected what was being plotted. It seems probable that some of them knew for certain and had been invited to take part in the revolt. And for those who wavered there was a compelling argument in Christophe's actions. For, although his brain remained clear, his temper grew more uncertain, its violence exacerbated by the cramps and rheumatic pains that racked his crippled body and the forebodings that tortured his mind.

Duncan Stewart remained within call, day and night. "I used often to converse with him for hours. He seemed sensible that he had used his people harshly and that he ought to have been more liberal with his soldiers; but he had a very correct knowledge of the character of the people he governed and how necessary occasional severities were." Certainly the consideration that he might have been too harsh in the past did nothing to mitigate his severity now. "He suffered much in body but very much in mind," Stewart wrote to Clarkson, "and his impatience became quite insupportable to all about him." It was a word that once neither Stewart nor anybody else in the kingdom would have dared to use – but now the restive cripple's paroxysms had become just that: insupportable.

His illness and his refusal to consider a regency council that might have mitigated the harshness of his rule or relaxed the old disciplines until he was well enough to enforce them again, exposed him to attack from four quite different directions. It could come from the moderates among his ministers and generals who hoped for bloodless reforms; or from the ambitious extremists who planned a revolution of violence and the death of the king; or from the discontented soldiery, typified by the 8th Regiment at Saint-Marc; or from whatever conspirators or hired killers President Boyer had in mind when he assured Admiral Popham that "Christophe's tyranny" would not last another year. As it turned out, it was with the 8th Regiment, and as a result of Boyer's threats, that trouble began.

After Boyer's rejection of Sir Home Popham's proposed mediation in April, and his failure to reply to the admiral's warning letter in mid-May, there had been no further contact, either direct or indirect, between the leaders of North and South. Sir Home, who had himself suffered two slight paralytic strokes within four months, was advised by his surgeon to return to England. In June he handed over his command, much to the regret of Christophe, who missed his friendly visits and began to brood more anxiously over the likelihood of war with the Republic. Early in September, while he still lay half bedridden at Sans-Souci, the July newspapers arrived from Paris carrying circumstantial stories about his death, as the result of a revolution aimed at setting up a Republic. The royal family, the reports said, was concealing the fact that Christophe had been assassinated until the Prince Royal was firmly on the throne.

Seeing Boyer's hand in these rumours, Christophe gave orders that Saint-Marc was to be provisioned immediately with everything that it would require to withstand a long siege. All the food, ammunition and equipment was carried over the mountains by the long-suffering 8th Regiment, driven on by the Saint-Marc commander, General Claude. Hard work and no pay were the tinder of their discontent; the flame that set it blazing was the news they picked up in Cap-Henry that their colonel, whom they had not seen since he was summoned for his interview with the king, had in fact been in Citadel-Henry for three months, imprisoned and fettered. They determined on mutiny.

The movement began among the non-commissioned officers and men, but it soon spread to all ranks of the regiment, although many of them were still sufficiently afraid of Christophe to try to hedge their commitment. One officer, for instance, sent his wife to warn Bazin, Comte de Mont-Rouis, of the imminent mutiny. But he took the precaution of sending her on foot across the rough roads of the Mornes de Saint-Marc, and he may also have known that Bazin had already left Les Verrettes where he had sent her, and had gone to join Romain, Prince du Limbé, the governor of the province of the Artibonite, at La Petite-Riviere. However, if the mutiny failed, he now had proof of his loyalty to the king.

Another officer, equally cautious but less resourceful, slipped out of Saint-Marc that same evening (Saturday, September 30) and rode to La Petite-Rivière, where he reported to Romain that a mutiny was timed to begin within a week. Romain hurried to Saint-Marc, arriving there on Sunday evening. On Monday morning he had the whole garrison paraded and reviewed them without giving any indication that he had heard of the plot. In the afternoon he summoned the officers to his quarters and there demanded point blank that they should tell him all they knew about talk of mutiny. Nobody would admit to any knowledge at all, but one of them whispered in private to a member of Romain's staff that the non-commissioned officers might be able to say something. He named one in particular, Regimental-Sergeant-Major Antoine, who, as everybody except Romain and his staff knew, was the ringleader of the conspiracy.

It was nightfall when the officer whom Romain sent to fetch Antoine arrived at the sergeant-major's quarters. He ordered Antoine to report to the governor immediately and then foolishly returned without waiting for the sergeant-major, who said that he needed to tidy himself before appearing in front of Romain. As soon as the officer left, Antoine gave the signal for instant action and, collecting as many of his supporters as he could find, raced to the arsenal for ammunition.

The men on guard at the arsenal were already won over, and Antoine issued weapons and ammunition to his followers as they rallied to him in the darkness. Meanwhile, General Claude had sensed an unusual atmosphere in the town and decided to ride out to inspect the fortifications. Coming upon a band of men from the 8th Regiment hurrying furtively through the streets, he challenged them and was shot and fatally wounded. The mutiny had begun.

Romain, still waiting in his quarters for RSM Antoine to report to him, heard the sound of shots and shortly afterwards learned that the garrison commander was dead. With the mutineers committed to violence, the small force of cavalry that he had brought with him from La Petite-Rivière was quite inadequate to master the situation. He led them at the gallop through the streets, forced a passage through the town gate and took refuge in one of the outer forts, which he put in a state of defence and at the same time sent a messenger to Sans-Souci, warning Christophe of the outbreak.

The mutineers found themselves in the embarrassing situation of having acted without deciding what they should do next. They consulted their officers and the lead was now taken by Major Constant Paul, the cautious conspirator who had sent his wife over the mountains the night before to warn Bazin. It is possible that Paul was already in President Boyer's pay; whether he was or not, his advice to the mutineers was to send a deputation to Port-au-Prince asking for the protection of the Republic. Three delegates were appointed and, as a proof of their *bona fides*, they were provided with a sack containing the severed head of General Claude. They left Saint-Marc at dawn on October 3 and, by hard riding down the coast road across the cluttered no-man's land, they arrived at Port-au-Prince during the morning of the next day.

That same day, Boyer sent three officers to Saint-Marc by sea, choosing this longer but safer route in case Christophe's loyal troops had already cut the Saint-Marc road. They carried money for the soldiers, a colonel's epaulets for Major Paul, and the assurance that Boyer would follow as soon as he had mobilised an army. Meanwhile Romain had captured another of the outlying forts and began to bombard the mutineers in the town, successfully resisting their attacks and hopefully waiting the arrival of Philippe

Guerrier, Duc de l'Avancé, who was hastening with six thousand men from the eastern borders of the province.

It was on Wednesday, October 4 that Christophe received the first news of the mutiny. He had spent the previous day discussing with Sanders (who had sailed in from Philadelphia a short time before) the plan to bring the Negroes of North America to Haiti, and had agreed to provide a ship and 25,000 dollars as a first contribution to the expenses of the project. Since losing the use of the right side of his body he had taught himself to write his name with his left hand; he told Sanders to draw up the proposals and bring them to him on Thursday and he would sign them himself as proof of the importance that he attached to them. He also ordered that a vessel in harbour at Cap-Henry, due to leave for Philadelphia on the 5th, should delay until the evening of the 6th so that Sanders could sail in it. But as the situation grew more threatening he cancelled the meeting with Sanders on the 5th; and on the 6th he issued the fateful order to the Duc de la Marmelade to send all available troops to Saint-Marc.

At Cap-Henry all through that afternoon, Marmelade conferred in the governor's palace with the officers of the garrison troops; for Marmelade was head of another of the conspiracies against Christophe – the conspiracy of the generals. The mutiny at Saint-Marc, which had erupted too early for Boyer's plans, had precipitated a crisis in their own. They were confronted with a decision that had to be made immediately. If they marched their troops to Saint-Marc to put down the mutiny, they would so strengthen Christophe's position that their own revolt would have to be postponed indefinitely. If they did not march, the southerners, already moving up to attack, would overrun the kingdom and, although Christophe's régime would be ended, they would have lost their own opportunity to take over power – for it was ambition, not hatred of tyranny, that inspired them.

There was only one possible course; they must seize power at the centre and at once. As night fell drummers paraded the streets, summoning all troops back to their barracks. When they were drawn up on their various parade grounds, their officers went out to harangue them. They told them that they had great news. The tyrant was to be deposed – some said he was dead already. Liberty was to return to the people, liberty and true independence. The words were not as important as the tone of voice, the mounting pitch, the sense of excitement, violence and change. The words had been used many times before, and by Christophe himself; now they could be used equally effectively against him, because they were words of turbulence and rage. The officers screamed the words at the soldiers; soon the soldiers began to scream the words back at them.

When they were told to break their ranks and reassemble on the place d'Armes to be addressed by the generals, they went on shouting, "Liberty! Independence!" as they flowed through the streets, brandishing their sabres and muskets and ordering the passers-by to return to their homes. It was thus that Sanders saw them as he went down to the quay to take the boat to Philadelphia, and instead fled back to his lodgings with the shouts of *à bas le Tyran! à bas Christophe!* ringing in his ears. William Wilson, too, returning from a friend's house, convalescent from a bout of yellow fever that had been almost fatal and had kept him in bed for six weeks, found himself surrounded by the wild-eyed soldiers. "Suddenly every door was closed; while the assembled military passed the night, some in consultation, others in dancing and riot, and many in mad efforts to excite their comrades to plunder. That night no one slept in the Cape."

On the place d'Armes those troops who were not already casting about the town in search of mischief listened to the speeches of their generals: the Duc de la Marmelade, flanked by Lebrun, Comte de Gros-Morne, and Prophète, commander of the King's Light Horse. Marmelade denounced the king, the monarchy, the nobility, all titles. "I am no longer Duc de la Marmelade," he shouted. "I am the General Richard you have always known!" To thundering cheers he continued: "No King! No Nobility! No Tyranny!" Tearing the cross of Saint-Henry from his tunic he threw it to the ground, and the other generals followed his example.

They were now committed. Nothing could save them from death if they did not succeed. In the morning they turned back Christophe's orderly officer at the city gates and then marched their troops out to Le Haut-du-Cap. There they took up position by the bridge over the river and waited through Saturday night. They had decided not to attack Christophe at Sans-Souci, since that might drive his remaining forces into a reluctant loyalty. It was better to wait and try to enlist them to the rebellion when they came, even more reluctantly, to suppress it.

It was late on Sunday afternoon before the Haitian Guard came in sight, dragging four cannon with them, and led by Joachim, Duc de Fort-Royal, Grand Marshal of the Palace, Grand Marshal of Haiti. Joachim wheeled the guns into position facing the rebels and then rode forward to read out the letter that Christophe had given him. This letter – and the rebels' response to it – had now become vitally important, for he saw that his men could scarcely resist an attack from the rebels and could certainly not deliver one; with only twelve hundred men he was facing at least five thousand.

As he approached the rebels he was greeted with shouts of "Go back or we fire!" followed by "Liberty! No Slavery! No King!" He reined in his horse and raised the letter for them to see. The shouting grew louder. There was nothing for it: he galloped back to his own men, drew his sword and ordered them to advance.

There was a volley from the rebel lines, thin, scattered, the ball whistling harmlessly overhead. The rebels were still shouting and now, from behind him, he heard answering shouts. *"Vive la liberté! Brisons les chaînes de l'esclavage!"* He swung round in the saddle and saw that his men had thrown down their weapons and were running with arms outstretched to the rebels. With them, intent on making his submission to the new rulers, was their commanding officer, General Riché. Joachim put spurs to his horse and headed back to Sans-Souci. It was growing late; he made the last stage of his journey in the forlorn blackness of the night.

After seeing the Haitian Guard off down the road to Cap-Henry, Christophe had returned to his room and slumped on the bed, making a pretence of dealing with papers and letters which his secretaries in their turn made a pretence of regarding as urgent. Nothing had urgency any more except the outcome of that afternoon's struggle down in the plain. Half his life had been spent in fighting, and for the greatest fight of his life he must be absent from the field, a useless cripple.

As dusk fell his mood became more sombre and when at last Joachim returned with the crushing news that even his personal guard had deserted him he received it without violence and without hope. "Since the people of Haiti no longer have faith in me, I know what I have to do," he said.

* *"Long live Liberty! Break the fetters of slavery!"*

He ordered servants to bring him warm water and clean linen. With their help he washed himself and changed his clothes, and was propped up in a chair to receive his wife and children. The gentle Marie-Louise led them into the room, fiery now, her eyes determined. Sometimes, in recent years, when he had reminisced to Admiral Popham about battles of the past, she would recount her own adventures when "she accompanied her husband, with her children on her back, often without any other food than wild fruit and berries, and generally exposed to the weather, sometimes half-clothed." Now she was prepared to join him in new wanderings, take to the mountains before Boyer's troops and the seditious generals, and raise the field hands as he had done nearly twenty years before. The gross Prince Royal, hopelessly unequipped to cope with the crisis that confronted them all, stood gawkily transfixed between two attitudes, habitual deference to his father and the conviction that he must not let the leadership pass to his mother and the two girls who comfortingly grasped her hands.

The decision still rested with Christophe. He said nothing of his plans, but told them of Joachim's grim news, urged them to take courage, embraced them, and gestured them to retire, taking his attendants with them. As they closed the door of his bedroom behind them, leaving him quite alone, he raised his left hand, holding the pistol that he had taken from beneath a cushion of his chair, and shot himself through the heart.

The family ran back into the room to find him already dead. The Prince Royal, drawing his own pistol, put it to his forehead and would have pulled the trigger, but his sister Améthyste snatched it from him, sobbing: "Is that how you ought to die? Go and avenge your father!" Some of the palace officials entered the room and began to weep but Marie-Louise rounded on them: "You cry, you wretches, and yet it was your cowardly flattery that killed the King!"

She was not long offended by the courtiers' expression of grief. News had already spread through the palace that the rebels had left Le Haut-du-Cap and were marching on Sans-Souci. Dupuy and Prézeau, the only two members of Christophe's staff who remained faithful after his death, gave money to some of the servants to carry the body, uncoffined and unshrouded, suspended in a hammock, out of the palace and up the mountain. As the queen and the two princesses followed, the remaining servants, the sentries and the field hands from the neighbouring plantations were already streaming through the palace apartments, looting whatever was portable, smashing all that was not.

It was a tribute to at least one of Christophe's virtues – his freedom from racial prejudice – that both Dupuy and Prézeau were mulattos. With their pistols drawn, they guarded the weeping queen and princesses as they followed the body through the queen's gardens to the rough road that led up to the Citadel. In the blackness they stumbled painfully along the steep paths, their way startlingly illuminated at intervals when gaps in the trees let through the glare of the fires that raged in the plain. The knife-edged flints underfoot slashed the women's thin shoes to ribbons and the men carrying the hammock grumbled and would have let it fall but for the threat of the pistols behind them.

They passed the martello towers that Christophe had recently built on the slopes below the Citadel to protect the plantations that were to supply it with food, and climbed the steep steps to the fortress's entrance. There the soldiers – and the prisoners whom they had already released – gave wild cries of joy at the sight of Christophe's body and clamoured to throw it over the precipice. But threats from Dupuy and Prézeau – and the thought that they were wasting time which could be more profitably employed in looting at the foot of the mountain – held them off. Dupuy and Prézeau took the body to a storehouse and, unable to find tools or sufficient men to dig a grave, buried it in a heap of quicklime, tipped there for one or other of the endless building operations that had now, quite unbelievably, indeed come to an end.

They hurried the royal ladies off to a place of safety until they could get them a safe-conduct from the rebel leaders; but in this they had no difficulty. Marmelade and his associates owed Marie-Louise many debts of gratitude for her kind-hearted intercessions with Christophe, which had become more and more frequent in recent years. The queen and the two princesses were taken to Le Cap under military escort, jeered at but securely protected, and lodged in a house under guard.

William Wilson had 200 dollars stolen from him on the night of the rebellion, but suffered no other hardship as a result of his connection with the royal family, except for the distressing experience a short time later of seeing his pupil the Prince Royal brought to Le Cap, "his interesting figure covered with dust and sweat, suffering regret for the death of his father, his mother's misfortune and his own". With Prince Eugène, the Prince Royal was put under house arrest for a few days and then transferred to the central prison, only two hundred yards from the College Royal where George Clarke lodged as well as taught.

The terrors and horrors of this period of anarchy and summary revenge so affected Clarke that he found it impossible to sleep. He was pacing up and down his bedroom at midnight on October 18 when he heard prolonged and piercing shrieks in the prison yard. They came from the sixteen-year-old Prince Royal who, with Prince Eugène, the Duc de l'Artibonite, the Duc de Fort-Royal and Baron Dessalines, was being bayoneted to death. The faithful Joachim, Duc de Fort-Royal, shouted until his last moment: *"Vive Henry Christophe, roi d'Haiti!"* The following night the fiery Vastey and seven others suffered the same torture and death. Most of them were buried in a pit hastily dug in a clump of trees near the hospital, but Vastey's body was contemptuously tipped into a disused well and the Prince Royal's was exposed on a dunghill and left there to rot.

The monarchy was destroyed but the rebels' triumph was short-lived. Boyer brought his army up to Saint-Marc, where Romain surrendered, and the southern forces continued their march northward. When the news of Christophe's suicide reached Boyer he was at Les Gonaïves. He proclaimed the incorporation of the former Kingdom of Haiti in the Republic of Haiti and the rebel generals, unable to face an army of 20,000 men, declared their support for the president.

By comparison with Christophe, Boyer was an unheroic figure. Wilson, who had the opportunity of observing him in a moment of crisis, described him as "extravagantly timid . . . His fears are so strong that he had not even the power of concealing them." He wasted little time in finding pretexts on which to court-martial and dispose of Marmelade and the other rebel leaders, but his rule was weak and the North soon relapsed into the same condition of lethargic indigence as the South.

Prince Sanders, who stayed on at Cap-Henry – renamed Cap-Haitien – for several months after the rebellion, wrote to Clarkson of the "absolute state of brigandage in which everything is". Two years later he spent six months in Haiti and reported sadly "the alarming torrent of licentiousness and disorder" which pervaded "the greatest portion of every class in society. . . . The people of the South part of Haiti who had lived under the governments of Pétion and Boyer were at the least calculation twenty years behind the people of the Kingdom in their habits of industry and their improvements in the arts, sciences and manners of civilised society." But now all Christophe's cherished projects were destroyed. "The numerous schools and academies which were established throughout the King's dominions are abolished, and most of the buildings themselves have been defaced or entirely torn down by these unprincipled barbarians."

He remarked that in the North a realisation was growing that the rebellion might have destroyed something of value. Even the field hands, though they could now laze most of the day away in the sun, were dimly aware of being the poorer for having lost the stern hand of the fierce figure to whom they superstitiously referred only as *l'homme*; and they would often speak of the rebellion and the death of the king as *le temps de notre malheur.** By a strange irony, a week after the king's death, his old friend Vincent, more loyal to him than he had thought, wrote from Paris to Clarkson about "my old friend Christophe, today the worthiest and surest supporter of the most just of causes" (Negro emancipation) and mentioned the last time he had seen him, when he was "the stern and upright commandant of Le Cap and La Petite-Anse".

Wilberforce, writing to Archdeacon Wrangham at Christmas, said, "I cannot mention Haiti without interposing a word or two concerning this same *tyrant*, as now that he is fallen it seems to be the fashion to call Christophe. If he did deserve that name, it is then compatible with the warmest desire in a sovereign for the improvement and happiness of his people; and I must also add that all the authentic accounts I have ever heard of him have led me to believe that he was really a great man, with but few infirmities." A year later, in a letter to James Stephen, he exclaimed, "Poor Christophe! I cannot help grieving at the idea of his character's being left to the dogs and vultures to be devoured."

When Boyer went to Cap-Haitien to take possession of his new dominion he was accompanied by young Captain Robert Sutherland, who renewed his acquaintance with the queen and the two princesses – now Madame and Mesdemoiselles Christophe once more – and in the summer of 1821 escorted them to England and found them lodgings in London. There they were able to draw on the £6,000 that Christophe had placed at Clarkson's disposal for the expenses of his journey to Paris in November 1819 and of which Clarkson had spent only £300. They also brought with

* *"The time of our misfortune."*

them some of the queen's jewels, which Sutherland let his associates know had been preserved thanks to his courage and ingenuity. He was a bumptious young man whose irritating manner may have been the cause of Wilberforce's reluctance to receive the queen and her daughters in his home (though Wilberforce pleaded it was because of his wife's indisposition, Clarkson attributed it to Wilberforce's reluctance to accept Negresses, even though formerly royal, as his social equals). In his self-appointed role as their protector, he arranged for them to stay with the Clarksons at Playford Hall for three or four weeks.

As time passed, the Clarksons became uncomfortably aware that their grateful guests enjoyed life in Suffolk so much that it was going to be difficult to get rid of them. Sutherland sent them a Negress to act as their maid – and would have followed her with a footman and coachman had not Clarkson refused to have them. He then busied himself with sorting out their financial affairs, much to the alarm of Clarkson and Wilberforce, neither of whom had great faith in the captain's ability or honesty.

The unfortunate Madame Christophe was at this time deluged by claims from creditors who had first sent their bills to Boyer (not unreasonably, since he had impounded both the public funds of the kingdom and as much as he could find of Christophe's private treasure) but had been told to address themselves to Christophe's family. There were outstanding accounts from London merchants for dresses and regalia, demands from Wilson and Clarke for compensation for the unexpired portion of their seven-year contracts, a claim from Stewart for medical fees, a plea from Prince Sanders for help with the expenses of his journey from Philadelphia. Many of the claims were exaggerated (Wilson accused Stewart of downright untruths) but in the end the ex-queen settled Stewart's claim and the others for reduced sums, Clarke and Wilson receiving £600 each.

The guests remained at Playford Hall until April 1822. They went back to London for a time and then to Hastings where the climate was more agreeable and kinder to Madame Christophe's rheumatism and Améthyste's delicate chest. But the deep warmth of Haiti was lacking from the south coast of England and in September 1824 they moved on to Italy, settling down finally in Pisa in a house that had been found them by the ever-faithful Vincent.

The sale of the jewels had brought them enough money to live in comfort and to make little journeys of exploration in their adopted land. Neither of the daughters married and Madame Christophe outlived both of them, Améthyste dying in 1832 and Athénaïre in 1839. Christophe's only remaining descendant was the son of the illegitimate Prince Eugène.

Towards the end of 1839 Madame Christophe wrote to Boyer:

A final and horrible misfortune has just crowned the calamities with which it has pleased Divine Providence to try me. The last of my daughters, Mme Athénaïre, has died of a cruel malady. In the state of isolation and abandonment in which I find myself, my thoughts and desires naturally turn to my dear homeland, the love of which has never faded from my heart. I feel the need to associate once more with people with whom I have ties of blood and who will not look on me as a stranger.

Your Excellency, I am sure, will appreciate such sentiments. You will understand that a woman like myself, bent under the weight of years and misfortunes, desires only to see her country again and will remain entirely apart from politics.

I furthermore make a formal undertaking to keep entirely aloof from any intrigue of that nature. I hope that your Excellency will consequently grant my sister, Mme Louis Pierrot, a passport to come to fetch me from Europe and will also send me one so that I may enter Haiti. In making this request, I venture to remind you of the gracious words which you were good enough to address to me on my departure, telling me to return one day to my country.

The prayers which I offer to Heaven for the prosperity of my country and for the conservation of your Excellency's person will become the more ardent when I have obtained that which forms the object of this letter. . . .

Marie-Louis, veuve de Henry Christophe.

The passport never came and in March 1851 Marie-Louise died, still lonely in a foreign land.

On the peak of La Ferrière within the walls of the deserted Citadel, the quicklime gradually subsided around the corpse of Christophe and, as the planks of wood with which the entrance to the storehouse had been boarded up mildewed and fell away, an arm and outstretched finger could be seen, pointing skyward. In time, the whole skeleton became visible and occasionally a visitor would make the increasingly difficult climb up the neglected paths to gaze upon the cadaver of the King of the Blacks. Under the triumphant republic, his reputation was denigrated, his name and monuments were erased like those of Akhnaton; but in 1847 he was at last given burial, lifted from the bed of lime and placed in a simple concrete tomb on the Citadel's place d'Armes. But even beneath the parade ground he was not allowed to sleep in peace. A prowler, seeking the treasure which legend said Christophe had hidden in the fortress, broke into the vault and, finding nothing else, took away a fingerbone as a souvenir. Others followed, until at last the crumbling walls of his stronghold, the rows of guns still alert in their embrasures, flanked by neat pyramids of cannonballs and rotted boxes from which trickled tiny avalanches of black gunpowder, continued to stand guard over nothing at all.

Appendices

Table of Events

June: Colonial Assembly rejects the declaration.

August: Buckman leads slave-rising in North Province.

September: Mulattos and whites of West Province join forces against revolutionaries and rebel slaves.

November: News that National Assembly has reversed its decision, leaving status of mulattos and free Negroes to discretion of Colonial Assemblies. Confederation of whites and mulattos in West Province breaks up in violence. Civil commissioners Mirbeck, Roume and Saint-Léger arrive at Le Cap.

December: Jean-François, Biassou and other slave leaders (among them Toussaint) offer submission in return for their freedom and better conditions for their followers. Colonial Assembly refuses to treat with them.

1792

March: Mulattos in West Province enlist Black slaves against the whites.

April: National Assembly again reverses decision, decrees equality for all freeborn men irrespective of colour.

September: Arrival of Sonthonax and other commissioners to enforce National Assembly's decrees.

1793

February: France declares war on Britain.

May: Rioting at Le Cap, which is ravaged by fire.

July: Christophe marries Marie-Louise Coidavid.

August: Sonthonax liberates all slaves in the colony.

September: *Colons* of South Province put themselves and their property under the protection of George III.

1794

June: Sonthonax and other commissioners return to France. Colony almost entirely taken over by Britain and Spain. Toussaint deserts from Spanish army to French.

October: Williamson, Governor of Jamaica, appointed Governor and Commander-in-Chief of the British-held parts of Saint-Domingue.

November: Christophe promoted major.

1795

July: Spain surrenders her part of the island to France by the Treaty of Bâle.

1796

March: Toussaint rescues Laveaux from the mulattos of Le Cap.

April: Laveaux appoints Toussaint Lieutenant-governor.

May: Sonthonax returns from France with Roume and others.

October: Simcoe appointed C-in-C British troops.

1797

February: Colonel Christophe distinguished in campaign against the rebels of La Grande-Rivière.

March: Sonthonax appoints Toussaint C-in-C French forces.

August: Toussaint forces Sonthonax to return to France.

1798

January: Nesbitt appointed C-in-C British troops.

March: Maitland arrives at Môle Saint-Nicolas, Nesbitt left dying at Madeira.

April: Maitland opens negotiations with Toussaint.

October: Last British troops in Saint-Domingue evacuate Môle Saint-Nicolas. Toussaint forces Hédouville to return to France.

1799

March: Christophe appointed commandant of Le Cap. Dr Edward Stevens appointed U.S. Consul-general.

June: Rigaud makes war on Toussaint.

1800

July: Rigaud escapes to France.

November: Toussaint arrests the only remaining civil commissioner, Roume, and sends him back to France.

1801

January: Toussaint invades and annexes the Spanish part of the island.

July: Proclamation of a new constitution under which Toussaint is appointed Governor-general for life.

October: Moyse's rebellion. France signs preliminaries of Treaty of Amiens.

November: Toussaint conducts public execution of the rebels.

December: Leclerc's expedition leaves Brest.

1802

January: French fleet arrives in Samana Bay.

February: Christophe refuses to allow Leclerc to land at Le Cap. Evacuates the town and sets it on fire.

April: Christophe submits to Leclerc.

May: Toussaint and Dessalines submit.

June: Leclerc arrests Toussaint and sends him to France.

October: Pétion and Clervaux mutiny, followed by Dessalines and Christophe.

November: Leclerc dies of yellow fever. Command passes to Rochambeau.

1803

April: Toussaint dies in captivity.

May: Renewal of war between France and Britain.

November: Rochambeau surrenders to Dessalines. French troops under General Ferrand continue in possession of Spanish part of the island.

1804
January: Declaration of Independence of the State of Haiti.
May: Napoléon named Emperor of the French Republic, his coronation set for December.
September: Dessalines acclaimed Jean-Jacques the First, Emperor of Haiti, crowned in October.

1805
March: Dessalines unsuccessfully invades Spanish part of the island.
July: Dessalines appoints Christophe C-in-C.

1806
February: U.S. Congress bans trade with Haiti, and renews the embargo annually until 1809.
October: Dessalines assassinated.
November: Christophe orders elections.
December: Christophe refuses offer of presidency, denounces mulatto intrigues, and marches south against Pétion.

1807
February: Christophe elected President of the State of Haiti.
March: Pétion elected President of the Republic of Haiti.

1808
October: Royal Navy seizes the corvette *Lord Mulgrave*.
December: British Order in Council removes restrictions on trade with Haiti.

1809
April: Rigaud returns from France. Pétion appoints him Governor of the South Province.

1810
May: Christophe confiscates cargo of the *Crown*, a British merchant vessel.
July: Christophe changes name of Cap-François to Cap-Henry.
September: Pétion offers to accept British sovereignty.
November: Rigaud tries to oust Pétion.
December: Christophe declares his official blockade of the Republic.

1811
February: Three British seamen killed in incident at Les Gonaïves.
March: Christophe declares Haiti a Kingdom.
April: Creation of the Order of Saint-Henry.
June: Christophe crowned as King Henry I
September: Rigaud dies.

1812
February: Royal Navy captures the corvette *Améthyste*.

March: Christophe opens new campaign against Pétion.

June: Pétion successfully organises desertion of some of Christophe's troops and mutiny of others; but fails to have him assassinated at Saint-Marc. U.S. declares war on Britain.

1813: Christophe fights back to former line of demarcation but makes no further attempt to invade the Republic.

1814

October: Lavaysse arrives at Port-au-Prince with proposals from the newly-restored French monarchy.

November: Christophe arrests Medina and orders his trial as a spy.

December: Lavaysse leaves Port-au-Prince for France.

1815

February: Christophe offers to incorporate the Republic in the Kingdom.

1816

January: British trader, Davison, arrested and allegedly tortured at Cap-Henry.

June: Pétion promulgates new constitution for the Republic, with himself as President for life.

September: Gulliver, first of the English teachers, lands at Cap-Henry.

October: New French mission, led by Fontanges, arrives at Port-au-Prince.

November: Fontanges's mission returns to France. Christophe publishes his *Déclaration du Roi* stating "our unshakable resolution either to live free and independent or to die".

1817

May: Pétion gives Methodists permission to open a school in the Republic.

1818

March: Pétion dies and is succeeded by Boyer.

August: Lightning explodes powder magazine at Citadel-Henry.

September: Clarkson interests Czar Alexander in Christophe's projects.

December: Christophe sets up Royal Chamber of Public Instruction.

1819

July: Christophe distributes lands to soldiers, preparatory to reducing size of the army.

November: Christophe asks Clarkson to explore possibilities of a treaty with France.

1820

February: Christophe accepts Admiral Popham's mediation with Boyer.

April: Boyer rejects mediation.

August: Christophe collapses at Limonade.

October 2: Mutiny of the 8th Regiment at Saint-Marc.
October 8: Christophe commits suicide.
October 18: Prince Royal and others bayoneted to death.

Notes

The full titles of books and authors quoted will be found in alphabetical order in the SOURCES *under* Books *and* periodicals, *and manuscript sources under* Manuscripts. *Abbreviations follow the form of author where possible or short-title where the author is anonymous in the case of printed sources; and for the three major manuscript sources Bib. Nat. is used for the Bibliothèque Nationale, Paris,* BM *for the British Museum and* PRO *for the Public Record Office, London.*

CHAPTER II

page 33.6–13, B., C.M. 57
 41.23–31, Sylvain, 113
 42.2–4, PRO, Adm. 1/245
 45.30–5, PRO, CO 245/1
 45.36–8, *Ibid.*, WO 1/61
 46.9–35, *Ibid.*, 1/62
 46.39 to 47.5, *Loc. cit.*
 47.38 to 48.25, Bib. Nat., ff. 12104
 49.21–4, Madiou, I, 238
 49.25, *Ibid.*
 50.15–18, BM, F.717(12), Tracts on Hayti
 50.22–3, Bib. Nat., n. af, 6847
 53.37 to 54.7, PRO, WO 1/67
 54.8 to 55.8, *Ibid.*, 1/69
 57.28 to 58.28, *Ibid.*, 1/71
 59.12–17, Rainsford, 11
 59.38 to 60.1, Madiou, I, 346
 60.11–12, PRO, CO 245/1
 60.26–31, Rainsford, 22
 60.32 to 61.13, PRO, CO 245/1
 61.37–8, *Ibid.*, WO 1/74
 63.32, Ardouin, IV, 177
 63.37, *Ibid.*, 176
 65.15–26, Madiou, II, 76
 66.37–9, *Ibid.*, 98
 67.2–4, Bib. Nat., ff. 12104
 68.30–3, Ardouin, IV, 375
 68.40 to 69.5, Placide-Justin, 341
 69.16–19, Lacroix, II, 29
 69.31, Ardouin, IV, 381
 70.35, Brutus, 43
 71.6, Schoelcher, *Toussaint*, 280
 71.13–16, Madiou, II, 116
 71.27–31, Gragnon-Lacoste, 193

CHAPTER II—*cont.*

page 71.32–3, Madiou, II, 116
     74.33, *Ibid.*, 122; BM, Add. MS. 38,074
     75.28–40, Madiou, II, 123

CHAPTER III

     78.1–4, Lacroix, II, 31
     78.20–6, Junot, II, 330
     79.40 to 80.3, Poyen-Bellisle, 98
     81.35–41, Lacroix, II, 262
     83.18-32, *Ibid.*, 78
     83.34 to 84.3, Leclerc, 62
     84.18–24, Lacroix, II, 70
     84.28 to 85.3, BM, 1196.i.36, Tracts on Hayti
     89.24–7, Hardy, 268
     90.4–23, Leclerc, 309
     90.32 to 91.4, *Ibid.*, 269
     91.12 to 92.17, *Ibid.*, 79
     92.21–6, Lacour-Gayet, II, 63
     93.23–34, Leclerc, 85
     94.3–11, *Ibid.*, 87
     94.25–7, *Ibid.*, 99
     95.13–16, Hardy, 271
     96.30–8, PRO, Adm. 1/252
     97.6–13, *Ibid.*, CO 318/19
     97.14–18, *Ibid.*, Adm. 1/252
     97.28–31, *Loc. cit.*
     100.31 to 104.39, BM, 1196.i.36, Tracts on Hayti
     105.4–8, Hardy, 284
     105.23–35, Boisrond-Tonnerre, 40
     106.37–9, Leclerc, 272
     107.17–23, *Ibid.*, 150
     107.25–7, *Ibid.*, 146
     107.28–33, *Ibid.*, 145
     108.14 to 109.5, *Ibid.*, 271
     110.21–30, Hassal, 7
     110.31–2, Norvins, III, 10
     111.5–6, Leclerc, 161
     111.9–12, Leconte, 97
     111.16–36, Leclerc, 334
     112.24–5, *Ibid.*, 168
     112.28–32, Napoléon, VII, 617
     113.2, Ardouin, V, 155
     113.18–33, Madiou, II, 269
     114.4–8, Leclerc, 180
     114.10–31, *Ibid.*, 180–96
     115.36 to 116.28, Métral, 152
     116.33 to 117.2, Leclerc, 199
     117.12–19, *Ibid.*, 201
     117.26.37, *Ibid.*, 207

CHAPTER III—*cont.*

page 118.3–10, *Ibid.*, 214
    118.35 to 119.8, *Ibid.*, 230
    119.24 to 120.2, Lacroix, II, 225
    120.11–26, *Ibid.*, 227
    121.1–14, Leclerc, 245
    121.22–8, Madiou, II, 337
    121.37 to 122.10, Leclerc, 256
    122.17–28, Norvins, III, 22
    122.33–6, Lacroix
    123.12–15, Lacroix, II, 232
    124.20 to 125.37, Norvins, III, 36
    126.14–36, Madiou, II, 347
    127.25–7, Junot, II, 342
    128.34–5, Madiou, II, 376
    131.31–2, *Ibid.*, 404
    132.35 to 133.9, Lemmonier-Delafosse, 66
    133.28 to 134.17, *Ibid.*, 70
    134.28, Fréminville, 147
    134.30 to 135.11, Lemmonier-Delafosse, 85
    136.3–33, PRO, Adm. 1/253
    137.8–14, Norvins, III, 2
    137.29–32, PRO, Adm. 1/253

CHAPTER IV

    140.12 to 143.12, PRO, Adm. 1/254
    143.28 to 144.8, *History of Island of St Domingo*, 304
    144.12 to 145.18, Placide-Justin, 420
    145.24–7, Ardouin, VI, 24
    146.27 to 147.8, Madiou, III, 185
    151.2–3, Ardouin, VI, 251
    151.32, *Ibid.*, 323
    153.7–14, *Ibid.*, 338
    154.4–6, *Ibid.*, 316
    154.10–11, *Ibid.*, 361
    154.27–30, *Ibid.*, 363
    154.35–9, *Ibid.*, 349
    155.4–8, *Ibid.*, 364
    155.39–40, Bonnet, 148
    156.1–6, Ardouin, VI, 456
    156.20–1, Saint-Rémy, 333
    157.20–31, PRO. Adm. 1/257
    158.12 to 159.5, *Ibid.*, WO 1/75
    160.20–3, *The Times*, 27 November, 1807
    161.7–9, PRO, WO 1/79
    161.26 to 162.8, *Loc. cit.*
    162.16–19, *The Gentleman's Magazine*, LXXVIII, 70
    162.20–4, PRO, WO 1/79
    164.24 to 173.20 (*passim*), PRO, Adm. 1/258
    173.29–37, *Ibid.*, WO 1/75

CHAPTER IV—*cont.*
page 174.11–17, *Ibid.*, Adm. 1/259
174.22–4, BM, OG.H.10/2, Hayti, *Gazette officielle*
175.38–9, PRO, WO 1/75
177.39 to 178.5, *Ibid.*, Adm. 1/261
178.8–14, *Ibid.*, WO 1/76
178.27–31, Ardouin, VII, 337
179.16–29, PRO, WO 1/75
180.1–14, *Ibid.*, 1/76
180.38 to 182.30, *Ibid.*, Adm. 1/261
183.30–40, *Ibid.*, WO 1/75
184.3 to 186.22, *Ibid.*, 1/76
186.25–32, *Ibid.*, Adm. 1/261
186.35–190.3, *Ibid.*, WO 1/76

CHAPTER V
192.33–9, Ardouin, VII, 412
193.4–7, Prévost, 157
193.30 to 194.13, PRO, WO 1/76
196.40 to 197.8, *Ibid.*, Adm. 1/263
198.19 to 200.17, *Ibid.*, WO 1/77
200.20–8, Ardouin, VII, 477
201.37 to 202.5, Leconte, 333
203.34–5, Brown, II, 196
204. 26 to 205.36, PRO, WO 1/77
208.22–8, Harvey, 185
210.33–41, BM, Add. MS. 41,266
211.4–18, Ritter, 73
211.33–4, Hérard-Dumesle, 83
213.14–19, Griggs, 39
214.38 to 215.3, PRO, Adm. 1/264
216.1–4, BM, Add. MS. 41,266
216.6–14, *History of the Island of St Domingo*, 419
216.37 to 217.7, *Ibid.*, 424
218.13–25, Ardouin, VIII, 88
219.22–6, *Ibid.*, 109
221.6 to 222.2, BM, 1196.i.36, Tracts on Hayti
222.33 to 223.2, Ardouin, VIII, 139
223.5, Bib. Nat., ff. 1203; Ardouin, VII, 513
224.6–11, BM, Add. MS. 41, 266
224.26–33, Southey, III, 590
224.41 to 228.40, BM, 1196.i.35, Tracts on Hayti
229.21–31, BM, Add. MS. 41,266
229.34–5, Borough Road T.C., Gulliver to Millar, 27 September, 1816
230.2–3, Brit. and For. Sch. Soc., Manual, Preface iii
230.23–5, *Ibid.*, 11
230.30–7, *Ibid.*, 10
231.28–236.3, *Déclaration du Roi* (BM, L.A.S.E.203)
236.8 to 238.31, PRO, WO 1/78
239.13–19, Brit. and For. Sch. Soc., *Report*, May 1817, 33

CHAPTER V—*cont.*
page 239.23–40, *Blackwood's Magazine*, IX, 269
    240.8–11, *Loc. cit.*
    240.17–23, Brit. and For. Sch. Soc., *Report*, May 1817, 34
    240.26–8, Methodist Magazine, XL, 557
    241.7–15, BM, 1196.i.35, Tracts on Hayti
    241.16–26, Brit. and For. Sch. Soc., *Report*, May 1817, 54
    241.28–9, Borough Road T.C., Daniell to Millar, 11 September, 1817
    241.39 to 242.5, *Ibid.*, Gulliver to Millar, 11 June, 1817
    242.21–6, *Ibid.*, 4 December, 1817
    243.1–9, *Ibid.*, Daniell to Millar, 14 August, 1818
    244.1–27, Harvey, 202
    245.26–9, *Report . . . on the Extinction of Slavery*, 224
    245.32–41, BM, Add. MS. 41,266
    246.10–11, Ardouin, VI, 68
    246.27–33, BM, Add. MS. 41,266
    248.18–250.3, *Blackwood's Magazine*, IV, 131
    250.15 to 252.19, BM, Add. MS. 41,266
    252.35 to 253.1, Wilberforce, *Correspondence*, I, 376
    253.4–5, Wilberforce, *Life*, IV, 355
    253.31 to 254.19, BM, Add. MS. 41,266
    254.34 to 255.3, St John's Coll., Camb., Clarkson to Turckheim,
        11 March, 1820
    255.6–27, BM, Add. MS. 41,266
    255.28–31, *Blackwood's Magazine*, X, 549
    255.41 to 256.2, Wilberforce, *Correspondence*, I, 384
    256.9–19, BM, Add. MS. 41,266
    256.37 to 258.20, Harvey, 226
    258.35, BM, Add. MS. 41,266
    258.39 to 259.4, *Blackwood's Magazine*, X, 551
    259.20–6, Ardouin, VIII, 426
    259.34–8, *Report . . . on the Extinction of Slavery*, 224
    260.4–14, Ardouin, VIII, 426
    260.22–3, BM, Add. MS. 41,266
    261.18–19, Leconte, 275
    263.23–7, Bonnet, 285
    264.6–31, St John's Coll., Camb., Wilson to Clarkson, 1 January, 1821
    265.15 to 271. 40 (*passim*), BM, Add. MS. 41,266
    272.7–10, *Blackwood's Magazine*, X, 549
    272.28–32, Schoelcher, *Colonies*, II, 155
    273.39–41, BM, Add. MS. 41,266
    274.11–12, Ritter, 62
    274.28 to 275.3, BM, Add. MS. 41,266
    275.14, Mackenzie, I, 143
    275.17–20, St John's Coll., Camb., Vincent to Clarkson, 17 October, 1820
    275.22–8, Wilberforce, *Life*, V, 82
    275.29–31, *Ibid.*, 108
    277.7–31, Lespinasse, 54

Sources

This list comprises only those sources from which I have drawn material for this book.

Manuscripts

Bibliothèque Nationale: ff. 8986-8, 12103-4; naf. 4372, 6846-7, 6864, 22101.

Borough Road Training College, Isleworth: Letters of Bosworth, Daniell and Gulliver.

British Museum: Add. MSS 37,870, 38,074, 38,229, 38,245, 39,824, 41,266.

Ipswich Central Library: Letter of Clarkson.

Public Record Office: Adm. 1/245-70, 50/137; CO 137/126-7, 245/1-3, 318/11-13, 19; HO 30/2; WO 1/59-79, 6/5.

St John's College, Cambridge: Letters of Clarkson, Mrs Clarkson, Vincent and Wilson.

I am most grateful to the Librarians of the above institutions for their help and permission to make use of the manuscripts, and to those of the Bibliothèque Nationale, the British Museum, the University Library, Cambridge, and the Huntingdonshire County Library for making printed works available to me.

Books and Periodicals

Adams, Henry, *History of the United States during the first administration of Jefferson* (New York, 1889).

Ambigu, L'.

American Historical Review, XVI.

Annual Register, The

Anthologie d'un siècle de poésie haïtienne (Paris, 1925).

Ardouin, Beaubrun, *Etudes sur l'histoire d'Haïti* (Paris, 1853–60).

Ardouin, Beaubrun, *Géographie de l'île d'Haïti* (Port-au-Prince, 1832).

B., C.M., *A Glimpse of Hayti and her negro chief* (Liverpool, 1850).

Barré de Saint-Venant, Jean, *Des colonies modernes* (Paris, 1802).

Beard, John R., *Life of Toussaint L'Ouverture* (London, 1853).

Blackwood's Magazine, IV, IX, X.

Boisrond-Tonnerre, Félix, *Mémoires pour servir à l'histoire d'Haïti* (Paris, 1851).

Bonnet, Guy-Joseph, *Souvenirs historiques* (Paris, 1864).

British and Foreign School Society, *Annual Reports*, 1815–22; *Manual of the System of teaching Reading, Writing, Arithmetic and Needlework* (London, 1816).

Brown, Jonathan, *History and present condition of St Domingo* (Philadelphia, 1837).

Brutus, Timoléon César, *L'homme d'airan* (Port-au-Prince, 1946).

C., F., [Carteau, Félix], *Soirées bermudiennes* (Bordeaux, 1802).

Candler, John, *Brief Notices of Hayti* (London, 1842).

Capefigue, Jean-Baptiste-Honoré-Raymond, *L'Europe pendant le Consulat et l'Empire de Napoléon* (Paris, 1839–41).

Castonnet des Fosses, Henri-Louis, *La perte d'une colonie – la révolution de Saint-Domingue* (Paris, 1893).

Chalmers (Colonel), *Remarks on the late war in St Domingo* (London, 1803).

Chateaubriand, François-René de, *Mémoires d'outre-tombe* (Paris, 1946–7).

Clowes, William Laird, *The Royal Navy* (London, 1897–1903).

Coke, Thomas, *A History of the West Indies* (Liverpool, 1808–11).

Debien, Gabriel, *Etudes antillaises* (Paris, 1956); *Plantations et esclaves à Saint-Domingue* [Université de Dakar, Section d'Histoire] (Dakar, 1962).

Descourtilz, Michel-Etienne, *Voyages d'un naturaliste* (Paris, 1809).

Dorsinville, Luc, *Jean-Jacques Dessalines et la création du drapeau bleu et rouge haïtienne* (Port-au-Prince, 1953).

Dubroca, Louis, *La vie de J.-J. Dessalines* (Paris, 1804).

Firmin, Anthénor, *M. Roosevelt et la république d'Haïti* (Paris, 1905).

Fortescue, John William, *History of the British Army* (London, 1899–1930).

Franklin, James, *The present state of Hayti* (London, 1828).

Fréminville, Christophe-Paulin de la Poix, chevalier du, *Mémoires* (Paris, 1913).

Furber, Holden, *Henry Dundas* (London, 1931).

Garran-Coulon, Jean-Philippe, *Rapport sur les troubles de Saint-Domingue* (Paris, an IV).

Gentleman's Magazine, The.

Gragnon-Lacoste, Thomas-Prosper, *Toussaint L'Ouverture* (Bordeaux, 1877).

Griggs, Earl Leslie, and Prator, C. H., *Henry Christophe and Thomas Clarkson: A Correspondence* (California, 1952).

Haïti, or renseignements authentiques sur l'abolition de l'esclavage et ses résultats à Saint-Domingue et à la Guadeloupe (Paris, 1835).

Hardy, (General) Jean, *Correspondance intime* (Paris, 1901).

Harvey, William Woodis, *Sketches of Hayti* (London, 1827).

[Hassal, Mary], *Secret history, or the horrors of St Domingo, in a series of letters written by a lady at Cape François to Colonel Burr, late vice-president of the United States, principally during the command of General Rochambeau* (Philadelphia, 1808).

Hayti, Royaume d', *Almanach Royal.*

Haytian Papers [trs. Prince Sanders] (London, 1816).

Hazard, Samuel, *Santo Domingo, Past and Present* (New York, 1873).

Hérard, Dumesle, *Voyage dans le Nord d'Haïti* (Les Cayes, 1824).

Herring, Thomas S., *Reminiscences of Hayti* (Portsmouth, 1833).

History of the Island of St Domingo, from its first Discovery by Columbus to the Present Period [attributed to Sir James Barskett] (London, 1818).

Inginac, Joseph-Balthazar, *Mémoires* (Kingston, Jamaica, 1843).

Jean-Baptiste, Saint-Victor, *Haïti, sa lutte pour l'émancipation* (Paris, 1957).

Juan, George, and Ulloa, Antoine de, *Voyage historique de l'Amérique méridionale fait par ordre du roi d'Espagne* (Amsterdam and Leipzig, 1752).

Junot, Laure [duchesse d'Abrantès], *The Home and Court Life of the Emperor Napoléon* (London, 1893).

King, Rufus, *Life and Correspondence* (New York, 1895–6).

Lacour-Gayet, Georges, *Talleyrand* (Paris, 1928–34).

Lacroix, François-Joseph-Pamphile, baron de, *Mémoires pour servir à l'histoire de la révolution de Saint-Domingue* (Paris, 1819).

Laujon, A. P. M., *Précis historique de la dernière expédition de Saint-Domingue* (Paris, 1805).

Leclerc, Victor-Emmanuel, *Lettres de Saint-Domingue* [ed Roussier] (Paris, 1937).

Leconte, Vergniaud, *Henry Christophe dans l'histoire d'Haïti* (Paris, 1931).

Lemonnier-Delafosse, Marie-Jean-Baptiste, *Seconde campagne de Saint-Domingue* (Le Havre, 1846).

Lespinasse, Pierre-Eugène de, *Gens d'autrefois – Vieux souvenirs* (Paris, 1926).

Levasseur, Arnaud, *Evènements qui ont précédé et suivi l'évacuation de Saint-Domingue* (Paris, 1804).

Logan, Rayford Whittingham, *The diplomatic relations of the United States with Haiti, 1776–1891* (Chapel Hill, 1941).

Louis, Marceau, *Maria-Luisa de Haiti* (Buenos Aires, 1953).

Mackenzie, Charles, *Notes on Haïti* (London, 1830).

Madiou, Thomas, *Histoire d'Haïti* (Port-au-Prince, 1847–8).

Magnac (Docteur), *La perte de Saint-Domingue, 1789–1809* (Paris, n.d.).

Malenfant (Colonel), *Des colonies, et particulièrement de celle de Saint-Domingue* (Paris, 1814).

Marcelin, Frédéric, *Choses haïtiennes* (Paris, 1896).

Mars, Louis, *La crise de possession dans le vaudou* (Port-au-Prince, 1946).

Methodist Magazine, XL, XLI, XLII.

Métral, Antoine-Marie-Thérèse, *Histoire de l'expédition militaire des français à Saint-Domingue* (Paris, 1841) ; *Histoire de l'insurrection des esclaves dans le Nord de Saint-Domingue* (Paris, 1818).

Montague, Ludwell Lee, *Haïti and the United States* (Durham, North Carolina, 1940).

Moreau de Saint-Méry, Médéric-Louis-Elie, *Description topographique de la partie française de Saint-Domingue* (Philadelphia, 1797–8).

Napoléon I, *Correspondance* (Paris, 1858–70).

Nemours, Auguste, *Histoire militaire de la guerre d'indépendance de Saint-Domingue* (Paris, 1928).

Norvins, Jacques-Marquet, baron de Montbreton de, *Mémorial* (Paris, 1896).

Notice historique sur les désastres de Saint-Domingue pendant l'an XI et l'an XII, par un officer français détenu par Dessalines (Paris, 1803) [republished in 1804 as *Détails sur quelques uns des évènements qui ont eu lieu en Amérique pendant les années XI et XII, publiées par un officier de l'état-major de l'armée*].

Paullin, Charles Oscar, *Commodore John Rodgers* (Cleveland, 1910).

Perkins, Samuel G., *Reminiscences of the insurrection in Saint-Domingo* (*Proceedings of the Massachusetts Historical Society*, 1886).

Placide-Justin, *Histoire politique et statistique de l'île d'Haïti* (Paris, 1826).

Poetical Epistle to the King of Hayti, A (London, 1817).

Poyen-Bellisle, Isidore-Henri de, *Histoire militaire de la révolution de Saint-Domingue* (Paris, 1899).

Prévost, Julien, comte de Limonade, *Relation des glorieux évènements qui ont porté leurs majestés royales sur le trône d'Haïti* (Cap-Henry, 1811).

Ragatz, Lowell Joseph, *The Fall of the Planter Class in the British Caribbean* (New York, 1929).

Rainsford, Marcus, *A memoir of transactions that took place in St Domingo in the spring of* 1799 (London, 1802).

Report from the Select Committee on the Extinction of Slavery throughout the British Dominions, 11 *August* 1832.

Revue de l'histoire des colonies françaises, t.XXXIII.

Revue des questions historiques, t.LXIV.

Ritter, Karl, *Naturhistorische Reise nach der westindischen Insel Hayti* (Stuttgart, 1836).

Rouzier, Semexant, *Dictionnaire géographique et administratif d'Haïti* (Paris, 1892).

Saint-Anthoine, Jean-Hippolyte-Daniel de, *Notice sur Toussaint Louverture* (Paris, 1842).

St Rémy, Joseph, *Pétion et Haïti* (Paris, 1854).

Schoelcher, Victor, *Colonies étrangères et Haïti* (Paris, 1843); *Vie de Toussaint Louverture* (Paris, 1889).

Southey, (Commander) Thomas, *Chronological History of the West Indies* (London, 1827).

Sylvain, Benito, *Etude sur le traitement des indigènes dans les colonies d'exploitation* (Paris, 1899).

Tansill, Charles Callan, *The United States and Santo Domingo* (Baltimore, 1938).

The Times.

The Trial between Mr Goodall (Admiral of Hayti), Plaintiff, and Mr Fletcher (Attorney-at-Law), Defendant, for Criminal Conversation with the Plaintiff's Wife (London, 1813).

Vastey, Pompée Valentin, baron de, *Political Remarks on some French Works* (London, 1818).

Venault de Charmilly, *Answer by way of a letter to Bryan Edwards Esq.* (London, 1797).

Victoires, conquêtes, désastres, revers et guerres civiles des français de 1792 à 1815 (Paris, 1819).

Wallez, Jean-Baptiste, *Précis historique des négociations entre la France et Saint-Domingue* (Paris, 1826).

Wilberforce, Robert Isaac and Samuel, *Life of William Wilberforce* (London, 1838).

Wilberforce, William, *Correspondence* (London, 1840).

Wimpffen, Alexandre Stanislas, baron de, *A Voyage to San Domingo* (London, 1797).

In addition to the pamphlets listed separately above, I have drawn on material contained in bound volumes at the British Museum under the following shelf marks: B.665; F.715–25; L.A.S.E.203; O.G.H. 10/2; 746.c.17; 935.e.10; 958.k.3; 1184.a.6; 1196.c.15; 1196.c.16; 1196.i.35; 1196.i.36; 1884.c.6; 8156.aaa.78; 8156.b.48; 8156.d.27; 8176.b.21; 8181.aa.12.

Index

The following general headings have been used: British and Foreign School Society; France – GOVERNMENT; Merchants and Merchant Houses; Saint-Domingue and Haiti – PHYSICAL, TOPOGRAPHICAL, etc, POLITICAL, SOCIAL, etc.

The definite article has been omitted from most geographical names. The biographical information is intended to supplement, not duplicate, details given in the text.

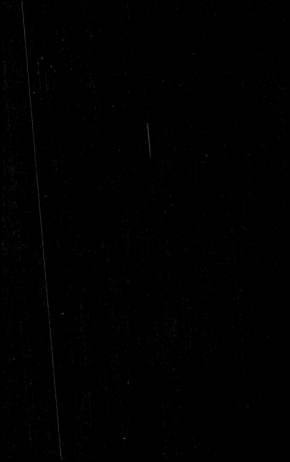

Date Due